PENGUIN BOOKS

a wolf in the kitchen

'LINDSEY BAREHAM
is one of those food writers – like Elizabeth David or Jane Grigson
before her – whose books have the power to change the way
people cook and eat' – *Sunday Times*

IN PRAISE OF THE POTATO
'I love this book. It is full of delicious recipes and good information'
– Elizabeth David

A CELEBRATION OF SOUP
'If I could buy only one book this year it would be Lindsey Bareham's
A Celebration of Soup' – Nigel Slater in the *Observer*

ONIONS WITHOUT TEARS
'Calm, measured, assured, sensible, clever, useful, amusing
and jam-packed with spot-on recipes. I am almost of a mind that
Lindsey Bareham's books are all that you need in a kitchen'
– Matthew Fort in the *Guardian*

THE BIG RED BOOK OF TOMATOES
'A book worth celebrating; inspiring and instructive in the wide world
of tomatoes' – Rose Gray of the River Café

ABOUT THE AUTHOR

Lindsey Bareham made her name as a restaurant critic and food-
writer. Twenty years of reviewing many of the best and some of the
worst restaurants provided her with a unique background for cookery-
writing. Her book on soup, *A Celebration of Soup*, was shortlisted
for the prestigious André Simon Award in 1993, and her most recent
book, *The Big Red Book of Tomatoes*, was shortlisted for the Glenfiddich
Food Book of the Year Award in 2000. She helped Simon Hopkinson,
founder chef and part owner of Bibendum, to write *Roast Chicken
and Other Stories*, which was winner of both the André Simon
Award and the Glenfiddich Food Book of the Year Award in 1995.

She is now a freelance food-writer and-broadcaster, and writes a
daily recipe column for the London *Evening Standard*; a selection
of these recipes has been published by Penguin in *Supper Won't
Take Long*. She is a regular contributor to *Woman's Hour* and
You and Yours on Radio 4.

a wolf in

the kitchen

easy food for hungry people

lindsey bareham

PENGUIN

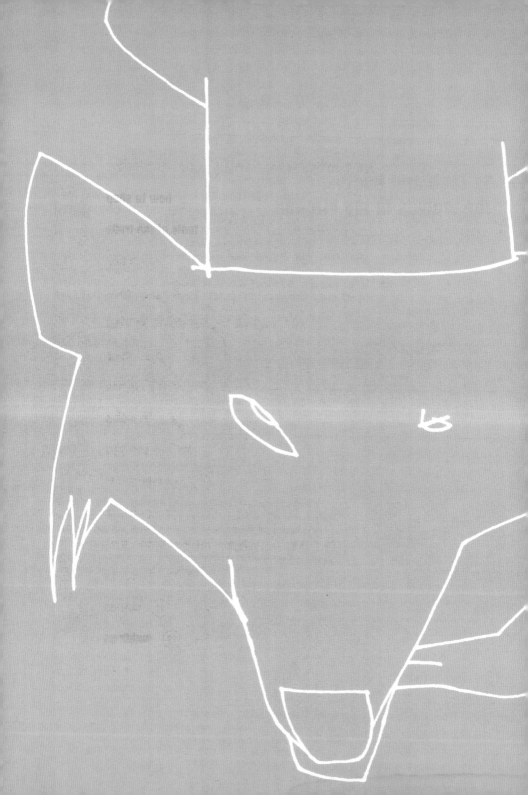

contents

are you a wolf?
why you should read
this introduction

No one reads introductions. But this book needs a few words to explain where it's coming from. It is a book about eating well every day of your life without a lot of fuss and bother. It is a book aimed at people who like good food – by which I mean food that tastes good, fills you up and keeps you healthy – but think they can't cook and haven't the time or inclination to learn.

This book isn't like other first-time cook books. And it's not like other student cook books. This is a realistic cook book, a book that tells you how to cheat and prosper. There are ideas for improving canned and packet convenience food but, of course, there are also many original recipes. There are tips on how to get the best from ordinary, basic and inexpensive food. It's a book to get you going, turn you on to making good meals for yourself and your friends. It is about laying in a few basic provisions so that you can always rustle up something decent to eat.

Cooking is about confidence. If you can fry an egg and boil pasta you can cook everything in this book. None of the recipes, however, should be regarded as being written in stone. If you haven't got an ingredient, use something else or leave it out altogether. After all, it's only food. You haven't got a camera crew in the kitchen. Most dishes are very quick to cook. Some are for one, some are for feeding the gang, some will last you several days. Few will require special equipment.

Wolf is not a sexist name. While this book was gradually taking shape in my mind, it seemed to me that Wolf summed up everything the book stood for: someone who is hungry, has a vast appetite and not much money. He or she also loves food and has high expectations but not very much experience of cooking. He or she doesn't want to spend much time planning what food to eat, shopping for it or cooking it. He or she does, however, enjoy eating, either alone, with a special friend, or with a gang of mates.

Food is what we live on. It is our fuel and it is also our pleasure. We seek different foods for different moods. Sometimes we want something to eat now and other times we are happy to plonk around in the kitchen in a mindless chopping-this-and-stirring-that sort of way. Sometimes, it is easier to make a big version of something – a soup, stew or stir fry – that can be heated up the next day or added to or altered into something quite different.

This cook book assumes no knowledge of cooking whatsoever but it isn't an idiot's cook book. Recipes are written in a helpful, step-by-step, user-friendly way. There are short cuts, but when care is needed to get something right, you aren't left in the lurch. There are no fancy culinary words. The book champions seasonal food – so much cheaper and easier to buy – and is realistic about time spent on shopping and then chopping. When unusual ingredients are introduced, they are explained thoroughly.

Learning how to eke out the budget and eat well without spending hours labouring over a hot wok becomes crucial once you are fending for yourself. You will soon discover that frozen pizza is mighty expensive (especially when it takes two to fill you up), that a diet of baked beans and biscuits quickly gets boring (and makes you spotty), and when the Cornflakes run out, mum won't be there to replace them. Or the bread, or the butter, or the milk. Having said that, if you start off with a good store cupboard and a few simple recipes up your sleeve, you'll be able to afford the occasional restaurant meal. If you are sharing, it is a good idea to work out a system for buying basics, and rotating the cooking, but initially you will probably want to be self-reliant.

Wolf is peppered with food to suit all occasions. There is quick food, very quick food, almost instant food, and food that cooks itself while you wander off and do something else. Many dishes are vegetarian.

So, if you want to learn how to have food on your fork in ten minutes, or how to spend ten minutes in the kitchen and come back to a feast an hour later, then this is the book for you. Learn how to eat well when you think the cupboard is bare, and learn how to eat like a lord on a pauper's budget. Learn how to shop well, economically and without waste.

Are you a Wolf who's hungry to learn?

Lindsey Bareham, September 2000

how to shop

As a general observation, I think it is a waste of space listing a whole load of ingredients that will transform your kitchen into a culinary haven from which you can conjure meals at the drop of a hat. Most people shop for specific meals or on impulse if they see a particular bargain such as twenty oranges for 10p or a kilo bag of rice for £1.

There is food shopping advice dished up all through this book. The book is divided up in terms of common ingredients that are easy to come by. Most of them, such as **canned tomatoes**, **sausages**, **rice** and **pasta**, are available throughout the year. Others, such as particular **fruits** mentioned in the pudding chapter, are seasonal and vary depending on the time of year. Some of them, **strawberries** and **grapes** for example, are available all year round but will have been imported from half way round the world. That means they will be expensive. The greatest key to good shopping is to buy in season. And I mean in *local* season. That is such a basic point to make but if you do most of your shopping in **supermarkets**, and most people do, it isn't always obvious.

It is worth knowing that many supermarket own-brand foods – rice, for example, canned soups and sauces, vinegars and oils – are often exactly the same as the well-known brand next to them on the shelf. Not always, but often. They tend to be several pence cheaper. Look out, too, for bargain counters, usually located at the end of the aisle and frequently touted towards closing time.

Don't miss out on your local shops: the **butcher**, **baker** and **fishmonger**. They are far more in tune with the seasons and many are still family-run, by people who live and breathe their produce. Get to know the family and seek their advice about seasonal specialities and discounts on food on the brink of being past its prime. I was brought up on yesterday's bread, often free, because my mum knew our baker, and I still buy soft tomatoes and other bruised fruit and veg for soups and sauces. The great advantage of buying **meat** from a butcher, is that you buy the quantity you want and can seek out inexpensive, slow-cook pieces of meat, such as belly of pork and ribs, and other bones and trimmings 'for the dog'. Chicken wings (only a few pence a pound) and chicken livers are fantastically good value. Another good thing to scrounge is a ham bone. Add it to a lentil or vegetable soup. **Street markets** can be even better value although you have to watch that what you want actually finds its way into your basket. Often there's the opportunity for haggling over the price, especially at the end of the day or when you want a lot of something.

Check out the possibility of a weekly **organic box scheme** home delivery. It will definitely be seasonal and could be very good value. Ask around in your locality or check out *The Organic Directory* published by the Soil Association with Green Books (tel 0117 9290661). There are fantastic bargains to be had at **Chinese, Thai** and **Japanese** food stores; big bags of dim sum, frozen prawns, rice, noodles, canned and dried soups and sauces, condiments, vegetables and fruit.

There are many ingredients that you will use time and time again. **Onions**, for example, feature in many savoury dishes from soups and stews to sauces for pasta. It makes sense, then, to stay stocked up with them. They keep for ages in a cool, dark place that isn't damp (they rot in the fridge). Buy various sized onions: big ones for dishes that require lots of onion (less peeling and less hassle to chop), and medium-sized ones for pasta sauces. **Red onions** cook faster than brown-skinned onions and **spring onions** cook even faster, although they don't keep so well (they sweat and then rot if kept in the fridge in their cellophane bags; the secret is to open the bag so they can 'breathe').

Garlic should never be kept in the fridge and if a green sprout starts developing within each clove, remove it because it tastes rough. **Pasta**, **rice** and other staples like **noodles**, **potatoes** and **eggs** are always useful to have in the store cupboard and are dealt with in their own chapters. Don't, for example, ever chuck out stale bread; there are countless wonderful ways of using it and several are included throughout the book. One extremely useful item for transforming leftover cooked food is a packet of soft **tortilla**, or **soft wrap** as some stores are now calling them. They keep, unopened, for ages in the cupboard. Once opened, seal the end of the pack and stash in the fridge; they keep perfectly well for several days. **Flour** and **butter** or butter equivalent will be used all the time.

Stock concentrates are vital for soups, sauces and for pepping up stews: **Knorr** and **Just Bouillon** chicken cubes, **Telma** chicken soup mix and **Marigold** vegetable powder (especially the organic variety) – the last two both available from Sainsbury's – are the best and won't ruin the flavour of your creations. A spoonful of **Marmite** (if you are vegetarian) or **Bovril** in a cup of boiling water will ward off hunger pangs.

Vinegar (**red wine vinegar** is the most useful; **balsamic** is surprisingly versatile), **vegetable oil**, for everyday cooking and **olive oil** for some dishes, **Dijon mustard** and **mayonnaise** (once opened, keep both in the fridge to avoid deterioration), **Tabasco** or another chilli sauce, **tomato ketchup** (and **HP**, perhaps) and **curry powder**, will get used all the time. The rest – **soy sauce** and **Thai fish sauce**, for example, and particular **curry spices** – you will build up as you go along. And don't forget **lemons**; they are extremely useful, along with a plastic bottle of pure lemon juice (the baking department of the supermarket) for emergencies. For more about lemons, *see* page 21.

Fresh herbs, particularly pots of **summer basil** for the window ledge or big bunches of **flat leaf parsley**, **coriander** and **mint**, from Cypriot food shops or some street markets or ethnic shops – *not* the supermarket – will make your food look and taste good.

Particular cuts of **meat** and **chicken** are recommended and explained for specific dishes, but as a general observation about quality, you get what you pay for. **Organic, free range** produce is always the best choice (reared on natural feed which isn't stuffed with hormones, pesticides and antibiotics), but it is likely to be quite a bit more expensive.

and then there's salt and pepper

An essential ingredient for me, something I use in almost every savoury dish I cook, is **black pepper**. To buy ready-ground black pepper is OK but it makes me sneeze – white pepper is even worse – and is never as powerful as grinding your own as you need it. So, invest in a good pepper grinder – a wooden one with a steel grinder – because it will last a lifetime. Buy black peppercorns as you need them; they are cheaper if you buy refill packs at the supermarket. Check out Asian and Oriental food stores which often sell big bags very cheaply.

I am a salt snob. I use **Maldon sea salt flakes** (*not* granules because they are too hard, even for a salt grinder) on my food; you use less and it's unprocessed and thus better for you. Then I use ordinary cooking salt in my cooking. Sometimes it really makes a difference to a dish if it is served with a crumble of sea salt, most of the time it doesn't. So I leave the choice up to you: most recipes merely specify 'salt and black pepper'.

tools of the trade

There are two ways to go here: either cheap and cheerful because everything will either get broken, burnt or lost, or the best you can afford and look after them. Remember, though, that good tools make light work. In reality, you will probably end up with a mixture of the two, along with a few of mum's rejects. I've divided tools into essentials and those, such as kitchen scales or a food processor, that will make life much easier but you can live without; items to put on your Christmas and birthday lists.

essentials

Knives: A good quality, well made cook's knife will eat into your budget but is well worth the outlay. Look after it and it will last a lifetime. You really need two: a small blade for small jobs and one with a decent-sized blade that can double as a carving knife. It is worth checking out Chinese supermarkets for inexpensive knives and cleavers. Some will be carbon steel which sharpen brilliantly but need careful looking after to avoid rusting. A bread knife is useful too; the serrated blade is good for slicing soft fruit and tomatoes.

Most knife-related accidents in the kitchen happen because the knife isn't sharp enough. So, buy a **knife sharpener** too. The simplest to use replicates a sharpening steel with two crossed steels set on springs. It's small and neat and sits on a work surface and works by sliding the knife through it. The best is the Chantry but it costs about £20. Aim to keep your knives so sharp they glide through an onion as though it were butter.

Saucepans etc: A large saucepan (approx 2½ litre) is vital. I recommend investing in a two- or three-tier, lidded steamer saucepan which doubles as a **colander**, casserole and serving dish. Look out for one in stainless steel with a heavy base. You will use it all the time. Alternatively, buy a large oven-proof casserole for stews and baking puddings, etc, which can double as a serving dish. A cast-iron version is more expensive but has the advantage that you can cook in it over the hob as well as in the oven. You will need a couple of ovenproof **baking dishes** (a deep one for shepherd's pie and macaroni cheese and a shallow one for gratins). Both can double as serving dishes. Ikea do brilliant pots and pans.

A **baking sheet** and at least one **oven pan** probably come with the oven. If you are buying new, choose heavy-duty versions that won't warp at high temperatures. A heavy duty, preferably non-stick (but not for long), large **frying pan** (about 25 cm across) or similarly wide-based pan, is almost vital. You also need a **small saucepan** for milk, baked beans etc, a **medium-sized saucepan** for pasta, rice and vegetables, and a wok.

Woks: If you can only afford one pan, then choose a wok. Its shape is extremely clever. It is curved so that liquid collects in the bottom and there is plenty of room for tossing ingredients thus enabling large quantities of finely sliced or chopped food to be cooked at the same time. You can use it for frying, steaming, poaching, braising, or to do just about anything, including making soups and frying eggs. It is perfect for making large quantities of tomato-based sauces. You can buy a specially designed shovel-cum-spatula or wide wooden spatula for use with a wok, and many come with a similarly domed lid.

The cheapest and best can be bought for a pittance in all Chinese stores. This sort of wok is made from thin carbon steel, rather than a westernized non-stick finish, and has a wooden handle. This negates the need to have an oven glove at the ready whenever you wok. The downside is that it needs to be seasoned before use (heated up with salt and beaten egg then rubbed with oil) and washed and dried immediately after use to prevent rusting. **Implements:** You need a **chopping board**. A large one, wooden or plastic, which you must scrub clean after use. Chinese supermarkets sell wonderful round wooden chopping boards that are so thick that they will last a lifetime and are too heavy to go missing. A **can opener** is vital as is, of course, a **corkscrew** and **bottle opener**.

You will find a **potato peeler** (all-steel swivel-head is fastest and sharpest) is essential; also a **grater** (box-style is sturdy and easiest to use) which is useful for grating all sorts of other things, such as carrots, onions, apples etc, as well as cheese. A **fish slice**, for lifting fried eggs and much more, is handy and so too is a **potato masher** (if you like mashed potato). A large **sieve**, either plastic or a well-made metal one, is useful for draining as well as sieving. Buy several different sized **wooden spoons** and at least one last-lick plastic **spatula**. A **balloon whisk** will save lumpy sauces as well as mixing eggs and other foods. You need **bowls** for mixing ingredients and one that is large enough for salads. A **pestle and mortar** is borderline essential for the Wolf. Use it for grinding and pounding anything from a clove of garlic to a mix of curry spices and fresh herbs. Choose a chunky black stone one from Chinese or Thai food stores.

You should always keep supplies of **tinfoil** and **clingfilm**, and **plastic bags** and **plastic boxes** are essential for storing food in the fridge/freezer.

not essential but useful

Kitchen scales and a **measuring jug** might seem essential, and do make following recipes easier, but you can do without. Both should be on your Christmas/birthday lists. Butter is marked off in 25 g sections on the packet and you can work out liquid quantities with a mug (usually 300 ml) or pint beer glass (600 ml), and empty yoghurt pots etc. A **rolling pin** is handy but a bottle is just as good. You will need a **metal tart tin** and a **deep flan tin** for some of the recipes in this book but neither is essential for everyday cooking.

A **heat diffuser**/simmer mat stops food catching and burning and spreads the heat evenly over the base of the pan; vital if your pans have thin bottoms and useful if you cook a lot of rice or favour slow cooking. Metal **tongs**, the sort with serrated sides for gripping food, are fantastically useful for lifting and turning. They go hand in hand with a cast-iron ridged **grill pan** with a black matt enamel coating. This gives meat and vegetables barbecue scorch marks. Remember to oil the food not the pan and get the pan very hot – several minutes over a high heat – before adding the food. Adjust the heat so the food doesn't burn and resist the urge to fiddle with the food. After several minutes it will have formed a thin crust and can be lifted and turned without tearing.

Many of the recipes in this book specify the use of a **liquidizer** or **food processor**. Either can be used since there is usually plenty of liquid in the recipes. To have one of these is useful but not essential and speeds up jobs that otherwise have to be done by hand. Although it is not so fast (or such a pain to wash up), a **hand-held liquidizer/mixer** is great for liquidizing jobs. Alternatively, a really useful and inexpensive gadget for puréeing and soup making is a large **Mouli-légumes** food press. It is a sort of sophisticated sieve-cum-masher and comes with three different-sized metal discs for puréeing. Its relative, the **Mouli-julienne**, comes with five blades of varying sizes for slicing and grating. Both are quick to take apart and easy to wash up.

and finally

A **pressure cooker** could solve most of your cooking needs; but it really needs another book. The same could be said for a plug-in **slow cooker** which you just leave cooking away all day. The casserole doubles as an oven casserole and serving dish. A **microwave** is useful for heating up ready meals, baked beans, coffee etc, and cooking baked potatoes quickly (but without the delicious crisp skin) but it shouldn't be regarded as a kitchen panacea. If you do, you probably won't be reading this book.

If you are moving into student halls, a bed sit, or a flat share, your facilities will be basic. You will probably be sharing the kitchen. If you are lucky you will get a hob and oven with a grill, microwave, fridge, kettle, toaster, and lockable cupboard. If you are unlucky, you might just have a hob – no oven – with a no-frying rule and you will need to keep food in your room. Shared kitchens mean you can't always cook when you want to and there always seems to be someone else's mess to clear up. A smart idea is to invest in a **toasted sandwich maker and contact grill** and keep it in your room along with a personal kettle. It comes with removable plates for easy washing, and it can be stored standing up out of the way, looking a bit like a handbag cum small metal briefcase. Apart from toasted sandwiches, you will be able to grill sausages, bacon, tomatoes, mushrooms.

reading list

For more basic cooking advice: *The Modern Cook's Manual* by Lynda Brown (Penguin) and *The ABC of AWT* by Antony Warrall Thompson (Headline). And Delia. For more recipes for quick food: *Supper Won't Take Long* by Lindsey Bareham (Penguin); *Real Fast Food*, *Real Fast Puddings* and *The 30-Minute Cook* by Nigel Slater (Penguin), *More Grub on Less Grant* by Cas Clarke (Headline), and *Marie Claire Food Fast* by Donna Hay (Merehurst). More about ingredients: *The Cook's Encyclopaedia* by Tom Stobart (Grub Street), and (if you are seriously hooked) *The Oxford Companion to Food* by Alan Davidson (OUP).

helpful tips

a note about quantities

The number of people the recipes feed varies wildly. Some are for only one, but the majority are for two, four or six, and there are several for feeding the gang. If you want to make a particular recipe for more or fewer people than recommended, either double or halve the quantities, increasing or decreasing the ingredients in proportion.

what if you don't own a food processor

The bulk of the recipes in this book are faster and easier to make with the help of a food processor. If you don't own one, you can purée and liquidize soft foods like cooked fruit or vegetables by passing them through a fine sieve, pressing down hard with a wooden spoon; be sure to scrape the underside of the sieve.

To make breadcrumbs without a blitzer, crumble the bread with your fingers until it is very fine. It is easier to do this with slightly stale bread.

For alternative equipment that does the various jobs of a food processor, *see* Tools of the Trade.

boiling water

Water comes to the boil faster if you don't add salt at the beginning. When you need to cook something in 'boiling salted water' – such as vegetables – add the salt as soon as the water boils. This little tip also avoids stainless steel pots and pans ending up with salt smears.

skinning tomatoes

Some recipes tell you to skin tomatoes. That is because the skin
will spoil the dish. To skin tomatoes, place them in a bowl of some
sort and cover with boiling water. Count to 20, prick a tomato with
a sharp knife and if the skin peels back immediately, drain the
tomatoes and splash with cold water (to stop them continuing to
soften – which they will do, considerably, and very quickly).
Remove the skin in sheets.

a chilli warning

Chillies are powerful enough to burn your mouth, eyes, and other
delicate or sensitive parts of the body. Be safe, be smart: always
wash your hands in soapy water immediately you've handled a
chilli. If you do have the misfortune to burn your lips or mouth with
raw chilli, drink milk, rub your lips with olive oil and, if you happen
to have any around, eat boiled rice. See page 214 for more
information about chillies.

Paprika, chilli, cayenne and pimenton are all powders made
from dried, ground chillies. They all vary slightly but are essentially
interchangeable. Paprika (from Hungary) and pimenton (from
Spain) are available in two strengths – either sweet ('soft') or hot;
both are intensely hot.

lemon zest

When lemon zest is to be eaten, I have always specified unwaxed
lemons. This is because most lemons are waxed and the skin may
contain shellacs, paraffin, palm oil, synthetic resins and, in some
countries, a range of fungicides to prevent the fruit from going
mouldy. Organic lemons are not waxed, nor are they treated with
fungicides. Consequently, they don't keep well.

1. the right cans

Canned food is hassle-free food. It shouldn't be regarded as the poor relation of the food world. Not if you choose your cans carefully, that is. Some canned products can be as effective as fresh, if not more so. Cans present few storage problems and all you have to do is open the can and eat.

Useful though canned food is on the occasions when you must-eat-now, there are a few little tricks that will vastly improve it. Take baked beans, for example, or canned tomatoes. And you will. If you turn to pages 60 and 186 you will see what I mean. Cans of curry or minced beef can be markedly improved by adding them to a finely-chopped onion that you've fried in a little oil until it is soft. The right cans could save your bacon. Buy a few extra next time you go shopping. They will always come in handy.

tomatoes

You are never very far from a meal with a can of tomatoes. Fortunately they are cheap and everywhere from the worst-stocked corner shop to Fortnum & Mason sells them. Whenever you see canned tomatoes on special offer, which they often are, stock up. But read the label. Like fresh tomatoes, all processed tomato products – and that includes bottles, tetrapacks and tubes of passata (sieved uncooked tomato pulp), creamed tomatoes, tomato paste and purée, as well as canned tomatoes – are surprisingly variable.

Price is a good indication of quality and it is usually worth paying a few pence extra for a good brand. Many of the very cheap ones are pretty nasty: heavy on liquid, thin on tomatoes, with an acidic, bitter metallic after-taste. The best are jam-packed with even-sized tomatoes in a thick juice made from puréed tomatoes. The widest variation is in cans of *chopped* tomatoes. Some canned tomato products contain genetically modified tomatoes. Some are organic. Keep an eye open for Italian tomatoes, but be warned; even those with Italian names don't always use Italian tomatoes. Of the supermarket own-brands, Tesco is by far the best.

As a general rule, avoid those that come with herbs. They might sound appetizing but dried herbs, which are usually used, will dominate the flavour of whatever you cook with an unpleasant mustiness. These cans will also be more expensive. Some recipes specify chopped canned tomatoes. They too are always a few pence dearer than whole tomatoes. Why not chop them yourself? I do.

What about Fresh Tomatoes?

All recipes that specify canned tomatoes can be made with fresh. Fresh isn't always better. Buy them very ripe, preferably during the summer and until late autumn when they are in season, and *don't* keep them in the fridge.

Everyone needs to know how to make a basic tomato sauce that can be varied to suit what is to hand and what the sauce is required for. For example, what about garlic? You may like to include one clove or a whole head. Which herbs to use? You may wish (or be forced) to use none. Or perhaps you want to *scent* the sauce with, say, thyme or rosemary, or to dominate it with chopped parsley or coriander. You may wish to have a thick sauce or a thin sauce, or a chunky sauce (soften a chopped onion in oil before adding all the other ingredients) or a smooth one.

Perhaps you want to add things to it – chilli, scraps of fried bacon, or red pepper, for example. Serve it with pasta, over boiled potatoes, cauliflower, beans or courgettes. Or layer it with slices of fried aubergine and bake in the oven with or without slices of mozzarella. Use it as a cook-in sauce for chicken or fish, or add a few black olives and call it Napolitana.

the ubiquitous tomato sauce

4 servings
15 minutes preparation
20 minutes cooking

ingredients

2 x 400 g cans of Italian peeled
   tomatoes
1 tsp sugar or 2 tbsp tomato
   ketchup
1 tsp dried thyme or oregano
2–4 tbsp vegetable oil (olive oil
   will give a richer flavour)
2 garlic cloves
1 bay leaf (optional)
1 heaped tsp salt
1 tsp black pepper

method

❶ Peel and finely chop the garlic.
❷ Place all the ingredients in a pan. Bring to the boil, lower the heat, then simmer for 20 minutes, breaking up the tomatoes with a spoon, until thick and syrupy. Remove the bay leaf.

NB: The longer you cook the sauce, the more concentrated the flavour and the thicker the sauce. Pass the tomatoes through a sieve to get a pip-free smooth sauce.

This soup is a perfect example of how a can of tomatoes and a few other store cupboard ingredients can be quickly transformed into an unbelievably delicious dish. Try it: all you need is a couple of pans and a sieve.

tomato and potato soup with thyme

method

❶ Peel, halve and finely chop the onion. Place in a medium-sized pan with the cooking oil and thyme, and cook over a low heat for a few minutes while you peel and chop the potatoes. Cut these into small even-sized chunks then rinse under cold water (to get rid of excess starch).

❷ Add the potatoes and 1 teaspoon of salt to the onions. Cover the pan and cook for 5 minutes. Pour on 500 ml water and bring to the boil. Cook until the potatoes are falling apart.

❸ Meanwhile, melt the butter in a frying pan and add the tomatoes, bay leaf, a generous seasoning of salt and pepper and ½ teaspoon of sugar. Simmer briskly, breaking up the tomatoes with a spoon, for about 5 minutes until the juices thicken.

❹ When the potatoes are ready, place a sieve over a second saucepan and pass the soup through the sieve, pushing everything through with the back of a spoon, scraping under the sieve so nothing is wasted.

❺ Remove the bay leaf from the tomatoes and pass the tomatoes through the sieve into the potatoes. Whisk both together, adjust the seasoning, reheat and eat.

2–4 servings
10 minutes preparation
20 minutes cooking

ingredients

1 large onion
2 tbsp vegetable cooking oil
1 tsp dried thyme
2 large potatoes, approx 500 g
knob of butter or margarine
400 g can of Italian peeled
   tomatoes
1 bay leaf
salt and black pepper
½ tsp sugar

The secret to this simple and delicious Mexican take on 'egg on toast' is making a really spicy tomato sauce and cooking it long enough so that it becomes thick. Fresh tomatoes give the cleanest flavour but canned tomatoes make a very acceptable alternative. There are countless variations on the theme of huevos rancheros but this basic recipe seems to me to be the best.

huevos rancheros

2 servings
10 minutes preparation
15 minutes cooking

ingredients

1 medium-sized onion
2 garlic cloves
1–2 green chillies
400 g can of Italian peeled
    tomatoes
2 tbsp vegetable oil
salt and black pepper
50 g mature Cheddar or
    Monterey Jack cheese
4 corn or flour tortillas
4 fresh eggs
1 tbsp chopped coriander

method

❶ Peel the onion and garlic. Split the chilli, scrape away the seeds and discard the stalk (*see* page 21). Roughly chop the onion and place in the bowl of the food processor. Blitz with the garlic and chilli until worked to a chunky paste. Add the tomatoes and their juices and blitz again until puréed. (If you don't own a food processor, *see* page 20.) Chop the tomatoes while still in the can and then stir the two sets of ingredients together.

❷ Heat 1 tablespoon of the oil in a frying pan over a medium heat. Add the tomato mixture. Season with salt and pepper. Simmer briskly, stirring frequently until the sauce is no longer watery and thickens enough to coat the back of a spoon. This takes about 12 minutes.

❸ Meanwhile, grate the cheese.

❹ When the sauce is ready, place a frying pan over a high heat. Roast the tortillas one at a time in the hot, dry pan, cooking for a few seconds each side until starting to brown and crisp. Set two of them on warmed plates and keep the other two warm (or cook them when you've eaten the first two).

❺ Use the second tablespoon of oil to fry the eggs, basting so the tops cook properly.

❻ Serve the tortillas with a share of the tomato spooned over the top. Place an egg on top, sprinkle with grated cheese and coriander.

peppers

If you've never checked out canned red peppers, often called pimientos, you'll be amazed at how neatly they are packed. They will have been cooked, peeled and (usually) seeded, and are preserved in an orange gloop – which should always be chucked. A can might contain one big one or several all curled inside each other. They can be sliced, chopped or chunked. They are great in sandwiches, and turn scrambled egg or cheese on toast into a treat. They can be quickly blitzed into a purée with or without a can of tomatoes, and used as the 'gravy' for mediterranean stews with chicken or lamb. Don't bother trying to stuff them.

The best processed pimientos are Spanish (*piquillo*). They've been roasted and are sold bottled in olive oil. Roasted piquillos cost about four times the price of standard canned peppers but have ten times the flavour. The oil they're bottled in is delicious. Similar, slightly cheaper, bottled roasted peppers are stocked by Cypriot foodstores and many supermarkets; Karyatis is a good brand. Three freshly roasted peppers are about the equivalent of a 400 g can and are interchangeable in all the recipes.

How to Roast Red Peppers

This can be done either under a very hot grill or in a very hot oven. Whichever way, place whole, unwashed peppers close to the grill or at the top of the oven. As the skin puffs and blackens, turn the peppers over. They are ready when all the skin is black. Remove to a bowl and stretch a piece of cling film over the top. Alternatively, shove into a plastic bag and fold over the end to seal. Leave for 15 minutes then peel away the blackened skin before cutting the pepper open and scraping away the white seeds and filament.

Peperonata is a soft and gooey stew of red pepper, onion and tomato, seasoned with garlic and a little wine vinegar, and fried in olive oil. This quick version is made with canned peppers and canned tomatoes and red onion. Red onion, incidentally, cooks faster than brown-skinned onions. Peperonata is also a good dish to remember when there is a glut of fresh tomatoes and peppers. In that case, roast or grill whole red peppers, peel very ripe tomatoes, and use a large Spanish onion. Either way, peperonata can be eaten hot or cold but I think it is at its best lukewarm. It is a great dish to make to last over several days (covered, in the fridge) because the flavours improve after a few hours.

It is excellent to come home to. Try it scooped up with crusty bread or slopped onto bruschetta (*see* page 59). With a fried or poached egg, or stirred into or with scrambled egg. With a few rashers of very crisp bacon, with crusty sausages, or chicken or lamb cooked any way you like. This recipe can easily be made in half quantities.

peperonata

8 servings
15 minutes preparation
20 minutes cooking

ingredients

2 large red onions
4 cloves of garlic
5 tbsp olive oil
salt and black pepper
2 x 400 g cans of whole red
   peppers (pimientos)
2 x 400 g cans of Italian peeled
   tomatoes
1 tsp honey or sugar
2 tbsp red wine vinegar

method

❶ Peel, halve and slice down the onion to make chunky half-moons. Peel the garlic and slice in wafer-thin rounds.
❷ Choose a spacious heavy-bottomed pan and cook the onion in the oil with a little salt over a gentle heat, cooking until very soft. Allow about 15 minutes.
❸ Meanwhile, remove the peppers from the tin and slice into strips. Drain the tomatoes and chop.
❹ When the onions are ready, add the garlic. Stir well and cook for a couple of minutes before you add the tomatoes. Season lightly with salt and generously with pepper. Add the honey or sugar and cook for several minutes, giving the occasional stir, until it looks more like a sauce than onions with chopped tinned tomatoes.

❺ Add the peppers and vinegar and continue cooking for about 10 minutes until you end up with a thick, creamy, jammy sauce but with the strips of pepper still distinctive. Taste, and adjust the seasoning. It's ready to eat.

How to Make Shortcrust Pastry

Sift 225 g plain flour into a mixing bowl. Cut 100 g cold butter or lard or a mixture of the two into pieces and then, using your fingertips, work it quickly into the flour until it resembles heavy breadcrumbs. Using a knife (or fork if you are superstitious), stir in 2–6 tablespoons of cold water a little at a time, until the dough seems to want to cling together. Knead together lightly to make a ball, dust with extra flour if it seems too wet, adding extra water if it seems too dry. To avoid shrinkage when the pastry is cooked, cover and leave for 30 minutes before rolling.

This looks stunning. Like a pale orange-red lemon tart.
It's smooth and creamy on the tongue and has the luscious just-set wobble
of the perfect quiche. Make it when you want to show off to non-meat-
eating friends. And when party time comes round, it could be your
contribution to the buffet. If you are feeling artistic, decorate the top with,
say, wafer-thin slices of skinned tomato. Glaze the tomatoes with a little
vinaigrette and scatter a few torn basil leaves over the top. The tart is at its
best eaten tepid or cold and is delicious with a salad of mixed leaves with a
garlicky vinaigrette. Or, try it with a few black olives and a wedge of feta
cheese. It will keep, covered, in the fridge for up to a week.

red pepper and tomato tart

8 servings

30 minutes preparation

**20 minutes cooking plus 45
minutes cooling**

ingredients

**350 g shortcrust pastry (see
page 29, or buy ready-made)**

knob of butter

**400 g can of whole red peppers
(pimientos)**

**400 ml passata or 400 g can of
Italian peeled tomatoes**

2 large eggs plus 1 egg yolk

100 ml double cream

salt and black pepper

method

❶ Pre-heat the oven to 350°F/180°C/gas mark 4.

❷ Dust a work surface with flour and roll out the pastry to
fit a 23 cm x approx 5 cm deep flan tin which you have
greased with the knob of butter. Trim the overhang and
use leftover pastry to plug tears.

❸ The pastry case needs to be part-cooked before the
filling is added. This is known as blind baking. The
uncooked pastry case is loosely draped with a sheet of tin
foil and then the base of the tart is covered with rice or
dried beans (or pebbles, if you can't find anything else
suitable) to stop the pastry rising. Bake the tart for 10
minutes, remove the foil and return the tart shell to the
oven for a further 5 minutes. Turn down the oven to
325°F/170°C/gas mark 3.

❹ Meanwhile, drain the red peppers, wipe away any stray
white seeds and blitz in the food processor. (If you don't
own a food processor, *see* page 20.) Tip into a measuring
jug (or something else that you know holds a pint of liquid)

and add sufficient passata or the puréed tomatoes to make up to 570 ml.

5 Whisk the whole eggs with the egg yolk, stir in the cream and season with salt and pepper. Add the eggs to the red pepper and tomato sauce and stir gently. Taste for seasoning; it will probably need more salt.

6 Carefully ladle the red pepper and tomato custard into the pastry case, letting it come right up to the rim. Transfer to the oven and bake for 20 minutes, or until the custard is just set but the centre is still slightly wobbly. Remove from the oven and allow to cool for at least 45 minutes, when it will set even more, before slicing in wedges.

beans

Baked beans are not the only canned beans. Red beans, white beans, green beans and black beans are amazingly versatile and are quickly turned into delicious hot and cold snacks, soups and main meals. Remember them too for hummus-style purées. The golden rule is to rinse away the rank liquid they all seem to be canned in.

A Word about Dried Pulses and Beans

Pulses and beans, and that includes lentils and split peas, chickpeas and the entire gamut of hard (as opposed to soft) green beans, might be cheap and convenient in cans but they are more nourishing, much better value and tastier if you cook them from dried. The down side is that most of them need soaking – in some cases overnight – and then lengthy cooking. Soaking for at least 2 hours and as long as overnight gives them an initial rehydration so shortens cooking time. It also helps them cook evenly. As a general rule, cook pulses and beans in plenty of water and don't add salt until they are tender. Red kidney beans, however, *must* be boiled for an initial 10 minutes to destroy toxins. Chuck out that water and start afresh. Red lentils (masar or masoor dhal) need no pre-soaking and cook to a purée within half an hour. Yellow lentils (toover, toor or arhar dhal) also require no pre-soaking but need to be cooked for an hour. The advantage is that they make a thicker, creamier purée. Chickpeas taste better if left overnight once they've been cooked. If possible, use some of the cooking water in whatever you're making; it has bags of flavour.

This is the sort of soup that will change your view about soup making. It is a store cupboard soup, something you can knock up almost as quickly as heating up a can or a carton. Let this be your first attempt at soup making and I predict you will be hooked. Follow with a toasted bacon sandwich. Bliss.

butter bean soup with thyme

method

❶ Peel, halve and finely chop the onion. Pour the oil into a medium-sized saucepan and add the onion. Cook briskly, stirring every so often, for about 6 minutes until the onion is slippery and beginning to colour.

❷ Meanwhile, peel and finely chop the garlic. Peel and chop the potato into small dice, rinse and shake dry.

❸ Stir the garlic into the onion and a couple of minutes later, increase the heat slightly and add the potato. Season with ½ teaspoon of salt and plenty of pepper. Add the thyme and curry powder, stir well and then add the hot stock.

❹ Tip the beans into a colander to drain and rinse with cold water. Shake dry and add to the pan. Bring the soup to the boil, then turn it down so it simmers, half-cover the pan and cook for about 15 minutes until the potato is tender.

❺ Pour the soup into a blender – you will probably have to do this in batches – and blitz until smooth. (If you don't own a blender, *see* page 20.) Pour back into the saucepan, stir in the mustard and lemon juice. Taste and adjust the seasoning with salt and pepper. Serve piping hot.

4 servings
15 minutes preparation
20 minutes cooking

ingredients

1 large onion
2 tbsp cooking oil
2 garlic cloves
1 large potato
salt and black pepper
1 tsp fresh chopped thyme or
    ½ tsp dried thyme
½ tsp curry powder
1 chicken or vegetable stock
    cube dissolved in 600 ml hot
    water
400 g can of butter beans
1 tsp Dijon mustard
squeeze of lemon juice

How to Make Vinaigrette

Get into the habit of making your own vinaigrette. It will taste better and is far cheaper than ready made. It can be kept in a screw-top jar in the fridge for a couple of weeks. Give it a good shake before using. In a bowl dissolve generous pinches of salt and sugar in 2 tablespoons of wine vinegar. Season with black pepper. Stir in 1 tablespoon of Dijon or another mild mustard (this adds flavour and thickens the vinaigrette). Gradually add about 7 tablespoons of vegetable oil or half vegetable oil and half olive oil, whisking constantly with a balloon whisk as you pour. It should end up very thick and glossy. Thin it slightly and help it homogenize by whisking in 1–2 tablespoons of water.

Quick, simple, delicious. Eat it on its own with crusty bread and a few crisp lettuce leaves or with one of the other extras listed at the end of the ingredients. This hearty salad is great to serve with burgers, sausages, chicken or lamb kebabs. It is also good piled into lightly toasted pitta bread pockets with a slice or two of ham or crisp bacon. It will keep, covered in the fridge, for up to a week. Just stir before eating.

bean salad with lemon garlic vinaigrette

method

❶ Tip the two cans of beans into a colander or sieve and rinse thoroughly with cold running water. Shake dry and leave to drip while you prepare everything else.

❷ Trim and finely slice the spring onions including all but the coarsest green stalks (or you could use a red onion: peel, halve it and then chop it very finely). Give the garlic clove a crack with your fist and the skin will flake away. Chop the garlic, sprinkle it with about 1/2 teaspoon of salt and use the flat of a knife to work it to a paste. Split the chilli, discard the stalk and scrape away the seeds with a teaspoon. Chop very finely. (*See* page 21.)

❸ Squeeze the lemon juice into a salad bowl. Add the garlic paste and season with black pepper. Gradually whisk in the olive oil – you want well over half as much oil as lemon juice – continuing to add more until it is thick and creamy.

❹ Pick the leaves from the parsley, coriander or mint and coarsely chop.

❺ Add drained beans, onions, chilli and parsley to the bowl. Season again with salt and pepper and toss thoroughly. Add one or more of the optional extras and toss again.

6–8 servings
15 minutes preparation
no cooking

ingredients

400 g can of haricot beans
400 g can of flageolet beans
bunch of spring onions
1 large clove of garlic
salt and black pepper
1 red chilli
1 large lemon
approx 6 tbsp olive oil
large bunch of flat leaf parsley
   or coriander or mint or
   mixture of two or three
OPTIONAL EXTRAS:
   quartered hard-boiled eggs,
   crumbled crisply grilled
   streaky bacon, chopped
   tomato, strips of ham,
   cooked frozen peas, stoned
   black olives, chopped fresh
   or cooked red peppers

The simplest way to serve this Mexican-inspired

vegetarian dish is to get everything ready and laid out in separate bowls so that people can stuff their own tortillas or pile up their own tostadas. The refried beans will keep, covered, in the fridge for up to a week. As soon as the beans cool, they stiffen up. Moisten with a little warm water to rectify matters.

refried bean fajitas with melted cheese

4 servings

30 minutes preparation

25 minutes cooking

ingredients

1 medium-sized red onion

2 plump garlic cloves

3 tbsp cooking oil

1 plump green chilli (approx 6 cm long)

2 x 400 g cans of red kidney or borlotti beans

¼ vegetable or chicken stock cube dissolved in 150 ml boiling water

1 tbsp tomato concentrate

salt and pepper

2 limes or small lemons

½ small cucumber

4 sticks celery with leaves

1 pack of 8 small wheat tortillas or 12 tostada shells

150 g grated Cheddar

8 tbsp Greek yoghurt

method

❶ Peel and finely chop the onion and garlic.

❷ Heat 2 tablespoons of the oil in a frying pan placed over a medium-low heat and stir in the onion and garlic.

❸ Trim and split the chilli. Discard the seeds and chop finely (*see* page 21). Add half the chilli to the onion and cook until onion and chilli are tender. About 10 minutes in total.

❹ Meanwhile, tip the beans into a sieve and rinse under cold running water. Transfer the drained beans to the bowl of a food processor and add the remaining chopped chilli, the stock and the tomato concentrate. Blitz briefly (or *see* page 20) to make a chunky, brown-red paste. Scrape the paste into the onion and reduce the heat to low. Season generously with salt and pepper and cook, stirring frequently, for 6 to 7 minutes. Taste and adjust the seasoning with salt and a squeeze of lemon or lime juice. Turn off the heat.

❺ Peel the cucumber, split lengthways and use a teaspoon to scrape out the seeds. Slice into half moons. Slice the celery finely and roughly chop any leaves.

❻ If using tortillas, smear a frying pan with a little of the remaining cooking oil and, when very hot, cook the tortillas for 30 seconds a side until puffy and golden.

Spoon a share of hot beans over each tortilla, top with grated Cheddar and celery and cucumber. Spoon over a dollop of yoghurt, sprinkle with coriander, roll up and eat (messily). If using tostadas, which are crisp and won't roll, pile all the ingredients on top of each other. You might like to use a knife and fork. Serve with lemon or lime wedges.

handful of roughly chopped coriander

lemon or lime wedges, to serve

chickpeas

Canned chickpeas, or *garbanzos* as they're called in Spain, are one of the most useful things to keep in the store cupboard. They're endlessly versatile and, like potatoes, are such a good vehicle for other flavours. Think of hummus with its kick of garlic, Indian channa masala with its sour tamarind gravy, and a steaming bowl of cous cous, its vegetable gravy dotted with chickpeas waiting for their dab of fiery harissa. The Spanish are past-masters at getting the best out of this knobbly pulse. It turns up in countless soupy stews, with pork and chorizo sausages, with spinach and tomatoes, and with lamb.

This would go well with a 'garnish' of crusty fried strips of lamb or chicken that have been soaked in lemon juice, crushed garlic and olive oil for half an hour.

moroccan chickpea salad

4 servings

15 minutes preparation plus
30 minutes marinating

15 minutes cooking

ingredients

1 large red onion

4 tbsp olive oil

3 plump garlic cloves

salt and black pepper

1/2 tsp ground cumin

1 tsp curry powder

1 tsp paprika or mild chilli
powder plus an extra pinch

400 g can of chickpeas

1 red pepper

large handful of flat leaf
parsley leaves

juice of 1/2 a large lemon

300 ml Greek-style yoghurt

method

❶ Peel and halve the onion and slice down the halves to make chunky half-moons. Heat a generous tablespoon of olive oil in a frying pan over a medium heat and cook the onion with a pinch of salt until soft and translucent.

❷ Meanwhile, peel the garlic, chop finely and sprinkle with a little salt and crush to a paste with the flat of a knife. When the onions are ready, add half the garlic, the cumin, the curry powder and the paprika or chilli powder. Cook for 1 minute stirring constantly. Using a spatula, scrape everything into a bowl.

❸ Tip the chickpeas into a sieve, rinse under cold running water, shake dry and add to the bowl. Stir well.

❹ Remove stalk, seeds and white filament from the red pepper and chop very finely. Coarsely chop the parsley. Add the pepper, parsley, lemon juice and remaining olive oil to the salad. Season, stir gently and leave to marinate for at least 30 minutes.

❺ Make the yoghurt sauce by mixing together the yoghurt and remaining garlic and season to taste. Stir the salad again and spoon the yoghurt over the salad. Dust the top with a little extra paprika.

In Spain they serve this as a tapas. Try it piled onto toast rubbed with garlic and dribbled with olive oil. Fry a couple of eggs and sit them on top. Alternatively, eat it with boiled rice and a dollop of Greek yoghurt or soured cream, scooped up with toasted pitta bread. This is also good with spicy sausages (merguez, chorizo or pepperoni), boiled new potatoes or nuggets of fried chicken or pork.

chickpeas and spinach

method

❶ Fill a large pan with water and put it on to boil. Pick over the spinach, removing any big thick stalks and any yellowing leaves. Wash thoroughly and shake dry. As soon as the water boils, add salt, then stuff the spinach into the pan and let it boil for a couple of minutes. Drain it and splash it with cold water so that it's cool enough to handle. Leave in a colander to drain.

❷ Meanwhile, peel and finely chop the onion and garlic. Heat the oil in a frying pan over a medium-low heat. Stir in the onion and garlic and cook, stirring every so often, until the onion is tender and beginning to brown in places.

❸ While the onion is cooking, split the red chilli in half, discard the stalk and white seeds and chop very finely. (See page 21.) Tip the chickpeas into a sieve and rinse thoroughly under cold running water.

❹ By now the spinach will be cool enough to squeeze between your hands to get rid of the remaining water. Shred it with a knife.

❺ Stir the cumin into the onion, let it cook for about 30 seconds then add the spinach, chickpeas and chilli or a few drops of Tabasco. Stir everything together, season with salt, pepper and lemon juice. Serve hot, cold or tepid.

4 servings
10 minutes preparation
10 minutes cooking

ingredients

500 g fresh spinach
1 small onion
2 garlic cloves
3 tbsp olive oil
Tabasco or 1 small red chilli
400 g can of chickpeas
1 tsp ground cumin
juice of ½ a lemon
salt and black pepper

A feeding-the-five-thousand kind of recipe. And it's all done in two pans.

pepperoni, pimiento and chickpea lash-up

6–8 servings

15 minutes preparation

20 minutes cooking

ingredients

750 g small new scrubbed
potatoes or big potatoes,
peeled and cut into chunks

2 large onions

3 tbsp cooking oil

2 large garlic cloves

2 x 400 g cans of chickpeas

400 g can of whole red peppers
(pimientos)

100 g pepperoni slices

700 ml bottle of passata

salt and black pepper

OPTIONAL EXTRAS:

large handful of young
spinach leaves, small bunch
of fresh coriander

method

❶ Boil the potatoes in plenty of boiling salted water, test with a sharp knife after about 15 minutes. Drain and keep warm.

❷ Meanwhile, peel, halve and slice the onions into chunky half-moons. Heat the oil in a large saucepan over a medium heat. When hot, stir in the onions. Cook, stirring often, for about 10 minutes until beginning to soften and turn golden.

❸ Meanwhile, peel and chop the garlic. Tip the chickpeas into a sieve or colander and rinse under cold running water. Drain the pimientos, halve lengthways and slice into thick ribbons.

❹ When the onions are ready, add the garlic. Cook for a minute then stir in the pepperoni, heating it through and separating the slices.

❺ Add the rinsed chickpeas, sliced pimientos and passata. Season with salt and pepper. Simmer together for 5 minutes. Add the cooked potatoes and, if using, the roughly chopped spinach and/or coriander. Serve with crusty bread.

The dip. **But remember it too in pitta bread, toasted** sandwiches, or on toast with roast peppers or tomatoes, and salad. Excellent with lamb kebabs. It will keep, covered, in the fridge for about a week.

hummus

method

❶ Peel and chop the garlic. Drain and rinse the chickpeas. Blitz both with the lemon juice, cumin, tahini, if using, and a little water if it seems rather dry. (If you don't own a liquidizer, *see* page 20.)

❷ With the machine still running, gradually add the olive oil. Season with Tabasco, salt and black pepper.

❸ Spoon the mixture into a bowl and serve with lemon wedges to squeeze over the top.

4 servings
10 minutes preparation
no cooking

ingredients

3 garlic cloves
400 g can of chickpeas
juice of 1 lemon
1/2 tsp ground cumin
1 tbsp tahini (optional)
5 tbsp olive oil
Tabasco
1/2 tsp salt, black pepper
lemon wedges, to serve

sweetcorn

Sweetcorn, which we always used to call corn on the cob, is good in omelettes, with pasta (try it with cooked frozen peas, a chopped fried onion and scraps of chilli), in any sort of hash, and is quickly turned into a soup with milk. Remember it for meal-in-a-bowl salads – with bulgar, rice or pasta – and team it with raw or roasted red pepper and hard-boiled egg. Although it has a gentle, undemanding flavour and is ideal comfort food, sweetcorn is very, very good with red hot chilli and other Thai seasonings. It is filling, high in carbohydrate and contains protein, dietary fibre, mineral salts and vitamins A, C and some of the B group.

Fresh Corn on the Cob

At the height of the season – late summer, early autumn – fresh corn on the cob is almost given away. Cook it on a ridged grill pan (without removing the husks if you cook it over barbecue coals) or in plenty of lightly salted water (test a kernel after 10 minutes) and slather with butter. Black pepper and salt are essential. If you want to cut the kernels off the cobs – either before or after cooking – stand the cob on its end and run a sharp knife down the length of the cob, turning as you finish each strip.

Sweetcorn goes well with chilli, coriander and coconut milk, and in this Big Soup, all these flavours come together in Thai-style. The soup is easily turned into a dish to eat with rice by adding chunks of skinned chicken (say 150 g per person) before the coriander is stirred into the soup. Simmer for 10 minutes, then taste and adjust the seasoning. Alternatively, or as well, add boiled small new potatoes, and green beans which you've cut in half and cooked for 2 minutes in vigorously boiling water.

thai-style sweetcorn chowder

4 servings
20 minutes preparation
20 minutes cooking

method

❶ If using a fresh red pepper, pre-heat the grill then proceed to roast it as described on page 27. Once the skin is peeled away, discard seeds and white filament. Chop into small dice.

❷ Meanwhile, keeping separate piles, peel and finely chop the onion, garlic and chilli. (See page 21.)

❸ Pour the cooking oil into a medium-sized pan placed over a medium heat. Cook the onion for about 6 minutes until it begins to brown. Add the garlic followed by the pepper (or pimiento), chilli and bay leaf.

❹ Meanwhile, using a potato peeler or very sharp knife, remove from the length of the lemon three 1 cm wide strips of lemon zest without any white. Drain the sweetcorn.

❺ Place three-quarters of the sweetcorn, the lemon zest, coconut cream, hot stock and 1 teaspoon of salt into the bowl of a food processor (see page 20). Season with pepper and liquidize until smooth. Pour the soup into the saucepan with the remaining sweetcorn. Reheat and add 2 tablespoons of lemon juice. Taste and adjust the seasoning with salt, pepper and Tabasco. Remove the bay leaf, then stir in the coriander and serve.

ingredients

1 large red pepper or 150 g canned or bottled roasted red peppers (pimientos)
1 large onion
1 big garlic clove
1 small red chilli
2 tbsp vegetable oil
1 bay leaf
1 unwaxed lemon
500 g of sweetcorn canned in water
200 ml carton of coconut cream (see page 221)
½ stock cube dissolved in 300 ml boiling water
salt and black pepper
Tabasco to taste
2 tbsp coarsely chopped coriander

Easy, quick and satisfying. It is very good with fried or poached eggs, served with a dusting of cayenne or another hot pepper or a sprinkling of Tabasco.

corn creole

4 servings
15 minutes preparation
15 minutes cooking

ingredients

1 onion

50 g butter

salt and black pepper

1 green pepper

500 g fresh tomatoes or 400 g
    can of Italian peeled
    tomatoes

350 g can of sweetcorn

cayenne pepper or Tabasco

100 g grated Cheddar cheese

method

❶ Peel and finely chop the onion. Over a medium heat, melt the butter in a pan that can hold all the ingredients. Add the onion, season with salt and pepper and cook for about 5 minutes.

❷ Meanwhile, split the pepper, discard the stalk and cut out the white filament and seeds. Rinse under cold running water to remove the last of the seeds. Slice into strips and cut across the strips to make dice. When the 5 minutes is up, add the pepper to the onion. Cook, stirring a couple of times, for a further 5 minutes or so, until the onion and pepper are tender.

❸ While that's going on, coarsely chop the fresh tomatoes or drained canned tomatoes. Tip the sweetcorn into a sieve to drain.

❹ Add the tomatoes to the pan, cook for 5 minutes and then add the sweetcorn. Season with salt, pepper and cayenne or Tabasco. Heat through, stir in the cheese, continue stirring until it is melted. Serve in bowls with a doorstep of very fresh white bread thickly spread with butter.

For a quick fix, serve this rolled up in a hot tortilla or pitta bread envelope. It is also good with rice, and an excellent addition to a vegetarian curry blow out, or as a side dish with any of the chicken or meat curries in the book.

spicy cauliflower and sweetcorn

method

2–4 servings
15 minutes preparation
20 minutes cooking

1 Half-fill with water a pan that can hold the cauliflower cut into florets and put on to boil. Trim away any leaves encasing the cauliflower, cut it in half and cut out the central stem. Divide the cauliflower into bite-size florets. Add 1 teaspoon of salt and the florets to the boiling water. Cover the pan and boil – you may need to adjust the heat – for 5 minutes or until the florets are half cooked. Drain.

2 Meanwhile, peel, halve and finely chop the onion. Heat the oil in a large frying pan and fry the onion over a medium heat until tender and beginning to brown.

3 While the onion is cooking, peel and finely chop the garlic and ginger. Sprinkle with ½ teaspoon of salt and pulverize with the flat of a knife to make a juicy paste. Trim, de-seed and finely chop the chillies (see page 21).

4 Add the garlic and ginger paste and chopped chillies to the onions and cook for a couple of minutes before adding the cumin and ground coriander. Cook for a further 5 minutes, stirring every now and again, and then add the sweetcorn. Cook, stirring often, for 2 minutes.

5 Meanwhile, chop the tomatoes. Add tomatoes, cauliflower florets and ½ teaspoon of salt and cook for 5 minutes, stirring every so often, while you beat the yoghurt until smooth. Stir it into the pan and simmer for 3–4 minutes until you have a rich, creamy-looking sauce. Taste and adjust the seasoning and sprinkle with the chopped coriander before serving.

ingredients

1 small cauliflower
salt
1 onion
2 tbsp cooking oil
1 plump clove of garlic
2½ cm piece fresh ginger
2 green or red chillies
1 tsp ground cumin
2 tsp ground coriander
**200 g canned or frozen sweet-
corn**
2 tomatoes
**3 heaped tbsp Greek-style
yoghurt**
**2 tbsp chopped coriander
leaves**

The best way to eat these fritters is straight from the pan.
They don't take long to cook but are even quicker to eat. Take it in turns to
cook or make omelette-size 'fritters'. Cut them into wedges and share them
round. They are very good with crisp rashers of bacon. In the States, this
combo would be served with maple syrup. Alternatively, you *could* keep
them warm in the oven to serve with, say, an already cooked roast chicken.

sweetcorn fritters

20–25 small fritters,
   12–15 big ones
15 minutes preparation
5 minutes cooking

ingredients

50 g flour
2 eggs, separated
150 ml milk
340 g can of sweetcorn
handful of coriander leaves
   (optional)
plump red chilli, approx 5 cm
   long (optional)
salt and black pepper
vegetable oil for frying

method

❶ Sift the flour into a mixing bowl. Add the egg yolks,
putting the whites into a separate mixing bowl or the bowl
of a blender with a whisk attachment. Use a wooden
spoon to stir the yolks into the flour, whilst gradually
adding the milk. Replace the spoon with a whisk and
whisk vigorously until the batter is smooth and has the
consistency of thick cream.

❷ Tip the sweetcorn into a sieve or colander and give it a
good shake to drain.

❸ If including coriander and chilli, coarsely chop the
coriander leaves. Split the chilli, scrape away the seeds
and remove the stalk. Slice into skinny strips then cut
across the strips to make tiny dice. (*See* page 21.)

❹ Stir sweetcorn, coriander and chilli into the batter.
Season with 1/2 teaspoon of salt and a generous
seasoning of pepper.

❺ Whisk the egg whites until they hold firm but not stiff
peaks. Fold into the batter until amalgamated.

❻ Heat a frying pan over a medium heat, swirl a little oil
round the pan and drop spoonfuls of batter into the pan.
Don't crowd the pan; you should be able to fit about 3 big
fritters or 5 or 6 small ones. Cook for 2–3 minutes until you
see little bubbles appearing in the fritters and when you lift
an edge you can see that the bottom is brown and the

fritter is beginning to set. Using a fish slice or blunt knife, quickly flip the fritter over and cook for a further 1–2 minutes. Eat immediately or keep warm in a single layer in a very low oven.

tuna

Tuna belongs to the same family as mackerel, sardines and sprats. Fresh tuna, unlike mackerel and the rest of the family, is stunningly expensive to buy fresh but a bargain in cans. Whether you buy it preserved in oil or in brine (which should be drained), it is very good flaked and stirred into a bowl of hot pasta or white beans (which have been rinsed and drained first), particularly if you add a few cooked frozen peas, too. It goes well with chilli and coriander, and acidic things like pickled cucumber (chopped in chunks) and capers. Try big chunks of it in a sandwich made with thin slices of cucumber and plenty of mayonnaise.

Inspired by the tuna and caper sauce which Italians serve with thin slices of cold roast veal (vitello tonnato), this is an excellent quick sauce with lots of uses. Try it stirred into hot rice, or spooned over hard-boiled eggs with sprigs of watercress and hot rice. Another idea is to serve it with a mound of lightly cooked green beans and new potatoes, or try it spooned over crustily fried chicken.

tonnato sauce

4–6 servings

5 minutes preparation

no cooking

ingredients

200 g can of tuna in oil

4 heaped tbsp mayonnaise

juice of 1 lemon

splash of Tabasco (optional)

salt and black pepper

50 ml sunflower oil

2 tbsp capers

method

❶ Place the tuna, 2 tablespoons of its oil, the mayonnaise (Hellmann's is best), juice of half the lemon, a few drops of Tabasco and a pinch of salt and pepper in a liquidizer. Blitz until smooth. (If you don't own a liquidizer, *see* page 20.)

❷ With the motor running, add the oil in a slow trickle until the mixture is thick yet pourable like salad cream. Taste and adjust the seasoning and thickness with extra lemon juice, oil (in a trickle), salt and pepper. Transfer to a bowl and stir in the capers which you have squeezed lightly to remove some of the juice.

Canned tuna is not the obvious choice for fish cakes but these have a surprisingly creamy and interesting flavour and a gorgeous crisp shell. Remember them when you have leftover mashed potato to use up.

tuna fish cakes

method

❶ If using fresh potatoes, peel and cut them into even-sized chunks. Rinse, then cook in salted boiling water until just tender. Make a stiff mash with butter and milk. Set aside to cool.

❷ Trim the spring onions and slice, including the green, very finely. Place them, together with the egg yolk/s, in a mixing bowl. Season generously with salt and pepper.

❸ Tip the tuna into a sieve and shake thoroughly to get rid of the brine. Break up the fish with a fork and add to the bowl.

❹ Squeeze the juice out of the capers and roughly chop. Add capers, parsley and mustard to the bowl. Add the cooled or leftover potato. Stir everything together very thoroughly. The mixture should be soft but cohesive.

❺ Form into 8 balls and flatten between your hands to make flat tops and straight sides. Lay out on a plate. If you chill the fishcakes for about 30 minutes, they will firm up and be easier to cook. Turn each one carefully in a little flour.

❻ Heat the oil in a frying pan over a medium heat. Cook the fish cakes in batches so they aren't crowded in the pan, reducing the heat slightly once the cakes are in the pan. Fry for 4–5 minutes on each side until golden brown and well crusted.

2–3 servings
15 minutes preparation
30 minutes cooking

ingredients

250 g leftover mashed potato
   or 4 medium-sized potatoes,
   a knob of butter and 2–3
   tbsp milk
6 spring onions
1 large egg yolk or 2 small
salt and black pepper
200 g can of tuna in brine
1 heaped tbsp capers
2 tbsp finely chopped flat leaf
   parsley
2 heaped tsp smooth Dijon
   mustard
2–3 tbsp flour
3–4 tbsp cooking oil

An any-time salad. Quick, simple and delicious. Eat with
bread and butter.

tuna and butter bean salad

2 servings

15 minutes preparation

no cooking

ingredients

400 g can of butter beans

185 g can of tuna in oil or brine

salt and black pepper

1 medium-sized tomato

1 tbsp capers

small bunch of parsley,
    preferably flat leaf

1 Little Gem lettuce heart

FOR THE VINAIGRETTE

1 medium-sized shallot or 4
    spring onions and 1 garlic
    clove

pinch of sugar

salt and black pepper

1 scant tbsp red wine vinegar

1 tsp Dijon mustard

4 tbsp olive oil or vegetable oil

method

❶ Tip the butter beans into a sieve or colander and rinse
thoroughly. Shake dry and tip into a mixing bowl.

❷ Drain the tuna and break it into chunks over the beans.
Season with black pepper and a little salt.

❸ Chop the tomato into quite small pieces. Give the
capers a good squeeze to get rid of most of their liquid.

❹ Pick the leaves from the parsley and chop coarsely: you
want a couple of tablespoonfuls. Add tomato, capers and
most of the parsley to the bowl. Shred the lettuce, rinse
and shake dry.

❺ Now make the vinaigrette. Peel and finely dice the
shallot. If using spring onions and garlic, trim the spring
onion and finely slice the white part. Peel and finely chop
the garlic. Dissolve the sugar and salt in the vinegar.
Season generously with black pepper, stir in the mustard
and then the shallot or onion and garlic. Vigorously beat in
the oil, added in a trickle. Pour the vinaigrette over the
bean mixture and toss well.

❻ Place the shredded lettuce in the bottom of a salad
bowl or on two plates, spoon the beans and tuna over the
top and garnish with the reserved parsley.

anchovies

I know what you're going to say. You don't like anchovies. They're
hairy (the tiny bones), very salty and expensive for what you get.
But, a little anchovy goes a long way and its flavour is both
powerful and addictive. It has an ability to accentuate other
flavours. A dish of pasta, for example, or potatoes, or, come to
that, toast, come to life with a hint of anchovy.

Pa amb tomaquet, which is the real name, is the secret to
tapas excellence. Make it with good crusty bread, good oil and a nice ripe
tomato. Like pizza, you can ring the changes with whatever you have to
hand – roasted red pepper, salami, ham, black olives, hard-boiled egg.

catalan tomato bread with anchovy

method

1 Split the ciabatta lengthways and cut in half to make 4
pieces. Grill the bread lightly on both sides. Coarsely chop
the anchovy fillets and mash them with a fork with a little
of their oil.

2 Cut the tomatoes in half crosswise and peel the garlic.
Rub the cut side of the toast lightly with garlic and then
vigorously with tomato, squeezing gently as you do, until
you are left only with the skin. Douse with olive oil and
smear with the anchovy paste. Eat immediately.

2 servings
10 minutes preparation
10 minutes cooking

ingredients

1 ciabatta loaf
4 anchovy fillets in oil
2 very ripe squashy tomatoes
1 plump garlic clove
3 tbsp extra-virgin olive oil

Bigoli is the name of a stubby wholewheat pasta with a fine hole running through it. The purpose of this little hole is to trap some of the dish's delicious sauce. You get a similar effect with quick-cook whole-wheat spaghetti which also has a hole running through the middle. The sauce is very easy to make and involves gently softening some sliced onions and mixing them with pounded anchovy and a generous slug of olive oil. The intensely savoury and piquantly salted slippery onions are mixed into the cooked pasta and tossed together so that every strand of pasta is coated. You will be surprised at how delicious this tastes.

bigoli with anchovy and onion

2 servings
15 minutes preparation
20 minutes cooking

ingredients

200 g bigoli or thick
  wholewheat spaghetti or
  another wholewheat pasta
1 large onion
6 tbsp olive oil
50 g anchovy fillets in oil
salt and black pepper

method

❶ Bring a large pan of salted water to the boil. Add salt but sparingly since anchovies are very salty. Now cook the pasta according to the instructions on the packet.

NB: A bit of judicious timing is necessary for this simple dish because you want the cooking of the onions – which need about 15 minutes to get them to the right state – to coincide more or less exactly with the cooking of the pasta. There are few things worse than overcooked wholewheat pasta.

❷ Peel and halve the onion through the root. Slice as finely as possible. Heat 2 tablespoons of the olive oil in a medium-sized, heavy-bottomed saucepan and stir in the onions. Cook them over a medium-low heat, tossing them around so they cook gently and evenly until transparent and beginning to flop but not brown. Allow 15 minutes for this.

❸ Meanwhile, chop the anchovy fillets and use a pestle and mortar, or the back of a wooden spoon, to pound them into a paste. Add the anchovy paste to the onions and cook gently for a couple of minutes, stirring the mixture constantly. Add the remaining olive oil to make a homogeneous sauce and season generously with black pepper.

❹ Drain the pasta, reserving a couple of tablespoons of the cooking water. Return the pasta and reserved water to the cooking pan. Toss together then stir in the sauce, mixing it thoroughly so that each strand of pasta is coated. Eat immediately.

This is the Swedish equivalent of macaroni cheese. Jansson, incidentally, was an opera singer, as famous for his singing as he was for his suppers and flirtations. This peasant-style casserole was his speciality. Leftovers, if there are any, are very good cold.

jansson's temptation

6 servings

20 minutes preparation

60 minutes cooking

ingredients

3 very large onions

2 x 50 g tins of anchovy fillets in oil

50 g butter

2 slices stale bread

1 kg potatoes (a waxy variety like Charlotte is best but any will do)

black pepper

300 ml double cream (or half double and half single)

method

❶ Pre-heat the oven to 425°F/220°C/gas mark 7.

❷ Peel, halve and slice the onions very, very thinly: this is important. Drain the anchovies and split lengthways. Use half the butter to liberally grease a large gratin dish or deep casserole.

❸ Cut the crusts off the bread, tear it into pieces and blitz in the food processor to make breadcrumbs. (If you don't own a food processor, crumble the bread very finely by hand.) Peel the potatoes and grate them (they should *not* be rinsed; the starch adds texture and holds the dish together), working quickly because they will discolour.

❹ Depending on which dish you are using, make one or two layers beginning with potato, followed by a lattice of anchovy, onions and potatoes. Season each layer lightly with black pepper. When you've finished, press the mixture down firmly and smooth the surface.

❺ Heat the cream and when it has reached boiling point pour it over the dish: the potatoes should be glimpsed, not smothered.

❻ Season again with black pepper, sprinkle over the breadcrumbs, dot with the remaining butter and bake for 20 minutes. Lower the heat to 400°F/200°C/gas mark 6 and cook for a further 30 minutes.

It is difficult to convey just how wonderful this dish tastes.
It looks marvellous, the tiny scraps of red chilli being caught up in the 'hair'
of broccoli florets, and the smell of the sauce as it is being prepared is
guaranteed to kick-start even the most jaded of palates. Quite why anchovy
goes so well with broccoli is mysterious but the salty intensity of the fish
brings out the best in this cabbagey vegetable. To expand this dish to feed
two or three, tip the whole lot into 200 g of cooked pasta which you've
tossed with a little olive oil.

broccoli with chilli and anchovy dressing

method

1 Bring a large pan of water to the boil. Add 1 teaspoon of salt.

2 Meanwhile, use a small sharp knife to cut all the broccoli florets off the main stalk. Divide the stalk into sections – depending on its thickness, it may need splitting – that will cook at the same rate as the florets. Drop the broccoli into the boiling water and cook until tender, allowing about 5 minutes for this. Drain, reserving 1 tablespoon of cooking water.

3 Peel the garlic and roughly chop. Chop the anchovy fillets. Trim and split the chilli, discarding the seeds. Slice the chilli in thin batons then chop into tiny dice. (*See* page 21.)

4 Make the dressing by pounding the garlic with a little salt to make a juicy paste. Incorporate the anchovy, pounding it with the lemon juice and hot broccoli water. Whisk in the olive oil to end up with a thick vinaigrette. Stir in the chilli and season with black pepper.

5 Tip the broccoli into a warm bowl and pour over the dressing. Toss thoroughly and eat immediately.

1 serving
15 minutes preparation
15 minutes cooking

ingredients

1 flourishing head of broccoli
1 big garlic clove
4 anchovy fillets in oil
1 red chilli
1 tbsp lemon juice
2 tbsp olive oil
salt and black pepper

frozen peas

Okay. You've spotted the deliberate mistake. Frozen peas don't come in cans. My theory is that frozen peas fall into the same category as all the cans in this chapter. We buy them, shove them in the freezer part of the fridge and forget about them until there's no fresh veg in the house. But think on. They have many uses.

It's hard to believe that something so delicious can be made so quickly and easily out of such mundane ingredients.

minted pea soup

4 servings
10 minutes preparation
10 minutes cooking

ingredients
1 small onion
500 g frozen minted peas
    or ordinary peas and 1 tsp
    mint sauce
1 chicken or vegetable stock
    cube dissolved in 600 ml
    boiling water
salt and black pepper
squeeze of lemon juice
4 drops of Tabasco
2 tbsp Greek yoghurt

method
❶ Peel and finely chop the onion. Place in a lidded pan with the peas and hot stock. Season lightly with salt and generously with pepper. Bring to the boil, establish a steady simmer, cover the pan and leave to cook for about 8 minutes until the peas are quite tender.

❷ Tip the pan's contents into the bowl of a food processor or liquidizer and blitz at high speed for a couple of minutes until smooth but still with some texture. (*See* page 20.)

❸ Pour the soup back into the saucepan, using a spatula to scape down the sides, and reheat. Taste and adjust the seasoning with salt, pepper, lemon juice and Tabasco. Spoon the yoghurt, if using, into the soup and stir a couple of times.

This is a simplified adaptation of a very fine, yet simple, early summer Venetian dish that is made with fresh peas and super-fine spaghetti called spaghettini.

spaghetti with buttered peas

method

1 Put a large pan of water on to boil. Add salt and the spaghetti and cook according to the packet's instructions until just tender (or *al dente* as they say in Italy). Drain the spaghetti, reserving about 3 tablespoons of cooking water. Cover the pan to keep the pasta warm.

2 While the spaghetti is cooking, peel, halve and finely chop the onion.

3 Melt the butter slowly in a medium-sized pan over a low heat and add the onion. Cook for 5 or 6 minutes until the onion is tender. Add the peas, a generous seasoning of salt and the reserved spaghetti cooking-water. Simmer, uncovered, for 5 or 6 minutes until the peas are cooked.

4 Divide the spaghetti between two deep soup plates, spoon the peas into the middle, add a knob of butter and, if you like, dust generously with freshly grated Parmesan. Eat.

2 servings
5 minutes preparation
15 minutes cooking

ingredients

200 g spaghetti
salt
1 medium-sized onion
50 g butter plus an extra knob
250 g frozen peas or petit pois
    with or without mint
freshly grated Parmesan
    (optional)

This pea purée is addictive. It goes well with simply
cooked white fish but is delicious with hard-boiled eggs, chicken or lamb
kebabs, or a few rashers of very crisp bacon.

pea dhal with white fish

4 servings

20 minutes preparation

20 minutes cooking

ingredients

250 g potatoes

1 onion

4 rashers of streaky bacon

50 g butter

250 g frozen minted peas

½ chicken stock cube
dissolved in 150 ml boiling
water

1 sprig fresh thyme or generous
pinch dried

salt and pepper

3 tbsp single cream, or natural
yoghurt or milk

400 g lemon sole fillets

flour, seasoned, for coating

lemon wedges, to serve

method

❶ First make the pea purée. Peel, dice and rinse the
potatoes. Peel and chop the onion. Slice the bacon into
skinny strips.

❷ Place half the butter in a medium-sized pan and stir in
the onion and bacon. Cook, stirring often, until the onion is
soft and golden and the bacon cooked. Add the peas, hot
stock, potato, thyme, a generous seasoning of salt and
pepper, and bring up to the boil. Simmer, half covered,
until the potato is tender.

❸ Purée the pea mixture in a blender (or see page 20) and
then stir in the cream, yoghurt or milk. Re-heat when
needed, stirring in a knob of the remaining butter. Taste
and adjust the seasoning.

❹ Just before you're ready to eat, dust the sole fillets with
flour. Melt the remaining butter in a frying pan and heat
until it foams. Fry the fillets in the hot butter for 1–2
minutes per side, until barely cooked.

❺ Divide the pea purée between the four plates and
arrange the sole fillets on top. Serve immediately with the
lemon wedges.

2. sandwiches and things on toast

It is very easy, particularly if you live on your own or are lazy about food, to more or less live on bread. Or, let's get it right, to live on toast. When I first had to fend for myself, my flat mates and I progressed from toast and Marmite (with toast and honey for 'pudding'), to baked beans on toast with badly cooked fried eggs and very fatty bacon toasted sarnies. I'm still addicted to toast.

These days I think more about the bread I buy and regard toast as an edible plate. I crush all manner of food such as cous cous and hummus or falafel, salad and Greek yoghurt into hot pitta bread envelopes. I make instant sweet and savoury 'pizzas' with toasted tortilla. I have adopted the Italian habit and now tend to go in the bruschetta direction (toast rubbed with raw garlic and dribbled with olive oil) or take the Spanish tapas route of pa amb tomaquet (rubbing garlicky toast with a very ripe tomato: see page 51). This delicious toast is then loaded up with everything (it's a great way of using up leftovers) from roasted red peppers and black olives to grilled mackerel.

It would be a great shame, however, if, in the midst of our honeymoon with other European food, we forgot our own heritage of 'something on toast'. Fashionable though bruschetta may be – and I don't want to get into a debate about the advantages of olive oil and a rub of garlic, against butter; or sourdough against sliced white – I just want to say a word in praise of the good old British savoury. I mean delicacies such as Welsh rabbit (or rarebit, as some people call it) and devilled herring roes on toast. In my book, these can be every bit as good as a River Café pugliese toastie. They are also quick, delicious and inexpensive.

Quite often you have to have a little fiddle with processed food to give it the necessary umph. We all do it, adding a handful of fresh herbs here and an extra grating of cheese there. Take baked beans. If you let them simmer gently for about 8 minutes until their juices thicken, and season them with plenty of freshly ground black pepper, a good shake of Tabasco, and perhaps a squeeze of lemon and pinch of celery salt too, they are far more delicious. I particularly like them on toasted, buttered muffins, rather than ordinary toast, because the dense, almost chewy texture of the dough with its strange not-quite crust, doesn't go soggy so quickly. With some very crisp rashers of bacon, some Cheddar grated over the top, and a poached egg, baked beans become the ultimate convenience supper.

But Heinz aren't the only canned beans and a white slice isn't the only bread. Cannellini beans, which is what you need for this recipe, look like naked baked beans and the lack of a sweet tomato sauce makes them a very versatile ingredient. Tortilla, which is the bread element in this recipe, is another handy thing to keep stashed next to your collection of canned beans. The opened packet keeps in the fridge for several days – the end tucked in so the bread doesn't dry out. An unopened packet keeps for ages in the store cupboard.

beans on toast

2 servings

15 minutes preparation

20 minutes cooking

ingredients

400 g can of cannellini beans

1 small red onion

1 small, slim aubergine

2 garlic cloves

handful of young spinach leaves

method

❶ Tip the beans into a sieve and rinse thoroughly with cold water. Shake dry.

❷ Peel and finely chop the onion. Trim the aubergine, quarter lengthways and chop in small kebab-sized chunks. Peel the garlic and finely chop. Shred the spinach.

❸ Place a medium-sized pan over a medium heat with 2 tablespoons of the oil and chopped onion. Stir as the onion softens. After 5 minutes stir in the garlic and as soon as you can smell it cooking, add the chopped aubergine, stirring constantly so that all the pieces get some of the oil. Season with salt, pepper and the thyme. Cook, stirring frequently for 6 or 7 minutes until the aubergine is tender. Add the passata or crushed tomatoes and simmer steadily for 5 minutes to thicken. Add the beans and re-heat. Taste and adjust the seasoning. Stir in the spinach and turn off the heat.

❹ Heat a frying pan. Add ½ tablespoon of the remaining oil and quickly fry the tortillas, one after the other (adding more oil), for about 30 seconds a side, until they puff slightly and crisp up. Transfer to two warmed plates.

❺ Add the last of the oil to the hot frying pan and fry the eggs.

❻ Divide the beans between the two tortillas. Cover with the grated Cheddar and place an egg on top of each tortilla. If liked, sprinkle a thin line of paprika, cayenne or Tabasco down the yolk and garnish with a few coriander leaves.

3 tbsp cooking oil

salt and black pepper

½ tsp thyme leaves or generous pinch of dried thyme

200 ml passata or 400 g can of Italian peeled tomatoes

2 tortilla

2 fresh eggs

50 g grated Cheddar

OPTIONAL EXTRAS

pinch paprika or cayenne pepper or dribble of Tabasco; a few coriander leaves

Most supermarkets sell very cheap but unattractively named 'economy mushrooms'. A 750 g pack could be the basis of several delicious meals, and mushrooms on toast is head of the list for quick suppers. They need nothing more than to be wiped, sliced, quartered or chopped, and then fried in butter. If there is garlic around, or parsley and lemon, preferably all three, then the mushrooms will be extra good.

This is the deluxe version with a full complement of flavour enhancers. Serve it as it is or with a few bitter salad leaves, such as watercress and frisée. A softly boiled or poached egg makes more of a meal of it.

mushrooms on toast

2 servings
10 minutes preparation
10 minutes cooking

ingredients

4 rashers rindless streaky
    bacon
bunch of spring onions
250 g (or more) small or
    medium-sized mushrooms or
    4 large flat mushrooms or a
    mixture of wild mushrooms
small bunch of flat leaf parsley
1 big garlic clove
large knob of butter
½ tbsp cooking oil
salt and black pepper
2 thick slices of country-style
    bread
50 g Philadelphia-type cream
    cheese (optional)
lemon juice

method

❶ Slice across the bacon rashers, cutting them into thin strips.

❷ Trim the spring onions, discarding only the toughest dark green. Slice thinly. Wipe away any dirt clinging to the mushrooms. Leave small mushrooms whole, quarter medium-sized mushrooms and slice large ones.

❸ Pick the leaves off the parsley stalks and coarsely chop – you want 2–3 tablespoons. Halve the garlic but don't bother to peel it.

❹ Melt the butter and oil in a large frying pan over a high heat. Add the bacon and toss around until beginning to crisp. Add the onions, reduce the heat slightly and, after a couple of minutes, add the mushrooms. Toss around for a few minutes until coloured all over. Season with salt and pepper and reduce the heat to low.

❺ When the mushrooms are just ready, toast the bread. Rub one side with the cut garlic. Spread thickly with cheese (if using) and place on a warmed plate. Squeeze lemon juice over the mushrooms, toss, add parsley, toss again and pile onto the toast. Eat.

Buck, as in rabbit, and I don't mean the furry variety. I'm talking here about posh cheese on toast, the dish that is often called by its gentrified name of Welsh rarebit. Think of the cheesy mixture as being like fondue, but instead of the Kirsch, garlic and white wine of a fondue, a rabbit has ale, mustard and Worcestershire sauce. Both are cooked in much the same way, by melting everything together and serving it piping hot while the rabbit is still on the move. The British version includes Cheddar, ale and cayenne, although milk could replace the ale. A Swiss version combines egg, cream, nutmeg and breadcrumbs with Gruyère. The full monty with a poached egg on top is called buck rabbit. This version of buck rabbit uses a ridiculously small amount of stout – the rest is for the cook. Good with salad.

golden buck salad

method

1 Grate the cheese and set aside

2 Place the butter, mustard, Worcestershire sauce, Tabasco and 2 tablespoons of stout or Guinness in a small pan and heat through. Add the grated cheese, stirring as it melts, but don't let the mixture boil. Remove the pan from the heat and leave to cool to room temperature. Then beat in the two egg yolks.

3 Pre-heat the grill. Toast the bread on one side. Leave the grill on.

4 Spread the untoasted side thickly with the cheesy mixture and lay out on the grill pan (laying out a sheet of kitchen foil first might be a wise precaution). Cook for a few minutes until blistered and bubbling. Dust with cayenne and eat.

2 servings
15 minutes preparation
10 minutes cooking

ingredients

75 g mature Cheddar or
**   Lancashire cheese**
25 g butter
1 flat tsp made English mustard
2 shakes Worcestershire sauce
2 shakes Tabasco
1 can of stout or Guinness
2 egg yolks
2 large, thick slices of bread
cayenne pepper

If you don't possess a toasted sandwich maker – and to the Wolf they are (almost) worth their weight in gold, *see* page 19 – this is how to make a deluxe cheese and ham toasted sandwich. It is unbelievably good; very filling, very rich and definitely worth the extra trouble of making a thick cheese sauce to serve with the sandwiches.

Make croque monsieur for a good friend and serve the sandwiches with a handsome bunch of watercress or a punnet of cherry tomatoes; both these make a superb sandwich look especially mouth-watering. The point about using Gruyère, incidentally, is that it goes molten-stringy in a deliciously voluptuous kind of way. However, Cheddar or another hard cheese will still taste good.

croque monsieur

2 generous snack servings

10 minutes preparation

10 minutes cooking

ingredients

100 g Gruyère cheese

150 ml double cream or Greek-
style strained yoghurt such
as Total

salt and black pepper

8–10 thin slices of white bread,
not too fresh

100 g thinly sliced ham

75 g butter

1 tbsp cooking oil

FOR THE CHEESE SAUCE

1 tbsp butter

1 tbsp flour

200 ml milk

method

❶ Grate the cheese on the small hole of the cheese grater. Put 2 tablespoons of it aside and mix the rest with enough cream or yoghurt to make a thick paste; leftover cream or yoghurt will go into the sauce. Season with salt and pepper.

❷ Cut the crusts off the bread and spread each slice with the paste. Put a slice of ham trimmed to fit on half the slices and close the sandwiches. Press together and cut each one in half diagonally.

❸ Next make the sauce by melting the butter in a small saucepan. Stir in the flour until smooth and then gradually add the milk whilst stirring constantly to avoid lumps. Bring to the boil, turn down the heat immediately and cook at a gentle simmer for several minutes. Season with salt and pepper and stir in the reserved cream or yoghurt, the mustard, if using, and the set-aside cheese. Cook until melted and smooth.

❹ To cook the sandwiches, heat half the butter and oil

until it is very hot. Fry half the sandwiches for a couple of minutes per side until crisp and golden. Drain on absorbent kitchen paper. Heat the rest of the butter and oil and fry the remaining sandwiches.

❺ Serve the sandwiches with a knife and fork, with the sauce in a jug.

salt and black pepper
1 tbsp smooth Dijon mustard
(optional)

tortilla toast

This is an idea rather than a recipe. Heat a frying pan. Swirl a little oil round the base and when very hot, add a tortilla. Let it puff, which it will do in places, then after about 30 seconds flip it over – it will be partially scorched brown – and repeat on the other side. This is the perfect base for making a delicious instant snack. Think layers of flavour. Something creamy such as hummus, tzatziki, raita or Greek yoghurt, a crunchy salad of tomatoes and cucumber and crisp lettuce or cous cous, and a topping of grated Cheddar cheese or egg (fried or hard-boiled and then chopped) and a sprinkling of chopped mint or parsley if you have it.

According to my local fishmonger, the season for herring roes is immaterial because they are frozen at sea and remain frozen until they emerge from the fishmonger's deep freeze and, for no particular reason, occasionally appear on the slab. It is springtime, during May, when you're likely to find big fresh herring for sale with their roes intact and, says my fishmonger, lots of them come from Canada. Soft herring roes, and the more grainy ones, too, are a treat we are in danger of forgetting. On the fishmonger's slab, they don't look particularly appetizing, and lie in their dish like large plump headless cream-coloured grubs. But powdered with cayenne-seasoned flour, they fry up beautifully. A crusty layer is essential and sets off their incredible creaminess and subtly strong flavour. The cayenne is important, too, adding a welcome piquancy, and they need plenty of salt and lashings of fresh lemon juice. The bread you choose to serve them on is important as well. Ideally, you want one with a dense crumb. The devil in the title, by the way, refers to the cayenne.

devilled herring roes on toast

2 servings
5 minutes preparation
5 minutes cooking

ingredients
500 g soft herring roes
3 tbsp flour
salt, cayenne and black pepper
1 tbsp cooking oil
1 lemon
4 slices densely textured brown
   bread
large knob of butter

method
❶ Trim away any dark sinews from the roes and lay out on a double thickness of absorbent kitchen paper. Pat dry thoroughly.

❷ Sift the flour onto a large plate or suitable surface. Season with salt, cayenne and black pepper. Roll each roe in the flour and shake off any excess.

❸ Heat the tablespoon of oil in a (preferably non-stick) frying pan and when it's obviously hot, add the roes in a single layer. They will instantly shrink and splutter, turn down the heat slightly but leave them to cook for 60 seconds without moving them. The objective of this initial very hot cooking is to get a nice crusty outer layer with sufficient heat almost to cook the roes inside.

❹ Use two forks or tongs to turn the roes and leave to

cook for a further 60 seconds, adjusting the heat so that they crisp without browning. Re-turn any roes that don't seem sufficiently cooked and cook for a further 60 seconds in total, or until firm and cooked through.

❺ Quarter the lemon – lengthways looks nicer. Toast the bread and butter generously while hot. To serve, load the roes onto the buttered toast and serve with lemon quarters; they need plenty of lemon juice, salt and pepper.

Regard this as more of a suggestion or a reminder than a recipe; you hardly need someone to tell you how to put together sardines on toast. Look out for sardines in olive oil. They cost a few pence more than those canned in other oils but are far better. They can be turned into a delicious pâté if you purée the fillets (split them first and remove the backbone) with a squeeze of lemon, a knob of warmed butter and plenty of black pepper. If you want to be posh, chill the pâté covered with a layer of melted butter and serve it with hot buttered wholemeal toast.

sardines on toast

1 serving
5 minutes preparation
2 minutes cooking

ingredients

120 g tin of sardines in olive oil
1–2 thick slices of wholemeal
    bread
butter
black pepper
½ lemon

OPTIONAL EXTRAS
    smooth Dijon mustard, 1 ripe
    tomato

method

❶ You usually get 3 plump sardines in a 120-g tin. Lift them out of the oil onto a plate and open them out like a book, then remove the backbone.

❷ Toast the bread, spread generously with butter and nudge the sardine fillets, cut side up, close to each other on the toast, breaking them up slightly with the back of a fork. Season generously with black pepper, squeeze over some lemon juice and dribble with a little of the olive oil from the can. Best eaten with a knife and fork.

❸ Alternatively, spread the buttered toast with a smear of mustard and/or cover with slices of tomato before you lay out the sardines etc.

The thing about garlic bread is that everybody loves it. It is great on its own, it will turn a salad or a bowl of soup into something special and it is wonderful with lamb kebabs, with hash (see page 166) or chili con carne (see page 192). This recipe uses a whole packet of butter but makes enough garlic butter for 3 French sticks or 4 ciabatta. If you only want to make one garlic loaf, then just scale down the quantities. Leftover butter (and cooked loaves) can be frozen. The garlic butter has many other delicious uses. Try it smeared on a pizza base hot from the oven – the sort sold in packs of three which are stiff enough to use as a frisbee – on baked potatoes and barbecued meat.

garlic bread

method

❶ Pre-heat the oven to 400°F/200°C/gas mark 6. Place the coriander or parsley in the bowl of a food processor. Blitz until finely chopped. Alternatively, chop by hand.

❷ Melt the butter in a suitable pan, add the garlic and cook over a low heat for 45 seconds. Season with salt and pepper. Stir in the coriander or parsley.

❸ Using a sharp knife, make diagonal incisions about 3 cm apart, as if you were slicing the loaf but without cutting right through. Take 3 or 4 sheets of tinfoil large enough to parcel each loaf separately. Place a loaf in the middle of each sheet. Spoon the garlic butter between the slices, encouraging it to soak into the bread, pour leftovers over the top of the loaves. Close up the parcels, tucking in the ends carefully to avoid leakage.

❹ Bake in the middle of the oven for 10 minutes. To achieve a crusted top, open the foil and bake for a further 5 minutes. Close the parcel again to keep the loaves warm.

6–10 servings
30 minutes preparation
15 minutes cooking

ingredients

50 g coriander or flat leaf parsley leaves
225 g butter
6 big garlic cloves, peeled and finely chopped
salt and black pepper
3 baguettes or 4 ciabatta
you will also need tinfoil

I prefer sirloin, rump or skirt (sometimes called feather steak, known as *onglet* in France, and only available from a proper butcher) for a steak sandwich. Not only do these cuts have more flavour, but they offer a good chew and thus provide essential textural contrast. To make it easier to eat, I like the meat carved into slices before it's loaded into the bread, and I like plenty of butter on the bread. I'd be happy with almost any white bread but it must be very fresh with a good crust and soft dough so that the hot meat will melt it slightly as its juices weep with each bite. Whether to add mustard (English or Dijon?) or creamed horseradish (or both) is a matter of taste and mood but, for my money, the addition of a buttery mound of juicy, soft onions (given a last-minute blast at a high temperature to get a few crisp edges and caramelized bits) is essential.

steak sandwich

4 servings
10 minutes preparation
30 minutes cooking

ingredients

2 large onions
25 g butter
salt and black pepper
2 x 225 g entrecote or rump
   steak, or 500 g piece of skirt
1–2 tbsp cooking oil
2 ciabatta, freshly baked
extra butter for spreading
mustard or horseradish

method

❶ Peel and halve the onions through the root. Slice as thinly as possible. Melt the butter in a frying pan over a low heat. When melted, stir in the onions so they're coated with the butter. Cook, stirring every so often, for 15–20 minutes until floppy but uncoloured. Sprinkle over ½ teaspoon of salt, stirring as the onions begin to look like sauerkraut – sort of sticky and forming into a clump. Cook for a further 5–10 minutes and then turn off the heat.

❷ Use your hands to smear the steaks with the oil. The best way to cook a steak is in a cast-iron, stove-top, ribbed grill pan (hereafter called a griddle) and the next best thing is a heavy-bottomed frying pan – grilling is not recommended. If using a griddle, *do not* oil the grill pan. Place griddle or frying pan over a high heat and get it very hot – allow a few minutes for this.

❸ Season one side of the steaks with salt and pepper and flip into the pan (seasoned side down) and leave untouched for 2 minutes (medium rare). Season the top of the steaks, turn and cook for 2 more minutes. It is difficult to give exact timings here: finger prodding is best – a slight indentation is left on the surface of a thick rare steak; medium-rare gives but finally resists; medium is bouncy, and well-done looks and feels tight. Remove the steaks to a warm plate and leave for a few minutes to rest while you finish off the onions.

❹ Turn the heat under the onions to very high, tossing them around for a couple of minutes until nicely crisp in patches. Halve the ciabatta, then split in half lengthways and butter liberally. Smear with mustard or horseradish. Slice the steaks thickly on a slight slant and load into the bread with a share of the onions. Eat fast.

'BLT', said Richard Branson, when asked to name his
favourite sandwich, 'but the bacon has to be very crispy.' It also has to be
thin rashers of streaky, and the pieces must be cut in half so that when you
bite into the sandwich, you don't drag the whole rasher out. A hazard of a
good BLT (bacon, lettuce and tomato) is that all the ingredients skid about
on a slide of mayo. Well, they should do. This is when you have to be
generous with everything, including the mayonnaise. Preferred lettuce
would be hearts of Little Gem, Cos or Romaine, which have flavour as well
as crispness, instead of the more usual Iceberg which can be tasteless.

the ultimate BLT

2 servings
10 minutes preparation
10 minutes cooking

ingredients

8 (at least) rashers of rindless,
   thin, streaky bacon
4 medium 'grown for flavour'
   tomatoes
2 lettuce hearts
4 drips Tabasco (optional)
4 tbsp mayonnaise
4 thick slices from the middle
   of a fresh country-style
   white loaf
butter
Maldon sea salt flakes and
   black pepper

method

❶ Pre-heat the grill to its highest setting. Cut the bacon
rashers in half and lay out on a grill tray. Cook until
completely crisp on both sides. Touch onto kitchen paper
to drain.

❷ Meanwhile, get everything else ready. Cut the core out
of the tomato (this is, after all, the *ultimate* BLT), cutting
round on the angle so it comes out like a pointed plug.
Halve the tomato and slice thickly. Slice across the lettuce
hearts, shredding them about 1 cm wide. Rinse and dry
thoroughly. Stir the Tabasco (if using) into the mayo.

❸ When the bacon is just about ready, toast the bread
until golden but not too brown. Spread lightly with butter,
and then generously with mayo, going right up to the
crust. Pile the lettuce on top of one half of the sandwich.
Cover with tomato pieces. Season lightly with salt flakes
and generously with black pepper. Arrange the bacon on
top and position the lid. Press firmly together with the flat
of your hand and slice in half with a sharp knife – not the
bread knife which will disrupt the contents. Keep the
second half warm under a napkin while you eat the first.

3. eggs

Eggs are one of the most complete and nutritious foods, and supply most of the vitamins, minerals and fats the body needs. Although low in fibre and carbohydrate, they are high in protein and calories. Wolves love eggs. They are quick to cook, versatile, easy to digest and the linchpin of countless dishes. They can also be made to stretch a long way.

It goes without saying that the best eggs come from hens that have been reared in the open on organically-produced feed stuff. **Organic free-range** eggs are produced in non-intensive systems and are the most expensive you can buy. Thereafter, egg prices spiral downwards. '**Free-range**' is one of those nebulous terms that inspires an image of free-roaming hens scratching around for their dinner but is more likely to mean that, although the poultry have access to the outside through small pop-holes, their feed is not much different from battery hens. **Barn and perchery** eggs are from hens that are reared in barn-like buildings. They move about freely, lay in nesting boxes and have natural light but no outdoor access. **Battery** eggs account for 85% of the eggs produced in the UK. The living conditions are known to be horrendous, with over-crowding and artificial light. They are given in-feed medication, growth-promoting agents, yolk colourants and animal wastes, including their own feathers, in their feed. The boxes are often labelled 'Farm Fresh' or 'Country' eggs.

Eggs have a shelf-life of three weeks from the packing date. Keep them in the fridge, pointed end down. The really important point is never to eat eggs that are past their 'best before date'. If your eggs aren't individually stamped with a 'best before' or laying date (unlikely), refrigerate them in their date-stamped box. Look out for eggs stamped with the 'Lion' quality mark which guarantees the eggs are laid in Britain and come from hens vaccinated against *salmonella enteritidis*. However, be aware of the salmonella risk when using raw or lightly cooked eggs.

The Basic Cooking Methods

TO BOIL a medium-sized egg or eggs, three-quarters fill a small saucepan with water. Bring the water to the boil. Add egg/s and cook for 5 minutes for a soft-boiled yolk, 8 minutes for just-set yolks and 12 minutes for hard-set yolks. Allow 1 minute less for a very fresh egg and 1 minute longer for a stale egg. Many eggs are now stamped with a 'best before' date (three weeks from laying) but a good tip is that if, when put into the water to boil, the egg 'sits up' rather than lies down on the bottom of the pan, it is definitely somewhat past its best. To peel the egg, crack the shell all over immediately it is cooked and hold under cold running water while you carefully peel away the shell. If you are not eating the egg immediately, stop the yolk from continuing to cook by returning it to the cooking pan and leaving it under cold running water for several minutes. It can remain in cold water until needed.

NB: piercing the pointed end of the egg shell will stop the shell cracking and the egg leaking. Adding salt to the cooking water will help seal a crack but isn't foolproof.

TO POACH an egg or eggs, half-fill a small saucepan with water. Bring to simmering point and add 1 tablespoon of vinegar. Crack one egg into a cup and slip the egg into the simmering water. If it nose-dives to the bottom of the pan, encourage it upwards by scraping under the egg with a wooden spoon. Once coagulated, add the second egg (it won't stick to the first egg), and keep the water at a gentle roll, cooking for 1–2 minutes until the white has set but the yolk is still soft. Remove one egg at a time with a slotted spoon and rest the spoon on absorbent kitchen paper to drain.

NB: fresh eggs give best results; old eggs that are close to their 'use by' date are most likely to sink and their white to spread and fragment.

TO FRY an egg or eggs **SUNNY-SIDE-UP**, melt a knob of butter, or enough oil to generously coat the base of a frying pan (or use a non-stick pan) placed over a medium heat. When hot, crack the egg/s directly into the pan. The white of fresh eggs will plump where it lands, the white of eggs close to their 'use by' date will spread and be thin. Adjust the heat so the egg fries steadily without turning crusty underneath. Tip the pan and splash some of the cooking fat over the yolk to encourage the top of the white and the yolk to cook. Reckon on about 2 minutes in total.

For **EGGS-OVER-EASY**, slide an egg slice under the egg and gently flip over. Cook for a further 30 seconds.

TO SCRAMBLE, crack at least 2 eggs per person, and no more than 12 at one time, in a bowl and beat them lightly with a fork. Season with salt and black pepper and cut a few scraps of butter over the top. Melt a big knob of butter in a suitably-sized pan, preferably non-stick, and place it over a low heat. Add the eggs and cook, stirring continuously with a wooden spoon, until the eggs begin to thicken and set. Bear in mind that the eggs will go on cooking after the pan has been removed from the heat. Take your time making scrambled eggs and add a splash of cream or more butter to make them richer, or a little milk to make them go further.

Scrambled eggs are good with a garnish of freshly snipped chives or parsley. A splash of Tabasco is another good addition, and so is grated Cheddar or another hard cheese. On toast. Scrambled eggs go particularly well with grilled tomatoes, or canned tomatoes simmered for 10 minutes. They go wonderfully with crisp bacon, grilled or fried mushrooms, and stirred into fried onion with or without tomato and/or red pepper. And, if your boat comes in, they are delicious with smoked salmon or trout.

TO RUMBLE is a forgotten way of cooking eggs that is a cross between scrambled egg and an omelette and is cooked in a frying pan. You're aiming for soft folds of egg and a moist, melting texture. Break 2 or more eggs per person into a bowl, season with salt, black pepper and Tabasco, if liked, and whisk with a fork until amalgamated. Melt a knob of butter and a smidgin of oil in a (preferably) non-stick frying pan and pour in the eggs. With a wooden spatula or spoon, gently push the egg mixture to the back of the pan, tipping the pan forward to allow the liquid, still uncooked egg to come to the front. Continue this process – pushing cooked egg to the back of the pan, and tipping the pan forward to allow uncooked egg to come to the front and into contact with the hot pan, adding (if you wish) a little more butter around the edges as you cook. The eggs are ready when they are firm, still moist and a little undercooked on the surface.

This is a wonderfully comforting dish of eggs buried in a creamy leek and cheese sauce, surrounded by a wall of mashed potato. Depending on your preference, the eggs can be soft-boiled and left whole, or hard-boiled and quartered. It is a good occasion to use the best organic eggs. The dish is covered with a cloak of cheese and breadcrumbs and baked until the top is crisp and golden. Don't attempt to serve this with anything remotely healthy. Frozen peas yes, salad no.

anglesey eggs

2 servings
15 minutes preparation
35 minutes cooking

ingredients

500 g floury ('old') variety of
potatoes, such as King
Edward
50 g butter plus an extra knob
200 ml milk
3 leeks
salt and black pepper
1 heaped tbsp flour
75 g grated Cheddar cheese
4 very fresh (organic) eggs
3 tbsp fresh breadcrumbs

method

❶ Pre-heat the oven to 400°F/200°C/gas mark 6.

❷ Peel the potatoes, cut them into even-sized chunks and boil in salted water until tender. Drain and mash with 25 g of the butter and sufficient milk – 1–2 tablespoons – to make a firm mash. Keep warm.

❸ Meanwhile, trim the leeks, slice them in rounds and wash thoroughly in cold water. Drain.

❹ Melt the second 25 g of butter in a medium-sized pan and add the leeks. Season with salt and pepper, and adjust the heat so the leeks soften without burning. Then sift the flour over the top and stir until integrated before gradually incorporating the remaining milk, while stirring constantly, to make a lump-free thick sauce. Simmer for several minutes before stirring in half of the cheese. Taste and adjust the seasoning.

❺ Meanwhile, put the eggs in a small saucepan and cover with water. For soft-boiled eggs, simmer for 4 minutes. For hard-boiled, cook for 7 minutes. Carefully crack the shell all over and leave under cold running water for a couple of minutes before peeling. Leave soft-boiled eggs whole. Cut hard-boiled eggs into quarters lengthways.

❻ Butter a soufflé-style dish and spoon in the mash leaving a decent-sized hole in the middle. Fill with the eggs and pour over the leek sauce. Mix breadcrumbs and remaining cheese together and sprinkle over the top. Cook in the oven for about 15 minutes until crusty and golden brown.

Instant munch. Try it bundled between two thickly-buttered door-steps. Cold omelette, incidentally, sliced, is delicious with a dribble of Tabasco. Try it in sandwiches, with rice or in egg fried rice (*see* page 135).

a quick cheese omelette

method

❶ Crack the eggs into a bowl, season with salt and pepper. If adding any of the extras, stir them in now together with most of the grated cheese.

❷ Heat a frying pan, preferably non-stick, over a medium heat, add a knob of butter and swirl it around. Turn up the heat, pour in the egg mixture and tilt the pan to spread it evenly. After a few seconds use a spoon or spatula to draw one edge of the omelette towards the centre, tilting the pan so that the uncooked egg runs into the space. When the eggs are set underneath but still slightly runny on top, tilt the pan away from you and use the spoon or spatula to fold the omelette almost in half. Slip it onto a plate, flipping to form a neatish roll. Scatter the last of the cheese over the top of the omelette. Eat.

1 serving
0 minutes preparation
3 minutes cooking

ingredients

3 fresh eggs
salt and black pepper
knob of butter
handful of grated Cheddar or another hard cheese
OPTIONAL EXTRAS
dollop of mustard and/or Greek yoghurt, crème fraîche or thick cream, shake of Tabasco, chopped parsley or chives

Spanish omelette is made with potatoes, onions and eggs, and cooked in olive oil. It should be cake-like, sturdy to cut but soft to eat. Inevitably, there are as many recipes for Spanish omelette as there are cooks to make it. It doesn't matter about exact quantities or ratio of potato to onion. What's important is that there are plenty of each. In Spain the potatoes are sliced and fried in masses of olive oil and the tortilla is eaten lukewarm or cold as a snack. This lighter version is made with potatoes that are boiled and then fried. The Wolf will eat it hot. Why wait?

tortilla (spanish omelette)

4 servings
20 minutes preparation
10 minutes cooking

ingredients

4 medium-sized potatoes, any
   variety
1 large onion, preferably
   Spanish
3 tbsp olive oil
4 large, fresh eggs
salt and black pepper
Tabasco

method

❶ Scrape or peel the potatoes, then rinse. Place in a pan and boil in salted water until tender. Drain and immerse in cold water for a couple of minutes to bring down the temperature then leave to drain and cool while you prepare everything else.

❷ Meanwhile, peel and halve the onion. Cut into small dice. Choose a deep, non-stick frying pan. Add most of the oil and cook the onions over a medium heat, stirring often, for 10–15 minutes until tender and lightly coloured.

❸ Meanwhile, crack the eggs into a bowl and season with salt and pepper and a few drops of Tabasco. Pre-heat the grill.

❹ When the onions are nearly ready, either thinly slice or dice the potato. Stir the potato into the onions, then tip the whole lot into the eggs.

❺ If the pan needs it, give it a quick wipe, then add the remaining oil, swirling it round the pan (and up the sides if the pan isn't non-stick). Return the pan to the heat and pour in the egg mixture. Smooth the top and cook for a couple of minutes until the base has set. Place the pan under the pre-heated grill and cook, keeping a beady eye on proceedings, until just set. To cook in the oven, pre-heat the oven to 300°F/150°C/gas mark 2, and cook for 10–15 minutes until set.

❻ Place an inverted plate over the pan and deftly turn upside down.

A frittata is a plump (flat) Italian omelette. It is the perfect way of using up leftover cooked pasta or for clearing out the remains of one or more packets.

pasta and cheese frittata

method

❶ If using dried pasta, bring a medium-sized pan of water to the boil. Add salt and the pasta and cook until tender. Drain. If using tagliatelle or other lengths of pasta, chop a few times.

❷ Meanwhile, beat the eggs and season with salt and pepper and a splash of Tabasco. Add three-quarters of the grated Parmesan. Cut the Cheddar into thin slices. When the pasta is ready, stir it into the egg mixture.

❸ Heat the oil in a non-stick frying pan (or swirl the oil up the sides if your pan isn't non-stick) over a medium heat and add half the egg mixture. Lay the cheese slices on top then pour on the rest of the egg. Cook over a low heat for about 8 minutes until the bottom is golden and the frittata firm but the top still unset. Finish the top under a hot grill. When set, sprinkle with the remaining Parmesan and return to the grill until golden.

2 servings
15 minutes preparation
20 minutes cooking

ingredients

approx 150 g dried pasta, any shape or size
4 large fresh eggs
salt and black pepper
Tabasco
50 g grated Parmesan
50 g mature Cheddar
1 tbsp cooking oil

Imagine, if you will, a thick and creamy, lightly curried onion sauce. The surface is covered with sunny soft-boiled eggs and it is served over boiled basmati rice with a garnish of chopped parsley or coriander. The flavours are subtle and gentle and it is eaten, curry style, with poppadoms and mango chutney. Superb in a comforting, vegetarian sort of way. And so simple to make. Definitely an occasion to splash out on some really good eggs.

Incidentally, kedgeree – which is the inspiration behind this delicious dish – is an Anglo-Indian pilau made with smoked haddock and curried basmati rice. It is usually decorated with hard-boiled eggs.

kedgeree eggs with poppadoms

4 servings
10 minutes preparation
40 minutes cooking

ingredients

3 large Spanish onions
50 g butter
salt and black pepper
1 tsp nutmeg, preferably freshly
    grated
1 flat tbsp flour
1 flat tbsp curry powder
500 ml milk
250 g basmati rice
6 large, fresh eggs
handful of coriander or flat leaf
    parsley leaves
poppadoms and mango chutney
    to serve

method

❶ Peel and halve the onions. Slice very thinly. Melt the butter in a large, heavy-bottomed frying pan or similarly wide-based pan placed over a medium-low heat. Stir in the onions and toss until coated in butter. Cook gently, turning often, until wilted, uncoloured and beginning to dry out. This will take about 20 minutes. Season with 1 teaspoon of salt, a good seasoning of pepper and most of the nutmeg. Stir in the flour and then the curry powder. Stir constantly until both have disappeared into the onions.

❷ Add the milk gradually, stirring constantly, to make a smooth, thick sauce. Bring to the boil, then turn down the heat immediately. Cook very gently, preferably using a heat diffuser mat so the sauce doesn't stick, for 30 minutes. Stir every so often. Taste and adjust the seasoning with extra salt and the last of the nutmeg.

❸ While the sauce is cooking, cook the poppadoms according to the packet's instructions. Place the rice and

500 ml water in a medium-sized saucepan, bring the water to the boil, turn down the heat immediately to the lowest setting, cover the pan and cook for 15 minutes. Turn off the heat, do not remove the lid, and leave for 5 minutes for the rice to finish cooking in the steam.

❹ At the start of the last 10 minutes of cooking, half-fill a medium-sized saucepan with water and put on to boil. Add the eggs and boil for 7 minutes. Drain the eggs and return to the pan, now filled with cold water. When cool enough to handle, gently peel them, setting them aside to drain on absorbent kitchen paper. Quarter the eggs lengthways and nestle them into the sauce, sunny side up. Sprinkle with the parsley or coriander and serve over the rice with the poppadoms and chutney.

Glamorgan sausages are really vegetarian rissoles. They could be described as reconstituted Welsh rarebit, because they use almost exactly the same ingredients. Although delicious with no accompaniment, they love a thick dipping sauce; say something creamy like Greek yoghurt laced with fresh herbs, or a well-flavoured fresh tomato sauce. Another good way of serving them is with a big bowl of peas, some new potatoes and lemon wedges.

For a treat, I recommend aïoli, the garlicky edition of mayonnaise, and the recipe following is for making it from scratch. For a super-quick cheat's version, peel, chop and crush 2 garlic cloves to a paste and stir into regular mayo. For extra authenticity, add a squeeze of lemon juice and a tablespoon of olive oil. Damn nice.

glamorgan sausages with aïoli

2 hearty snack servings
30 minutes preparation
15 minutes cooking

ingredients

FOR THE SAUSAGES
175 g Caerphilly or Lancashire cheese
1 large bunch of spring onions
275 g wholemeal bread
3 eggs
2 tsp made English mustard
3 tbsp chopped flat leaf parsley
1 tbsp freshly snipped chives
1 tbsp freshly snipped basil
salt and black pepper
flour for dusting
oil for frying

method

❶ Grate the cheese. Trim the spring onions, removing only the very coarse green part, then finely slice. Take the crusts off the bread, tear into pieces and blitz in a food processor to make crumbs (or, if no machine, crumble finely by hand). Set aside 4 tablespoons of the crumbs.

❷ Crack two of the eggs into a mixing bowl and whisk with a fork until smooth. Separate the remaining egg, placing the white in a shallow bowl and add the yolk to the whole eggs. Stir in the mustard and then the cheese, breadcrumbs, spring onions and herbs and a generous seasoning of salt and plenty of black pepper. Mix everything together to make a firm and not unduly wet mixture.

❸ Whisk the egg white until floppy. Have a little flour and the reserved breadcrumbs ready in separate bowls. Pinch off small handfuls of the mixture and shape into fat little sausages.

4 Dip each sausage first in flour, then egg white and then press them into the breadcrumbs. Fry in batches in hot oil until golden brown. Drain on absorbent paper and eat immediately; or they can be kept warm in a low oven.

5 To make the aïoli, have all the ingredients at room temperature. Peel and pulverize the garlic with a little salt, removing any green shoots, and beat with the egg yolks. Add the olive oil in a thin stream while beating continuously. Add a little lemon juice, then more oil, adding alternately until you arrive at a thick, glossy mayonnaise. Taste and adjust the seasoning with pepper.

FOR THE AÏOLI

2 (or more) large garlic cloves

2 egg yolks

approx 275 ml olive oil; an occasion for extra virgin

juice of 1 lemon

black pepper

Slightly stale bread is what you need for this surprisingly delicious dish. It is made in almost exactly the same way as a traditional sweet b and b pudding but in this case the buttered bread is toasted in the oven, rubbed with garlic and used to sandwich feta cheese, spring onions and mint. The egg custard is seasoned with salt instead of sugar and made with Greek yoghurt. As it cooks, the custard soaks into the bread and rises only slightly, thus allowing the toast and its final topping of grated Parmesan to get nicely crusted.

It is tempting to fall on this hot from the oven but it will be at its best when allowed to cool slightly and is particularly good when eaten cold, cut in slabs like moussaka. It needs no accompaniment but goes very well (and further) with a fresh tomato sauce and a crisp green salad, or minted peas and Jersey Royals tossed in butter and parsley. To upgrade the dish, serve it with a dollop of pesto (*see* page 88).

savoury bread and butter pudding

4 servings
20 minutes preparation
20 minutes cooking

ingredients

12 thin slices stale ciabatta or
   24 thin slices stale baguette
approx 25 g butter
1 tbsp olive oil
3 large eggs
200 g Greek yoghurt
200 ml milk or single cream
salt and black pepper
nutmeg
100 g feta cheese
bunch of spring onions

method

❶ Pre-heat the oven to 325°F/170°C/gas mark 3.
❷ Halve the slices of ciabatta and spread thinly with butter. Use half the olive oil to smear a baking tray and lay out the pieces of bread. Slip the tray into the oven.
❸ Crack the eggs into a mixing bowl and whisk lightly. Mix together the yoghurt and milk or cream and stir into the eggs. Season generously with salt, pepper and freshly grated nutmeg.
❹ Chop the feta into small cubes. Trim and slice the white and tender green part of the spring onions. Finely chop the mint.
❺ By now the bread will have dried out slightly, taken on some colour and crisped up. Remove from the oven. Use the remaining oil to smear round an earthenware or porcelain gratin dish about 20 x 25 cm. Rub one side of

each piece of toast with the garlic and lay out half the slices in the dish. Sprinkle over the feta, spring onions and mint. Season again with a little salt, plenty of pepper and freshly grated nutmeg. Cover with the remaining toasts, roughly approximating sandwiches. Season again. Slowly pour over the egg mixture, letting it soak into the sandwiches, more or less immersing them. Grate over the Parmesan in a thick blanket.

6 Cook in the middle of the oven for 20 minutes until the custard has set but still has a slight wobble and the Parmesan and some of the bread is temptingly crusted.

20 mint leaves
1 plump garlic clove
25 g piece of Parmesan

4. pasta

Most Italians eat dried pasta and unless fresh is made by an expert (as opposed to a supermarket), dried pasta is the thing to buy. The Wolf is tempted to live on pasta. It is cheap, and quick and easy to prepare. It is extremely filling and doesn't require much to make it tasty. It is also widely available, stores without taking up much space and lasts indefinitely. Anyone can cook it. Well, they can if they know how, and packets aren't always much help.

All pasta, except ready-cooked lasagne and cannelloni which cook in their sauces, should be cooked in plenty of boiling salted water. Stir it once when it has come back to the boil and then leave it alone. Some people add a splash of olive oil to the water; it is supposed to stop the pasta sticking together. Many pasta dishes need a little of the pasta cooking water added after the pasta has been cooked and drained; this helps to lubricate it and stop it sticking. Therefore, check the recipe carefully before draining away all the water.

Don't overcook pasta. It should be tender but still have some bite – known as *al dente*. If you are not sure of your timing – say you are going to the pub and want to eat the minute you get back – begin the pasta as normal, let it cook for a minute or two as soon as it has come back to the boil, then turn off the heat, clamp on the lid and leave it until you return. It will be perfect after 15 minutes and will stay hot for 45 minutes.

It's a good tip to cook double the amount of pasta you need: next day it can be re-heated in boiling water or made into a salad with, say, a can of drained sweetcorn, tuna and tomatoes. (You can do the same with rice.) Leftover pasta can also be the starting point for a minestrone-type soup, or it can be stirred into and heated up by a tomato-based or other gloopy sauce.

Good Things to Go with Pasta

There is no beginning and no end. When the cupboard is bare, try it with a knob of butter and some grated cheese, or with a splash of olive oil and a handful of chopped herbs; it is worth keeping a bottle of decent (by which I mean expensive) olive oil for this occasion. Another good idea is to stir a squeeze of sun-dried tomato paste into a dollop of yoghurt, and stir that in.

One of my favourite almost instant pasta suppers is made by adding frozen peas to chopped spring onions which have been softened in butter. Add a scoop of yoghurt or cream and it's a job done. Another good quick pasta sauce is made by mashing a can of tuna with finely chopped garlic, a dollop of mayonnaise and a few chopped tomatoes.

Many of these more or less instant 'sauces' don't even need to be cooked because they will be warmed by the hot pasta whilst stopping the pasta from burning your mouth.

Tomatoes go with pasta (almost) like peaches go with cream and there are many ways of preparing them together. Whether you use fresh tomatoes, canned tomatoes or one of the other prepared tomato products like passata, they take only a few minutes to cook into a sauce. When you add the tomato to a fried onion and/or garlic, the sauce becomes more interesting. Adding a few sliced mushrooms, or a chopped courgette, or a grated carrot, or a can of red peppers, it becomes even more interesting. A few scraps of leftover chicken, chunks of sausage, or a handful of minced meat, added when the onions are tender, turn it into something really substantial.

Pasta almost negates the need for meat. Meat sauces have their place, of course, but the almost chewy texture of pasta means it isn't a big deal if it isn't included. When it is, you don't need much of it and minced or finely shredded meat is more appropriate than big chunks of it, however lean.

Almost any cheese goes well with pasta, including very soft cheese like feta and mozzarella. Freshly grated Parmesan is, of course, almost an essential. In addition to the ubiquitous tomatoes and onions, vegetables, such as courgettes, aubergines, cauliflower and broccoli, go wonderfully well with pasta.

Pesto: Our New Best Friend

Pesto, we all now know, is a green pasta sauce sold in little bottles. It comes from Liguria in Italy. It is stirred into hot pasta for an instant meal and if there is some fresh Parmesan to grate over the top it will be even better. Pesto is good with potatoes, with gnocchi (*see* page 165), with tomatoes (soup, sauces, salads etc), with white beans and smeared onto toast (particularly bruschetta – *see* page 59). It goes with white fish, chicken and lamb. It can be diluted to make salad dressings and sauces for cous cous. It looks stunning, it (should) smell gorgeously pungent and it (should) taste wonderful: all at once creamy, hot and aromatic.

Unfortunately, pesto is often very disappointing. As a general rule, the more you pay for it, the better it will be. It is, however, *no trouble* to make. I promise. And when you've made it once, you will probably go on making it because home-made pesto will always taste more powerful, more interesting and more delicious whatever the quality of the ingredients you use. It goes without saying that the better the ingredients, the better the pesto.

Traditionally, pesto is pounded in a pestle and mortar but is quickly made in a food processor. Start by tossing about 3 tablespoons of pine kernels around in a hot frying pan until golden in places. Peel 3 cloves of garlic. Blitz both in the food processor with the leaves from a big bunch of basil (at least 60 g, preferably 90 g) and a little salt and black pepper. When it becomes a thick grainy paste and with the motor still running, gradually add about 7 tablespoons of olive oil in a thin stream. When the mixture is thoroughly amalgamated – you may need to scrape down the sides of the bowl a couple of times – transfer to a dish. Stir in at least 3 tablespoons of freshly grated Parmesan.

Pesto will keep, covered with a film of olive oil, in the fridge for several days.

Purists would disagree, but you can use other tender green leaves to make 'pesto'. Try watercress or rocket. Or half basil and half mint. You could make it with toasted almonds instead of pine kernels. Don't turn it into a dog's dinner but don't get trapped into thinking the recipe is written in stone. In a way it *is*, but you can experiment, making the best of what's available.

Pasta Shapes

At the last count, and new ones are patented every year, there were 652 pasta shapes, and there is a purpose behind every one of them. Spaghetti is still the market leader in Italy, followed by penne – the short stubby one. Rounded, long pasta such as spaghetti is good for liquid sauces that cling; penne and other short chunky pastas are good for liquid sauces that can slime through the middle, and flat tagliatelle-type pasta and wide ribbons are good for tomato sauces that sit on their surfaces. Tiny pasta and very thin pasta is good in soup.

Pasta is made with durum wheat flour and water. Egg pasta, when egg yolk replaces water, and the ratio of egg to flour is endlessly variable, is noticeably silky and can be very rich. *Also see* Noodles, page 105.

This is an incredibly quick, simple and delicious pasta dish. The wise Wolf will always have the necessary for it in the store cupboard. Hot pasta is bathed in olive oil flecked with scraps of garlic: it is hot and addictive. If you add chilli flakes – another classic combination – it becomes fiery hot and, some say, me included, it is even better. A hunk of crusty bread, a green salad and a glass of red would turn this modest dish into a feast. Did you know, incidentally, that chilli is addictive? It also gives you an adrenaline rush.

spaghetti with garlic or chilli or both

2 servings
15 minutes preparation
15 minutes cooking

ingredients

250 g spaghetti or spaghettini (thin spaghetti)
4 plump garlic cloves
1½ tsp chilli flakes (optional)
6 tbsp olive oil
salt and black pepper

method

❶ Bring a large pan of water to the boil. Add salt and then the pasta and cook until *al dente*, allowing about 12 minutes for this. Drain, saving about 2 tablespoons of cooking water.

❷ Meanwhile, peel the garlic and finely chop. In a small frying pan, combine the garlic and olive oil and cook the garlic over a low heat until pale brown. Do not let it darken or it will be bitter. If adding the chilli flakes, do so now.

❸ Warm a large serving bowl (boiling water works a treat) and add the reserved cooking water, garlic (and chilli flakes), oil and the well-drained pasta. Toss gently and season to taste with salt and pepper.

They have a neat way of making macaroni cheese in Trinidad. They don't bother with cheese sauce but get the same creamy result by whisking egg with milk and chopped canned tomatoes. The top is covered with a thick layer of breadcrumbs, chopped parsley and more cheese. It emerges from the oven with a gorgeously crusted top and sets so firm it can be cut like a cake. Eat on its own or accompany it with a chilli-hot tomato sauce. The pie is often eaten warm in Trinidad and is also very good cold. It will keep, covered, in the fridge for several days. Perfect picnic or lunchbox food. The Angostura or HP sauce, incidentally, give it extra oomph.

west indian macaroni pie

method

1 Pre-heat the oven to 350°F/180°C/gas mark 4.

2 Put a large pan of water on to boil. Add 1 teaspoon of salt and the macaroni and cook according to the instructions on the packet until *al dente*.

3 Meanwhile, use a knob of the butter to smear generously a gratin dish that can hold about 1.5 litres. Crack the eggs into a mixing bowl and whisk. Add the milk. Season with salt, pepper and the Angostura or HP, if using. Drain the tomatoes and chop. Grate the cheese.

4 Add tomatoes and 150 g of the cheese to the eggs. Stir together then add the drained macaroni. Mix thoroughly and tip the mixture into the buttered dish. Smooth the surface. Break the bread into chunks and blitz to make breadcrumbs (crumble finely by hand if you don't have a blender). Chop the parsley. Mix remaining cheese, breadcrumbs and parsley together and spread over the macaroni. Dot with butter. Bake in the oven for about 20 minutes until the top is golden-brown and the macaroni has set.

4–6 servings
10 minutes preparation
10 minutes cooking

ingredients

300 g macaroni
salt and black pepper
25 g butter
2 eggs
300 ml milk
1 tsp Angostura bitters or
   1 tbsp HP sauce (optional)
400 g can of Italian peeled
   tomatoes
225 g mature Cheddar cheese
100 g bread without crusts
small bunch of parsley

In Naples they sell basil in small bunches held together with an elastic band and usually with the root still attached. The leaves are noticeably larger, thicker and darker than the puny pot plants we've grown used to. Their aroma and flavour is strong and pungent. You can buy real Italian basil from enlightened greengrocers and mature basil from Spain at Marks & Spencer. Its strength will truly enhance this quick pasta supper.

fettuccine with cherry tomatoes and basil

4 servings
15 minutes preparation
15 minutes cooking

ingredients

300 g fettuccine
3 tbsp olive oil
large knob of butter
2 x 300 g punnets of cherry tomatoes or very ripe tomatoes
1 tbsp balsamic vinegar, or 1 tsp sugar dissolved in 1 tbsp red wine vinegar
salt and black pepper
1 heaped tsp chopped thyme leaves
2 garlic cloves, preferably new season
50 g Niçoise-style small black olives (approx 35)
15 g bunch of large-leaf basil
freshly grated Parmesan

method

❶ Pre-heat the oven to 400°F/200°C/gas mark 6.

❷ Bring a large pan of water to the boil. Add salt and then the pasta and cook until *al dente*. Drain, retaining about 1 tablespoon of the cooking water, and toss with 1 tablespoon of olive oil and the butter. Transfer to a warmed serving bowl that can also accommodate the tomatoes.

❸ Meanwhile, remove the stalks from the tomatoes, rinse, shake dry and place in a small metal oven pan that can fit them in a single layer. Whisk together 2 tablespoons of olive oil and the balsamic vinegar (or the sugar and vinegar mix), adding a generous seasoning of pepper and the thyme. Pour this over the tomatoes and toss thoroughly. Place the tray in the hot oven and cook for about 10 minutes until most of the tomato skins have burst and the flesh is soft and beginning to weep. If you prefer, or if you are halving the quantities to feed 2, cook the tomatoes under the grill pre-heated to its highest setting.

❹ While the tomatoes are cooking, peel the garlic, chop it finely and sprinkle with ½ teaspoon of salt. Use the flat of a knife to work it to a juicy paste. Smack the olives with a heavy weight to split and stone them.

❺ Tip the tomatoes and their juices into a warmed bowl,

stir in the garlic paste followed by the stoned olives. Shred or tear the basil over the top. Leave, covered, for 10 minutes or so for the flavours to develop then pour the tomato sauce into the pasta. Toss loosely and serve with freshly grated Parmesan over the top.

There are times when it is worth shelling out for good convenience products. In this simple pasta supper, ready-made hollandaise sauce turns this pasta into a treat.

macaroni with peas and cherry tomatoes

method

❶ Bring a medium-sized pan of water to the boil. Add salt and the macaroni and cook according to the packet instructions. When the macaroni is almost done, add the peas and turn up the heat so that the water returns to the boil as quickly as possible. Boil for a further 3–4 minutes until the peas are tender. Drain well into a colander then return to the pan. Add the hollandaise and stir.

❷ Meanwhile, remove any stalks from the tomatoes and place in a small frying pan that will hold them in a single layer. Add oil and vinegar, sprinkle with thyme, season with salt and pepper, and give the pan a good shake to mix everything up. Cook under a hot grill, shaking the pan every so often, for about 10 minutes or until most of the tomatoes have popped and split their skins. Tip the tomatoes and juices into a bowl to cool.

❸ Serve the macaroni risotto-style dusted with Parmesan, with the tomato salad on the side.

3–4 servings
10 minutes preparation
15 minutes cooking

ingredients

250 g macaroni
300 g frozen peas
200 g M&S hollandaise sauce
250 g cherry tomatoes
2 tbsp cooking oil, preferably olive oil
1 tbsp red wine vinegar
½ tsp dried thyme
salt and black pepper
2 tbsp freshly grated Parmesan

Spaghetti alla carbonara is one of those seemingly simple dishes that are easy to get horribly wrong. It doesn't involve many ingredients and the most important are fresh eggs and decent streaky bacon.

The idea is to cook the pasta *al dente* and then, at the last minute, to toss it with beaten raw egg mixed with thick cream, tiny specks of garlic and very crisp scraps of bacon. The egg is warmed rather than cooked and holds the garlic and bacon in a delicious cream that clings to the strands of pasta. If the eggs were to end up solid like scrambled eggs the whole point of the dish is lost. Wolf might not be able to lay his hands on organic, free-range eggs with gorgeous big, sunny yolks, so a little compensation is added in this recipe. Smooth, creamy Dijon mustard (*so* useful; *see* How to Shop) lifts the flavour of unremarkable eggs and has a similar thickening and silky effect as cream.

Traditionally, carbonara is made with spaghetti. However, short, chunky penne or rigatoni makes the actual eating more convenient (particularly if your fork technique leaves something to be desired) with the added advantage that the creamy egg can slide inside as well as around the pasta.

All you may wish for with this is a salad of floppy green leaves to mop up any egg left at the bottom of the bowl. Crusty bread with decent butter and plenty of red wine would be good too.

almost carbonara

2–3 servings
10 minutes preparation
15 minutes cooking

ingredients

2 fresh eggs plus 1 fresh egg yolk
1 scant tbsp smooth Dijon

method

❶ Bring a large pan of water to the boil. While that is happening, with a wooden spoon beat the whole eggs, egg yolk and mustard or cream or yoghurt and season with a pinch of salt and several grinds of pepper. Chop the bacon into thick matchsticks.

❷ Add 1 teaspoon of salt to the boiling water together with the pasta and ½ tablespoon of olive oil to the boiling water. Return to the boil, stir once and cook according to packet instructions until *al dente*.

❸ About 10 minutes before the pasta is ready, heat the rest of the olive oil in a frying pan and cook the bacon gently so it releases most of its fat, then turn up the heat until both bacon and fat are very crisp.

❹ Peel the garlic and chop very finely. Add this to the bacon right at the end of cooking, stirring quickly for a few seconds until aromatic. Don't let the garlic brown.

❺ When the pasta is ready, drain it thoroughly and tip it back into the saucepan. Combine immediately with the hot bacon, its oil and the garlic, then pour in the egg mixture. Stir to coat the pasta evenly so that the heat of the pasta cooks the egg slightly. Finally, add the Parmesan. Serve immediately in warmed bowls.

mustard or 2 tbsp thick cream or Greek-style yoghurt
salt and black pepper
100 g rindless streaky bacon, smoked by preference
1 tbsp olive oil
250 g spaghetti or penne
2 garlic cloves
2 tbsp freshly grated Parmesan and more to serve

If ever you needed an excuse to add dried oregano to your supplies then this is it. Think of the dish as a pasta version of Napolitana pizza: tomato sauce, molten mozzarella and oregano, but with the flavours underpinned by a kick of garlic and hint of chilli. This is perfect Wolf food: delicious, simple to make, quick and easy to eat. Inexpensive. And something to share with friends. The sauce, incidentally, can be prepared up to a day in advance; it will keep, covered, in the fridge, or could be frozen.

baked tagliatelle with tomatoes

6 servings

15 minutes preparation

30 minutes cooking (slightly longer if making the tomato sauce from scratch)

ingredients

2 Italian mozzarella cheeses, preferably buffalo milk, about 250 g each

4 tbsp olive oil

2 garlic cloves

1 dried chilli

2 tsp dried oregano

salt and black pepper

750 ml bottle of passata

400 g egg tagliatelle

25 g butter

6 tbsp freshly grated Parmesan

method

❶ Coarsely chop the mozzarella, put in a deep dish and pour over 2 tablespoons of the oil. Peel and finely chop the garlic and add that too, together with the whole chilli, 1 teaspoon of the oregano, and a generous grinding of pepper. Toss then leave to marinate for at least 30 minutes.

❷ Pour the passata into a saucepan and simmer vigorously for 5–10 minutes until thickened. You can improve the flavour, and turn it into more of a sauce by adding it to a chopped onion and garlic clove that you've fried in 1 tablespoon of olive oil. A bay leaf is a good addition and you may need to add 1/2 teaspoon sugar or 1 tablespoon tomato ketchup as well as salt and pepper.

❸ Towards the end of the marinating time, bring a large pan of water to the boil. Pre-heat the oven to 350°F/180°C/gas mark 4. Oil a shallow oven-proof dish. Cook the tagliatelle in the boiling water with 1 teaspoon of salt, until *al dente*. Drain, reserving a couple of tablespoons of cooking water. Return the pasta immediately to the cooking pan and toss with some of the reserved water, remaining olive oil and butter. Mix well, then add the hot tomato sauce – remembering to remove the bay leaf if used – and Parmesan.

❹ Remove and discard the chilli from the mozzarella and add the mozzarella and juices to the pasta. Toss thoroughly, and if the pasta seems too dry, add some more of the reserved cooking water. Taste, adjust the seasoning and pour into the prepared oven dish. Sprinkle the remaining oregano over the top, cover with foil and bake for 10 minutes. Remove from the oven and let the dish sit for a few minutes before serving.

Soft slippery lasagne bathed in a creamy cheese sauce
sandwiching slices of pepperoni and roasted red pepper sounds like hours
of work. It isn't; it is put together in minutes. Serve with buttered crusty
bread and a huge salad. All the ingredients were bought from Sainsbury's in
cans, cartons or packets. The cheese sauce and lasagne, sold in a flat
pack, is found in the fresh pasta and pasta sauce chill cabinet.

red pepper and pepperoni lasagne

4 servings
15 minutes preparation
20 minutes cooking

ingredients

250 g fresh lasagne sheets
1 garlic clove
1 tbsp vegetable cooking oil
**400 g can of Italian peeled
   tomatoes**
salt and black pepper
**½ tsp sugar or 1 tbsp tomato
   ketchup**
**2 x 300 g carton of 4-cheese
   sauce**
**400 g can of peeled red
   peppers or 3 Karyatis
   roasted red peppers**
large knob of butter
100 g pepperoni slices
2 tbsp freshly grated Parmesan

method

❶ Pre-heat the oven to 400°F/200°C/gas mark 6.

❷ Transfer the lasagne from the packet to a dish and cover with boiling water. Leave for 5 minutes. Drain.

❸ Meanwhile, peel and finely chop the garlic. Heat the oil in a frying pan and add the garlic, chopped tomatoes, a generous seasoning of salt and pepper, and the sugar or ketchup. Cook briskly for about 5 minutes until thickened and sauce-like.

❹ Tip the cheese sauce into a small saucepan and warm through. Drain the peppers, split down one side and slice into strips. Smear butter round the base and sides of a large, approximately 2-litre capacity gratin-style dish.

❺ Smear a little of the cheese sauce over the base of the dish. Then, peeling the slices of lasagne apart, make layers: a layer of lasagne, more cheese sauce, tomato sauce, slices of red pepper and pepperoni, another layer of lasagne, more cheese sauce etc, continuing until everything is used up except for the final two layers which should be the last layer of lasagne and a generous spreading of cheese sauce. Season the top with black pepper and strew with the Parmesan. Dot with any remaining butter.

❻ Cook in the oven for about 20 minutes until the top is golden-brown and the sauce is bubbling round the edge.

Cauliflower cheese is not the only way to cook the vegetable once described as cabbage with a college education. It goes very well with tomato, either fresh or canned, and can stand up to other powerful ingredients such as chilli and black olives.

orechiette and cauliflower

method

❶ Fill two large pans with water and put on to boil.

❷ If using a whole cauliflower, remove the outer leaves, cut in half and divide into bite-size florets. Add 1 teaspoon of salt and the cauliflower florets to the boiling water in one pan and 1 teaspoon of salt and the pasta to the other. When the water returns to the boil, adjust the heat so it simmers. Cook the cauliflower for 3 minutes, drain and keep warm. Cook the pasta according to the packet's instructions until *al dente*, drain (retaining some of the cooking water), toss and cover to keep warm.

❸ Meanwhile, peel, halve and thinly slice the onion. Heat the olive oil in a large, heavy-bottomed frying pan or similarly wide-based pan and cook the onion for about 8 minutes until tender and beginning to colour.

❹ Split the chilli, scrape out the seeds and chop finely. (*See* page 21.) Chop the anchovies. Add both to the pan and stir fry for a minute or two until the anchovy melts into the onions. Add the tomatoes. Break them up with a wooden spoon and simmer, uncovered, for about 6 minutes, until thick and sauce-like. Stir in the cauliflower. Cover the pan and cook for 5 minutes.

❺ Bash the olives with something heavy to crack them open. Remove the stones and discard, then tear the olives in half. Coarsely chop the parsley. Add both to the sauce. Taste and adjust the seasoning with salt and pepper. Stir the sauce into the drained pasta and serve with the Parmesan.

4 servings
15 minutes preparation
20 minutes cooking

ingredients

1 cauliflower or 500 g cauliflower florets
salt and black pepper
050 g orechiotte or concoreous pasta
1 large onion
3 tbsp olive oil
1 red chilli
4 anchovy fillets
400 g can of Italian peeled tomatoes
about 15 black olives
15 g bunch of flat leaf parsley
4 tbsp freshly grated Parmesan cheese

Students and other financially-challenged persons used to live on spaghetti Bolognese. Most of the time it was rubbish. The sauce, which is really called ragù, should be cooked for hours so it finishes up intensely flavoured, very thick and barely recognizable as a meat sauce. My hybrid version, which is made with minced lamb as opposed to beef, ends up with the desired texture, colour and rich flavour within an hour of cooking rather than the three hours needed with the authentic method. The Florentine bit refers to spinach. This gives the sauce colour and gives you your greens. Leave it out if you like. Ragù improves if it is left overnight. Instead of pasta, try it over cous cous or with rice (and a handful of separately cooked green beans). Or use it to make lasagne or stuff cannelloni.

spag bol florentine

4–6 servings
15 minutes preparation
60 minutes cooking

ingredients

**4 rashers of rindless streaky
   bacon
1 tbsp cooking oil
40 g butter
1 medium-sized onion
2 carrots
2 sticks of celery
500 g minced lamb
salt and black pepper
big glass of red wine or
   ½ chicken stock cube
   dissolved in 250 ml boiling
   water**

method

❶ Chop the bacon. Heat the oil and half the butter in a heavy-bottomed pan over a medium heat and cook the bacon, removing it when crisp.

❷ Meanwhile, peel and finely chop the onion and the carrot. Trim the celery and finely chop (including the leaves, if there are any).

❸ Add the onion to the pan and fry for a couple of minutes before adding the carrot and celery. Cook for 5 minutes, stirring a couple of times, then add the meat. Turn it around as it changes from pink to brown. Season generously with salt. Add the wine or stock and increase the heat to medium-high. Cook, stirring occasionally, until all the liquid has evaporated.

❹ Add the milk and nutmeg. Stir frequently, and when the milk has almost entirely disappeared (it takes about 10 minutes) add the passata.

❺ Return the bacon to the pan. Bring to the boil then turn

down low and cook at a gentle simmer, uncovered, for 35 minutes.

❻ Half-fill a medium-sized pan with water and put on to boil. Meanwhile, wash the spinach and drain. Stuff the spinach into the boiling water, add salt and cook for a minute or so until floppy. Drain in a colander and roughly chop against the side. Add the rest of the butter to the pan in which the spinach was cooked, stir in the spinach and let everything amalgamate. Stir the buttery spinach into the ragù for the last 5 minutes of cooking.

❼ Cook the spaghetti according to the packet instructions. Taste the ragù, adjusting the seasoning with salt, pepper and a squeeze of lemon juice. Serve over the drained spaghetti.

150 ml milk
grated nutmeg
250 ml passata (or 400 g can
of whole tomatoes puréed
and sieved)
100 g spinach
500 g spaghetti
squeeze of lemon juice

When it comes to cooking chicken livers – and you
should because they are so good and so easy – the best treatment is short
and sharp. It doesn't pay to get fussy with them, either. An excellent method
is to fry them quickly in a little hot olive oil, squeezing lemon juice over them
as they turn crusty. The whole process should only take a couple of
minutes. Eat them cooked like this with very buttery mashed potato and lots
of slippery, caramelized onion, or scooped up into a sandwich with a
handful of watercress or young spinach leaves.

This is a classic Italian recipe. Pappardelle, which is like wide tagliatelle, is
often teamed with tomato sauces. That's because plenty of sauce can cling
onto the ribbon noodles.

pappardelle with chicken livers and tomato

4 servings
15 minutes preparation
30 minutes cooking

ingredients

350–400 g chicken livers
2 plump garlic cloves
1 small onion
½ tsp fresh rosemary leaves or
    a generous pinch of dried
3 good-sized sage leaves
2 tbsp olive oil
1 glass of red wine
400 g can of Italian peeled
    tomatoes
salt and black pepper
500 g pappardelle
knob of butter
freshly grated Parmesan

method

❶ Rinse the livers, pat dry with kitchen paper. Remove
any stringy membrane or discoloured parts. Cut into
2½ cm pieces.

❷ Lightly crush the garlic in a little salt with the flat of a
knife and flake away the skin. Peel the onion and chop
very finely. Finely chop the rosemary until it resembles
green dust. Shred and finely chop the sage leaves.

❸ Heat the oil in a large frying pan or similarly wide-based
pan over a medium heat. Add the garlic and cook for two
minutes without letting it brown. Discard. Add the onion
and cook until soft. About 8 minutes.

❹ Add the prepared livers, rosemary and sage, and cook,
stirring for 2–3 minutes, until the livers are browned all
over. Remove the livers to a plate. Turn up the heat, add
the wine, stir vigorously as it bubbles, allowing it to reduce
by half. Add the tomatoes, breaking them up in the pan,
and cook for 10–15 minutes until the sauce becomes
noticeably thick and jammy. Taste for salt and pepper.

5 Meanwhile, cook the pasta according to the packet's instructions until *al dente*, tender but firm to the bite. Drain the pasta, retaining a little of the cooking liquid, then toss with the butter in a warmed serving bowl.

6 Return the livers to the pan and heat through for a minute or two. Pour the sauce over the pasta, toss and serve with freshly grated Parmesan.

Along the Amalfi coast, where this dish originates, spaghetti alla vongole is a summer speciality made with luscious, densely textured tomatoes, plenty of new-season garlic and parsley, and little clams fresh from the sea. But no matter. This all-season version is pretty good, too. All the ingredients can be fished from your well-stocked store cupboard or you can pick them up from a halfway decently stocked corner shop.

corner-shop spaghetti vongole

2 servings

10 minutes preparation

20 minutes cooking

ingredients

200 g spaghetti

salt and black pepper

1 medium-sized onion

1 plump garlic clove

1 tbsp olive oil

400 g can of Italian peeled
   tomatoes

splash of Tabasco

pinch of sugar

squeeze of lemon juice

65 g bottle of clams in brine

1 tbsp chopped flat leaf parsley

method

❶ Bring a large pan of water to the boil. As soon as it boils, add 1 teaspoon of salt and the spaghetti. Cook according to the packet instructions until *al dente*. Drain (retaining a little of the cooking liquid), toss and then cover to keep warm. This should neatly coincide with the time needed for cooking the sauce.

❷ Peel, halve and chop the onion. Peel the garlic and slice in wafer-thin rounds or chop quite small.

❸ Heat the oil in a large heavy-bottomed frying pan or similar shallow pan over a medium heat. Add onions and garlic and cook, stirring around frequently and adjusting the heat as necessary, until the onion is soft and beginning to colour. Allow 10 minutes.

❹ Add the tomatoes, season lightly with salt and generously with pepper, and simmer vigorously, bashing them with a wooden spoon to break them up. Cook until the tomatoes 'melt' into a thick, juicy sauce. Taste and adjust the seasoning with a little Tabasco, sugar and lemon juice if you think it needs it.

❺ Tip the clams into a sieve to drain and then stir them into the tomato sauce. Warm through and then stir the drained spaghetti into the clam sauce. Stir most of the chopped parsley into the sauce and sprinkle the last of it over the top. Serve very hot from the pan.

5. noodles

The difference between noodles and pasta is that noodles are flat or rounded like spaghetti and cut into long lengths whereas pasta can be almost any shape. Noodles come in various widths and thicknesses and, like pasta, are made with flour and water, and sometimes egg yolk, too. European-style noodles, which we tend to think of as pasta, are usually made from wheat flour, whereas oriental and Asian noodles, which is what we usually mean when we talk noodles, are generally made with white rice flour.

There are, inevitably, exceptions in both cases. Some Italian pasta, for example, is made with chestnut flour or chickpea flour. Some Chinese noodles are made with starches extracted from corn, mung beans and soy beans, and some Korean noodles are made with sweet potato starch. Chinese egg noodles, which are often flavoured with monosodium glutamate and oriental fish sauce, look glossy and very yellow. They tend to be sold in wavy sheets and taste quite different from Italian egg pasta. Japanese noodles are always distinctively packaged, either in flat packs which store easily and neatly, or held in a bundle with ribbon. They are made from wheat flour, rice flour or buckwheat flour, or a combination of flours. Green noodles, called chasoba, are made from buckwheat flour flavoured with green tea.

Chinese, South-east Asian and Japanese noodles are all available fresh from ready-meal chill cabinets at most supermarkets (although they are cheaper and better at indigenous shops) but there is a far greater choice if you buy them dried. All of them – except some of the more rarefied noodles – are cheaper than pasta and many dried noodles only need to be soaked in boiling water for about 10 minutes before they are ready to eat. Another advantage of noodles over pasta is that they can be prepared and kept waiting. They are brought back to life, as it were, by a brief soaking in boiling water.

And don't forget, when cooking noodles, never to add salt to the water. Use soy, tamari and oriental fish sauce to provide the essential, last-minute seasoning. Noodles are perfect for stir fries, soups and stews. They are quick, inexpensive and fun. Use them often. Experiment with dishes such as finely sliced raw chicken with diagonally sliced spring onions and sliced carrots simmered in stock (made with a cube or Japanese dashi). Pour the whole lot over ready-soaked hot rice noodles. Season with soy sauce and toasted sesame oil. Get noodling.

How to Noodle

CHINESE EGG NOODLES: made with wheat flour and egg yolk, look like thin spaghetti, sold in nests, fresh or dried. Noticeable egg flavour. Use them in soups and stir fries, or deep fry. Cook dried noodles in boiling water for 4 minutes, fresh for 1 minute, rinse in cold water and drain. Cover until needed, re-heat in boiling water.

WHEAT NOODLES: pale and almost tasteless, staple of Chinese diet, and eaten throughout South-east Asia. Sometimes flavoured with prawn or crab. Look like pale, thin, fragile spaghetti, sold in coils, fresh or dried. Cook dried in boiling water for about 4 minutes, fresh for 2 minutes, rinse in cold water and drain. Good with strong flavours. Perfect for stir fries.

FRESH RICE SHEET NOODLES: slippery ribbons cut from glossy, white, fresh rice sheets. Try them, Cantonese-style, wok-tossed with thinly sliced beef or chicken, bean sprouts and soy, or make Vietnamese pho soup, flavouring the stock with scraps of chicken or duck and root vegetables. Buy from Asian food stores, sold flat-pack in plastic bags. Buy ready sliced or in sheets, then cut to required width.

RICE VERMICELLI: semi-transparent in dried state, pure white when soaked. Looks like white wire wool. Also known as **Chinese rice sticks** or **rice stick noodles.** Soak in boiling water for about 6 minutes, rinse in cold water and drain. Perfect for stir fries (sometimes packaged as **stir fry noodles**), use them pre-soaked or dried, when they puff to approximately four times their original size. Add to soups, boiling for at least 2 minutes, remembering that they will absorb liquid.

BEAN THREAD VERMICELLI: looks like wiry white knitting yarn. Snip it with scissors then soak for a few minutes in boiling water until soft, gelatinous and transparent. Or deep fry direct from the pack. An alternative to rice vermicelli.

RICE STICKS: semi-transparent when dried, pure white when cooked. Look like white tagliatelle. Soak in warm water for 15 minutes, or boil for 3–5 minutes. Ideal for soups, add to stir fries.

SOBA: lightly flecked, pale beige flat Japanese noodles made from buckwheat and wheat flour. Pale green chasoba noodles have been flavoured with green tea powder. Drop fresh into boiling water and boil for 2 minutes. Drop dried into boiling water, add 1 cup of cold water, return to boil, add another cup of cold water. Repeat 2–4 times depending on the thickness of the soba, allowing about 6 minutes in total. Drain, rinse in cold water. Use hot in soups or cold (very common in Japan) with a dipping sauce made from miso or soy with dashi and mirin (sweetened Japanese rice vinegar).

UDON: plump, large, white, glossy Japanese noodles. Slippery texture so known as slurping noodles in Japan. Also available made from brown rice flour. Soak fresh in boiling water for 3–4 minutes. Drain then rinse in cold water. Twice. Cook dried udon like dried soba. Perfect for soups.

SOMEN: thin, white Japanese noodles made from hard wheat dough moistened with sesame seed oil. Delicate, elegant taste. Traditionally eaten cold or in a warm broth with, for example, beancurd. Cook dried somen like dried soba; entire process takes about 2 minutes.

STORE CUPBOARD STANDBYS: Yutaka range of Japanese noodle dishes. Sold in flat cellophane packs with colourful photos of the finished dish which include Udon noodles stir fry, Udon noodles with soup, and Yakisoba noodles. Ready in 2 minutes. Very cheap. Stocked by Sainsbury's. Also check out **Sharwood's** bottled stir-in sauce for noodles. Add a few scraps of bacon or pepperoni, fried with a couple of sliced mushrooms.

How to Add Pzazz to Noodle Dishes

BLACK BEAN SAUCE: dried and salted black beans mixed with soy sauce, sesame oil, chicken stock and rice wine. For authentic intense savoury tang. Best comes from Chinese and Asian stores. Is similar to **yellow bean sauce**; both are sometimes mixed with chilli.

DASHI POWDER: Japanese stock made with seaweed and bonito flakes. Use in Japanese-style noodle soups for authentic flavour.

HOISIN SAUCE: thick, sweet and sour, chilli-hot pungent sauce made from fermented soy beans. Gives instant injection of flavour.

INSTANT MISO SOUP: made from fermented soy bean. Use in place of stock for Japanese-style noodle soups.

MISO: thick, salty, fermented soy bean paste. Use like soy sauce or stock.

ORIENTAL FISH SAUCE: known as nuoc nam in Vietnam, nam pla in Thailand. Off-puttingly smelly but highly addictive, giving dishes a deep savoury flavour. Use sparingly but often.

SESAME SEEDS: cheap and nutty. More flavour if you toss them briefly until lightly golden in a hot wok. Add at the last moment or use to coat strips of meat. Excellent with vegetable and noodle stir fries.

SOY SAUCE: use in place of salt for last-minute seasoning. Light soy sauce is thin and fresh, dark soy sauce is thicker and stronger in flavour but lighter in salt. Japanese soy sauce, shoyu, is sweeter, lighter and more refined.

TAMARI SAUCE: Bovril-like sauce made from fermented soy beans and sweet rice wine (mirin); the Rolls Royce of soy sauces with a well-rounded flavour.

TOASTED SESAME OIL: use to marinate meat or as a last-minute seasoning. Expensive but a little goes a long way and worth it.

WASABI: sold in green tubes that resemble toothpaste, and is the bright green fiery-hot equivalent of mustard meets horseradish. Mix with soy for dipping sauce for noodles or vegetable noodle dishes. A great seasoning.

This is a stunningly simple store cupboard Thai-style
noodle soup-supper with plenty of interesting flavour in the coconut milk
gravy and good textural contrast from the nuts and shredded spring onions.
If, however, you were to fry up a few squares of tofu or some scraps of
chicken to perch on the top, that would be good, too.

sesame peanut noodles

method

❶ Three-quarters fill a large pan with water and bring to
the boil. Do not add salt. Add the noodles and soak or
cook according to the packet instructions. Drain and cover
to keep warm.

❷ Meanwhile, peel the garlic, chop and crush with a pinch
of salt.

❸ Heat the oil in a medium-sized pan and stir fry the garlic
paste for a few seconds. Add the stock. Grate or crumble
the creamed coconut into the stock and stir to dissolve.
Stir in the peanut butter. Simmer, stirring constantly, for 2
minutes. Add the fish sauce and season with black
pepper.

❹ Meanwhile, trim and finely slice the spring onions. Tip
the peanuts into a food processor and blitz until finely
chopped. (If you don't own a machine, crush with a rolling
pin or a bottle.)

❺ Heat a frying pan over a medium heat and stir fry the
sesame seeds for 1 minute. Tip the seeds into a large
bowl. Add the toasted sesame oil, vinegar, soy sauce, half
the spring onions and drained noodles. Toss to coat.
Divide the noodles between 4 deep bowls. Spoon over the
peanut sauce. Garnish with spring onions and crushed
peanuts.

4 servings
15 minutes preparation
20 minutes cooking

ingredients

250 g rice sticks or brown rice
    Udon noodles
2 garlic cloves
salt and black pepper
1 tbsp vegetable oil
½ stock cube dissolved in
    300 ml boiling water
100 g creamed coconut (see
    page 22)
2 heaped tbsp Whole Earth
    crunchy peanut butter
1 tbsp oriental fish sauce
bunch of spring onions
2 tbsp salted peanuts
1 tbsp sesame seeds
1 tbsp toasted sesame oil
1 tbsp rice wine vinegar
2 tbsp soy sauce

This is a great dish to knock up quickly when you're starving and want an instant carbohydrate hit with attitude. It goes with almost anything, oriental or not, but is a great base for piling on added value in the shape of cooked chicken, fish, mushrooms, or greens such as courgettes, bok choi or another of the Chinese greens, and broccoli.

chinese noodles with bean sprouts

2–4 servings

15 minutes preparation

15 minutes cooking

ingredients

250 g Chinese wheat noodles or Chinese egg noodles

2 Spanish onions

5 cm ginger

1 plump garlic clove

1 red chilli

salt

350 g bean sprouts

3 tbsp sesame oil

3 tbsp soy sauce

2 tbsp roughly chopped coriander leaves

3 shakes of toasted sesame oil (optional)

method

❶ Fill a large pan with water and put on to boil. Place the noodles in a second pan.

❷ Meanwhile, peel, halve and slice the onions. Peel the ginger, slice thinly lengthways, then into thin batons; cut these into 5 mm pieces. Peel the garlic and chop finely. Trim and split open the chilli, scrape out the seeds and slice into thin batons. Chop into small flecks. (See page 21.)

❸ By now the water will be boiling. Add ½ teaspoon of salt and fling in the bean sprouts. Bring back to the boil and cook for 30 seconds until plump and glossy. Place a colander over the noodle pan and drain the bean sprout water onto the noodles. Boil for 5 minutes, drain and cover to keep warm.

❹ Heat a wok over a high flame, and when very hot, add 2 tablespoons of the oil and swirl it round the wok. Add the onion, tossing for a few minutes allowing some edges to brown. Lower the heat, keep tossing, and cook for about 6 minutes until the onions begin to soften and change colour. Add the ginger, garlic, chilli and 2 tablespoons of soy sauce and stir fry for a few minutes. Add the bean sprouts, the remaining 1 tablespoon of oil and 1 tablespoon of soy sauce, then stir in the drained noodles. Toss to amalgamate, adding the coriander and toasted sesame oil.

Although I have used minced pork for this quick and simple
stir fry, you can also use minced chicken or a mixture of pork and chicken.
Or make it with sausage meat. Either way, it is economical and very
satisfying.

ants climbing trees

method

❶ Combine the pork, light soy sauce, sugar, cornflour and
chilli bean paste and leave to stand for 20 minutes.

❷ Pour boiling water over the noodles in a heat-proof
bowl and let stand for 3–4 minutes until tender and
transparent. Drain.

❸ Making separate piles, trim and finely chop 1 spring
onion and finely slice the green part only of the other. Trim
and split the chilli, scrape out the seeds and chop it very
finely. (See page 21.)

❹ When the meat is ready, heat the oil in a hot wok and
cook the chopped whole spring onion and chilli for about
30 seconds. Add the pork mixture and stir fry for 2–3
minutes, then add the noodles and mix well. Add the
chicken stock and dark soy sauce and bring to the boil.
Cook for a few more minutes until the liquid has all but
disappeared into the noodles. Scatter with the sliced
spring onion greens and serve.

4 servings
10 minutes preparation
10 minutes cooking

ingredients

250 g minced pork
2 tbsp light soy sauce
1 tbsp sugar
1 tsp cornflour
1 tbsp chilli bean paste or
    brown bean sauce with a
    shake of Tabasco
200 g bean thread vermicelli
2 spring onions
1 small red chilli
3 tbsp peanut oil
¼ chicken stock cube
    dissolved in 100 ml boiling
    water
1 tbsp dark soy sauce

There are times when there is nothing better than slurping a big bowl of slippery noodles. I haven't quite developed the Japanese passion for eating them cold but smart and distinctive buckwheat soba noodles are delicious in this typically simple Japanese noodle soup-supper. Any noodles would do for this but ready-cooked noodles would turn it into an almost instant dish.

soba noodles with mushrooms and chicken

2 servings
20 minutes preparation
20 minutes cooking

ingredients

5 cm piece fresh ginger
2 plump garlic cloves
salt
4 spring onions
½ chicken stock cube
    dissolved in 300 ml boiling
    water
2 chicken breasts (see page
    179)
6 medium-sized mushrooms
150 g soba Japanese buck-
    wheat noodles
squirt of wasabi (see page 108)
½ tbsp soy sauce

method

❶ Peel the ginger, slice into thin rounds, then batons and finally into tiny dice. Peel the garlic and chop very small. Sprinkle the two with a generous pinch of salt and use the flat of a knife to work together to form a smooth, juicy paste. Trim the spring onions and slice white and green very thinly, separating into two piles.

❷ Place half the ginger and garlic paste into a pan with the chicken stock. Add the skinned chicken breasts and bring slowly to simmer over a medium–low heat. Once simmering gently, cook for 10 minutes.

❸ Meanwhile, wipe the mushrooms and slice, preferably quartered through the stem to keep some semblance of the original shape. Add to the pot and cook for a further 10 minutes.

❹ Remove the chicken and use two forks to shred the fillets. Return the flesh to the pan with the green spring onion, cover and turn off the heat.

❺ Meanwhile, fill a large pan of water and bring to the boil. Do not add salt. Add the noodles and cook according to the instructions on page 107, or cheat and gently simmer for 10 minutes. Drain and tip into the soup pan along with the white spring onion and the rest of the ginger and garlic paste.

❻ Mix the wasabi into the soy sauce and stir that in too. Taste and adjust the seasoning if necessary. Divide between two bowls and, if you're game, eat with chop sticks.

A quick, vibrantly flavoured vegetable noodle dish to share with a friend. You will, however, need to have a few Thai staples in the store cupboard.

courgette and bok choi noodles

method

❶ Place the noodles in a pan or bowl and cover with boiling water. Leave for 15 minutes. Drain.

❷ Trim the courgettes, split in half lengthways then slice on the slant in chunky pieces. Quarter the bok choi lengthways and halve the quarters. Peel and finely slice the ginger then cut it into batons. Finely chop the garlic. Split the chilli, scrape out the seeds and finely chop (*see* page 21). Mix the fish sauce and soy sauce with an equal amount of water. Coarsely chop the herbs.

❸ Heat a wok or large frying pan over a high heat, swirling it round the pan, then add the ginger, garlic and chilli. Stir fry for a minute or two until the garlic is golden. Add the courgettes and bok choi and keep tossing for 2–3 minutes until the leaves of the bok choi are wilted and the stalks tender but still crunchy. Stir in the drained noodles. Toss to heat. Add the chopped mint and coriander, toss again and serve.

2 servings
15 minutes preparation
10 minutes cooking

ingredients

100 g rice stick noodles
2 medium-sized courgettes
2 small bok choi
2.5 cm piece fresh ginger
1 large clove of garlic
1 small red chilli
3 tbsp oriental fish sauce
2 tbsp soy sauce
handful of mint leaves
handful of corinader leaves
2 tbsp cooking oil

This is a cross between a Vietnamese-style noodle

soup-supper and a Thai stir fry. Like many noodle dishes, it is light on meat and high on flavour.

pork noodles with wilted spinach

4 servings

15 minutes preparation

10 minutes cooking

ingredients

1¼ chicken stock cubes
    dissolved in 600 ml boiling
    water
salt and black pepper
300 g fresh rice noodles (or
    reconstituted dried)
bunch of spring onions
1 plump garlic clove
1 small red chilli
5 cm piece fresh ginger
100 g young spinach leaves
200 g pork escalope
1½ tbsp sesame oil
2 tbsp dry sherry or rice wine
handful of coarsely chopped
    fresh coriander leaves
soy sauce to serve

method

❶ Bring the chicken stock to the boil in a medium-sized pan. Taste and season with salt and pepper. Add the noodles and simmer for a couple of minutes. Turn off the heat and cover the pan.

❷ Trim and slice the spring onions, including all but the damaged or very tough green ends. Peel the garlic and chop finely. Split the chilli, scrape out the seeds, slice into thin batons and chop into tiny specks. (*See* page 21.) Peel the ginger and grate or slice into very thin small batons. Bunch the spinach up in your hand and slice through it a few times to shred coarsely.

❸ Slice across the grain of the escalopes, cutting the meat into 3 cm long ribbons.

❹ Heat a wok or large frying pan over a high heat. When hot, add the oil and swirl it round the pan. Lift the wok off the heat, add the prepared spring onions, garlic, chilli and ginger, and stir fry for a few seconds before returning to the heat. Continue cooking for about 60 seconds, reducing the heat so nothing burns, then add the strips of meat. Toss around for a couple of minutes, again adjusting the heat so the food cooks quickly but without burning.

❺ Add the sherry or rice wine and allow to almost boil away until sticky. Stir the shredded spinach into the pan, tossing everything around for a few moments as the spinach wilts. Remove the pan from the heat.

❻ Scoop the noodles into deep bowls, sprinkle with

coriander but reserve about 1 tablespoonful. Pour the stock over the noodles and arrange the meat and spinach mixture on top.

❼ Garnish with the remaining coriander and serve with soy sauce, forks and spoons.

A Vietnamese noodle supper to share with friends. Easy, delicious and filling.

noodles with lemongrass pork kebabs

method

❶ Soak the bamboo skewers in cold water for 20 minutes.

❷ Remove the tough outer leaves and tough green tops from the lemon grass. Finely chop then grind the tender inner stalk. Peel and finely chop the shallot and garlic. Stir together the fish sauce, soya sauce, sugar and oil in a spacious bowl until the sugar is completely dissolved. Add the lemon grass, shallot and garlic.

❸ Thinly slice the meat into long strips, cutting against the grain. Soak the meat in the lemon grass marinade for at least 1 hour, covered and refrigerated.

❹ Slide 2–4 slices of pork onto each skewer so the meat is flat with the skewer going through the slices several times.

❺ About 15 minutes before you are ready to eat, soak the noodles in boiling water. Drain and toss with the coarsely chopped coriander. Cook the kebabs in a hot non-stick frying pan until the edges crisp, about 1 minute a side. Slide the meat off the sticks and toss with the noodles.

4 servings
20 minutes preparation plus
1 hour soaking
10 minutes cooking

ingredients

2 stalks lemon grass
1 large shallot
2 large cloves of garlic
50 ml oriental fish sauce
1 tbsp soy sauce
1 tbsp sugar
2 tbsp cooking oil
500 g pork tenderloin
200 g rice stick noodles
handful coriander leaves
you will also need 16 bamboo
**   skewers**

Once you start noodling, it becomes obvious how noodles can be used to make simple and painless suppers for yourself and your friends.

sesame chicken with udon noodles

4 servings

15 minutes preparation

15 minutes cooking

ingredients

200 g Udon wheat noodles

3 tbsp toasted sesame oil

3 tbsp soy sauce

6 carrots

1 large onion

1 chicken stock cube dissolved in 500 ml boiling water

500 g chicken meat (see page 179)

2 garlic cloves

1 tbsp vegetable oil

1 tbsp flour or cornflour

1 tbsp sesame seeds

method

❶ Three-quarters fill a large pan with water and put it on to boil. Do not add salt. Add the noodles and cook according to the packet instructions; they take about 4 minutes in total. Drain, toss with 1 tablespoon of toasted sesame oil and 1 tablespoon of soy sauce.

❷ Meanwhile, peel and trim the carrots and slice diagonally into chunky pieces. Peel the onion, cut in half and slice down the halves to make chunky half-moons. Place carrots and onion in a medium-sized pan with the stock. Boil with the pan half covered for about 8 minutes until the carrot and onion are tender.

❸ While the vegetables are cooking, cut the chicken into bite-size chunks and place in a bowl. Peel and finely chop the garlic. Smear the chicken with the rest of the toasted sesame oil and the garlic.

❹ When the vegetables are nearly ready, heat a wok over a high flame. Add the tablespoon of vegetable oil and swirl it round the wok. Add the chicken and stir fry briskly, adjusting the heat as necessary, for about 5 minutes until the chicken is half cooked. Sift the flour over the top, stir it in thoroughly and then scoop the vegetables out of the pan into the wok. Stir fry for a further few minutes, adding a little of the stock, the rest of the soy sauce and the sesame seeds.

❺ Divide the noodles between deep bowls, moisten with some stock and spoon the meat and veg over the top. Serve with extra soy sauce and toasted sesame oil.

Kashgar is the name of a medieval settlement on the north-west frontier of China famous for its huge bazaar. Here, a friend tells me, you can watch the noodle makers at work while slurping on a bowl of robustly flavoured noodles such as these. It is a good idea to use a can of chopped tomatoes for this recipe as it produces a thicker, richer sauce.

kashgar noodles

method

❶ Peel, halve and slice down the onions to make chunky half-moons. Quarter the red peppers lengthways. Scrape away seeds and white filament and cut into chunky dice. Peel and finely chop the garlic.

❷ Cut the meat across the grain into strips approximately 4 cm x 1 cm

❸ Heat a wok over a high heat and when very hot, add the oil and swirl it around the pan. Add the onions and peppers and stir for about 2 minutes until the onions are transparent but not softened. Add the garlic and cook for 30 seconds. Push the mixture up the side of the wok away from the heat, add the meat and cook until sealed on all sides. Stir onions and garlic back in.

❹ Add the cumin and allspice, cook for 1 minute, then stir in the tomatoes. Reduce the heat slightly, cover the pan and simmer for 5 minutes. Taste and season with salt and pepper to taste.

❺ Meanwhile, half-fill a large saucepan of water and bring to the boil. Add salt and the noodles and cook for 2 minutes until just tender. Drain thoroughly.

❻ Divide the noodles between 4 deep soup bowls, spoon over the lamb and eat.

4 servings
20 minutes preparation
15 minutes cooking

ingredients

2 medium-sized red onions

2 red peppers

2 big garlic cloves

300 g boneless shoulder of
    lamb or neck fillet

3 tbsp sesame or peanut oil

1½ tsp ground cumin

1 tsp allspice

400 g can of chopped Italian
    peeled tomatoes

salt and black pepper

450 g thick fresh Chinese
    wheat noodles (or soaked
    dried noodles)

6. stir fries

Wok cooking is one-pan cooking. And one-pan washing up. For most people, wok means stir fries but you can, in fact, steam, poach, braise or do just about anything in it, including frying eggs and making soups and stews. The curved design of a wok means it is ideally suited for stir fries and it is great fun tossing the food around so that nothing burns and everything gets a blast of heat. The actual cooking of a stir fry is fast and furious. All the work, the chopping and slicing, assembling of sauces and seasonings, has to be done before the cooking starts. And once it is done, a stir fry needs to be eaten immediately. If it is to be accompanied by rice or noodles, or anything else for that matter, it must be ready before the wok is heated.

Almost anything goes with stir fries. It is a great way, for example, of using up leftovers: that single carrot or the lonely piece of chicken that is about to go past its eat-by date. It is also a great way of making vegetables go further without seeming mean.

Don't fall into the trap of thinking that stir fries are always made with Chinese or with South-east Asian flavourings. Use fresh ginger, garlic, chilli and spring onions by all means but remember that soy sauce isn't the only liquid seasoning. A splash of apple juice, for example, or honey mixed with lemon juice or regular vinaigrette can all be used to season and flavour stir fries. The best stir fries, whether they are entirely vegetarian or include meat or seafood, are a mix of textures and flavours. Once you understand the basic rules – see the How to Stir Fry Properly check list on the page opposite – the wok will become your key to almost instant good food.

The pros and cons of wok buying are explored in detail on page 16 but if you don't own a wok, it doesn't actually matter. All these recipes can also be cooked in a large frying pan or a similarly wide-based saucepan.

How to Stir Fry Properly

- Prepare all ingredients before you start cooking. Have everything laid out ready to go like a fast-order chef. That includes pre-mixing sauces, measuring out bottled sauces and having all other seasonings to hand.
- If you are adding noodles or rice, be sure to have them soaked and drained, or cooked, before you start stir frying.
- Heat the wok until it is shimmering with heat before you add the oil. Immediately swirl the oil around the wok and then start adding food. Constantly adjust the heat, up when you add more food, down as it begins to cook, as well as keeping the food on the move. Use the uppermost part of the wok which is furthest away from the heat to rest cooked food when you add new ingredients.
- Don't try to stir fry too much food at once. Build up the ingredients, adding them in order of length of time of cooking. Cabbage and spring onions, for example, need very little time, whereas carrots, however thinly sliced, and other dense foods such as aubergines, take longer. All the food must come into direct contact with heat otherwise it will steam rather than fry.
- If you are not following a recipe, be sensible about adding ingredients in the right order so that everything ends up tender or *al dente*, as appropriate, when the dish is finished.
- Use nuts and seeds to add texture and flavour.

What about Ready-made Stir Fry Sauces?

As you become more experienced at stir fry cooking, it will become second nature to make your own sauces to flavour your stir fries. A splash of soy sauce, Tabasco or another chilli sauce and a little stock (made with a cube), a few drops of toasted sesame oil and rice wine vinegar work wonders for flavour. But there is a wide range of other oriental and South-east Asian bottled sauces such as oyster sauce, fish sauce and black bean paste now widely available in supermarkets; *see* page 108. Numerous packets, sachets and bottles of so-called stir fry pastes and sauces will inject flavour with minimum effort. Try out a few and see what you think. I'd particularly recommend The Merchant Gourmet range that includes Cantonese black bean stir fry paste, Szechuan chilli, ginger and garlic stir fry paste, Thai spicy basil stir fry paste and red and green Thai curry sauces. The Blue Dragon range is good, too, and great value. Although they are relatively inexpensive and tasty, you will spend far less in the long run and produce better stir fries if you make your own sauces.

My favourite seasoning trinity is a mixture of finely chopped garlic and chilli together with wafer-thin slices of peeled fresh ginger, with a handful of coriander added at the end of cooking, mixed with a little water to add moisture. That is really all you need for a tasty stir fry.

Not only do the cooking smells of this healthy almost-vegetarian dish fill the house with mouth-watering smells, it is also an extremely quick and easy dish to make. It manages to be both fresh and filling, lively on the tongue and a welcome mixture of textures. The dish looks pretty; the silky strands of red onion flop against the bright green of the quickly cooked broccoli and a shock of broken white 'angel hair', the whole thing flecked with specks of red chilli and golden sesame seeds.

sesame broccoli with noodles

method

❶ Place the noodles in a bowl and cover with plenty of boiling water. Leave for 10 minutes while you prepare the rest.

❷ Now prepare all the other ingredients. Peel the onions, halve them and then slice lengthways to make chunky wedges. Peel the garlic and slice in wafer-thin rounds. Split the chillies, scrape away the seeds and chop finely. (See page 21.) Chop the anchovy fillets.

❸ Remove the florets from the broccoli stalk and, where necessary, divide into bite-size pieces. Trim the broccoli stalk and slice into 1 cm thick rounds, then halve the rounds.

❹ Heat the wok over a high flame, add the oil, swirling it round the pan. Add the onion, tossing for a couple of minutes until it flops slightly then add the garlic and broccoli stalks. Keep the food moving, adding the florets 30 seconds later with the anchovy and chilli. Reduce the heat slightly. After 5–6 minutes of continuous tossing, drain the noodles in a sieve and add them to the pan with a couple of tablespoons of water if the noodles are catching on the bottom. Stir fry for 30 more seconds, sprinkle over the sesame seeds and tip into a bowl/s. Season with soy sauce and toasted sesame oil if available.

2 servings
15 minutes preparation
10 minutes cooking

ingredients

75 g rice vermicelli/stir fry noodles

2 medium-sized red onions

2 plump garlic cloves

2 small red chillies

4 anchovy fillets

400 g broccoli

3 tbsp sesame or vegetable oil

1 heaped tbsp toasted sesame seeds (see page 108)

soy sauce and toasted sesame oil to serve

Remember this quick lone supper next time you have a few leftover boiled potatoes to use up. The secret ingredient that turns this delicious combination of food into something really special is nutmeg. In an ideal world, you will be grating from a whole nutmeg directly into the pan. Its curiously exotic flavour has a magical effect. Serve with a well-buttered doorstep and a glass of milk.

potato, bacon and cabbage stir fry hash

1 large serving
10 minutes preparation
10 minutes cooking

ingredients

2–3 medium-sized leftover
   cooked potatoes or
   equivalent (or more)
4 rashers of rindless streaky
   bacon
½ small green cabbage
2 tbsp cooking oil
salt and black pepper
nutmeg, preferably freshly
   grated
1 tbsp chopped flat leaf parsley
   or chives (if possible)
1 or 2 eggs

method

❶ Slice across the pile of rashers to make short strips of bacon. Chunk the potatoes. Halve the cabbage through the core then cut away the core. Shred the cabbage across the halves.

❷ Heat the wok over a high flame, add 1½ tablespoons of the oil, swirling it round the pan. Add the bacon, tossing for 1–2 minutes, adjusting the heat so it begins to crisp without burning. Add the potato, keeping the food moving for a further couple of minutes then add the cabbage. Increase the heat and toss for another minute or so until the cabbage begins to wilt. Season with salt and pepper and add the nutmeg. Toss constantly for 30 seconds, adding the parsley or chives right at the end of cooking, then transfer to a warm plate.

❸ Add the remaining oil to the wok and fry the egg or eggs. Plonk on top of the vegetables and eat.

I was once asked to come up with interesting ways of cooking Spam and hit upon the discovery that if you chop it and fry it, it turns gorgeously crisp and un-Spam-like. It was the chef at my local Thai restaurant who suggested using it instead of pork in this quick and simple stir fry. I defy you to recognize the end result as Spam. You could, of course, use raw pork or chicken or turkey sliced into strips.

spam pad khee mao

method

❶ Place the noodles in a bowl and cover with plenty of unsalted boiling water. Leave for 10 minutes while you prepare everything else.

❷ Peel and chop the garlic. Split the chillies, discarding seeds and stalks, and chop finely, see page 21. Pound garlic and chillies with 1 tablespoon of cooking oil to make a paste – quickly and easily done in a mortar.

❸ Cut the Spam into chunks or batons. Finely shred the spring greens or cabbage, having cut out and discarded any dense stalk.

❹ Drain the soft noodles and shake dry. Mix 1 tablespoon of the paste, the oyster and fish sauce and soy sauce in a bowl. (The rest of the paste can be kept, covered, in the fridge for a week.)

❺ Heat the wok over a high flame. Add the remaining oil and swirl it round the wok, going up the sides. Add the liquid in the bowl and almost immediately add the Spam, tossing it around in the sauce, then add the noodles, and then the spring greens or cabbage. Cook for 2 more minutes whilst constantly tossing around the contents of the pan. Add the coriander leaves and eat.

1–2 servings
10 minutes preparation
10 minutes cooking

ingredients

50 g rice noodles

2 garlic cloves

4 red or green chillies

2 tbsp cooking oil

200 g can of Spam

approx 250 g spring greens or green cabbage

1 tbsp Chinese or Thai oyster sauce

1 tbsp Thai fish sauce (nuoc nam)

1 tbsp soy sauce

a few chopped coriander leaves to serve (optional)

The distinctive hot, sour, sweet and creamy flavours of Thai food come together in this simplified Thai-style stir fry. The cleanest strongest flavours shine through if you make your own green Thai curry paste or buy it fresh from a Thai grocery. A packet version will give very good results too and you can always add extra chilli and lemon juice.

thai-style stir fry

2 servings

10 minutes preparation

15 minutes cooking

ingredients

100 g rice noodles

1 tbsp cooking oil

225 g lean chicken, turkey or pork fillet

1 medium-sized red onion

6 spring onions

1 tbsp Thai green curry paste (see page 215)

2 tbsp white wine

½ tsp sugar

1 scant tbsp soy sauce

½ chicken stock cube dissolved in 100 ml boiling water

200 ml carton of coconut milk or 50 g block of coconut cream dissolved in 150 ml hot milk (see page 221)

salt

a few coriander leaves

method

❶ Place the noodles in a bowl and cover with plenty of unsalted boiling water. Leave for 10 minutes, then drain and mix with half the cooking oil. Cover to keep warm.

❷ Slice the meat thinly across the grain. Peel and slice the red onion into half moons. Trim and slice the spring onions quite thinly on the diagonal.

❸ Heat a wok and add the rest of the cooking oil with the green curry paste, meat and red onion. Stir fry over a medium heat for a few minutes until the meat firms and changes colour and the onion wilts slightly. Add the white wine (or white wine vinegar would do), sugar, soy sauce and spring onion. Stir as it bubbles then add the stock and coconut milk. Boil hard for a few minutes to thicken and concentrate the sauce. Taste and season with salt if necessary.

❹ Serve over the noodles garnished with chopped coriander.

There are several ways to go with prawns cooked like
this. I like them as they are, eaten against a mound of plainly boiled basmati
rice. They are delicious used as a scoop for a creamy dip such as garlicky
mayonnaise or tzatziki and chased with a hunk of well-buttered crusty bread.
Or try them with angel hair pasta slicked with a spoonful of olive oil.

There couldn't be a much simpler or more delicious quick supper than
this one.

chilli prawns with lemon and coriander

method

❶ Trim and split the chilli. Discard the seeds and slice into
skinny batons and then chop across the batons to make
tiny dice. Peel and chop the garlic as finely as possible.

❷ Tip 1 tablespoon of oil into the prawns and use your
hands to smear it all over them. Sprinkle the garlic and
chilli over the prawns and mix thoroughly with your hands
so that all the prawns are flecked with red and white. (Now
see page 21.)

❸ Roughly chop the coriander leaves.

❹ Place a wok or large frying pan over a high heat and
when very hot add the remaining oil. Swirl the oil round the
pan. Use a wooden spatula or similar to scrape the
prawns, chilli and garlic into the pan, and stir fry
constantly for a couple of minutes, adjusting the heat
slightly so nothing burns, and taking care because the
chilli will give a whoosh of fumes that might make you
catch your breath. Squeeze over the lemon juice, toss
again as the juice turns syrupy and evaporates slightly.
Turn off the heat, drop the coriander into the prawns.
Season with salt and black pepper. Toss again and serve
immediately.

2 servings
10 minutes preparation
3 minutes cooking

ingredients

1 red chilli
2 large garlic cloves
3 tbsp cooking oil
200 g cooked and peeled
  prawns
handful of coriander leaves
juice of 1 large lemon
salt and black pepper

Here's an idea for doing something a bit different with a small quantity of lean lamb. It is one of those quickly cooked lash-ups, when all the chopping and slicing is done while the potatoes bubble away in the background. The marinated meat and leeks release wafts of the most wonderfully tempting cooking smells which get even better when some finely chopped mint is stirred into the pan.

lamb with leeks and mint

2–3 servings
25 minutes preparation
10 minutes cooking

ingredients
225 g boneless leg of lamb steaks or 2 meaty lamb chops
3 tbsp olive oil
juice of 1 small lemon
1 plump garlic clove
450 g new potatoes
150 g French beans
3 leeks
about 30 mint leaves
salt and black pepper

method
❶ Trim any fat from the meat and discard. If using chops, cut the meat off the bone in one big piece. Slice into long, thin strips. Place the meat in a bowl and pour over 2 tablespoons of the oil, the juice from half the lemon and the garlic which you have chopped, then pulverized in a little salt with the flat of a knife. Use your hands to smear this all over the meat.
❷ Scrape the potatoes, cut into large bite-sized chunks. Place in a pan of boiling water with 1 teaspoon of salt and cook until tender to the point of a sharp knife. Drain.
❸ Put a second pan of water on to boil. When the water is coming up to the boil, cut the stalks off the beans (don't bother to remove the pointy end: that's edible). When the water is boiling vigorously, add 1 teaspoon of salt and the beans. When the water comes back to the boil, count to 30, then drain immediately.
❹ Trim the leeks and slice in thin rounds, discarding only the toughest green part. Place in a colander and rinse thoroughly under running water. Finely chop the mint.
❺ Heat the wok over a high flame, add the remaining tablespoon of oil and swirl it round the pan. Tip in the meat and its marinade and immediately start tossing it around in the pan. Cook, keeping the meat on the move

constantly, for about 2 minutes until it has changed in colour from pink to brown, then add the leeks. Keep stir frying, adding most of the mint after a couple of minutes when the leeks have flopped and their juices started to dry up. Season generously with salt and pepper, reduce the heat slightly, squeeze over the last of the lemon juice. Toss a few times and then add the potatoes and beans to the pan. Add the last of the mint, toss again and when everything is nicely hot, serve and eat immediately.

Gnocchi are dumplings made with flour or potato. Both, sold in longlife packs, are very useful store cupboard standbys. This dish ends up risotto-like, the starch from the gnocchi slightly thickening the white wine juices and is all at once light but very satisfying. Serve it with ciabatta or another crusty bread and some decent butter. Extremely moreish.

potato gnocchi with peas and prawns

2 servings

10 minutes preparation

15 minutes cooking

ingredients

400 g gnocchi di patate

125 g bunch of spring onions

50 g butter

150 g frozen peas

salt and black pepper

large glass of white wine or
 ¼ chicken stock cube
 dissolved in 150 ml boiling
 water

200 g cooked and peeled large
 prawns

2 tbsp chopped mint

2 tbsp freshly grated Parmesan

method

❶ Put a medium-sized pan of water on to boil. Add the gnocchi and 1 teaspoon of salt and return to the boil. The gnocchi are done when they've all risen to the surface. Drain.

❷ Meanwhile, trim and finely slice the spring onions. Melt the butter in a wok or large frying pan and soften the spring onions. After about 5 minutes add the frozen peas. Season with salt and pepper and cook for 2–3 minutes until the peas are tender and the onions very soft.

❸ Add the wine or stock, stir well and add the gnocchi. Bubble steadily for several minutes to reduce slightly and thicken, then stir in the prawns. Cook until the prawns are hot. Taste and adjust the seasoning with salt and pepper then stir in the chopped mint.

❹ Serve in bowls with a generous grating of Parmesan.

This is a classic Chinese stir fry. Delicious over rice

(which should be cooked and ready before you start stir frying).

beef with oyster sauce

method

1 Cut the steak in half lengthways, then into thin slices 5 cm wide and 5 mm thick, cutting against the grain. Mix the beef with the soy sauce, 2 teaspoons of sherry or rice wine, the toasted sesame oil and cornflour. Let it sit for 20 minutes.

2 Meanwhile, peel the garlic and lightly crush it to a paste with a little salt. Peel, halve and slice the onion.

3 Heat a wok or deep pan until it is very hot. Swirl in the oil and, when very hot and smoking, add the beef and stir fry for 3 minutes. Remove the beef and drain off all but 1 tablespoon of oil.

4 Reheat the wok, stir fry the garlic and onions for 3 minutes or until the onions are wilted and lightly browned. Pour in the chicken stock, remaining sherry or rice wine and sugar and bring to the boil over a high heat. Add the oyster sauce, mix well, return the beef and cook for 1 more minute. Serve immediately.

4 servings
15 minutes preparation
    plus 20 minutes
    marinating
20 minutes cooking

ingredients

450 g rump, entrecôte or skirt
    steak
1 tbsp light soy sauce
2 tsp dry sherry or rice wine
2 tsp toasted sesame oil
2 tsp cornflour
3 garlic cloves
2 medium-sized onions
3 tbsp vegetable oil
¼ chicken stock cube
    dissolved in 75 ml boiling
    water
1 tsp sugar
3 tbsp oyster sauce

A very basic Chinese-style stir fry. Quick and delicious.

Chicken can be used just as easily; you will need three large breasts.

ginger turkey noodle stir fry

3–4 servings

20 minutes preparation

20 minutes cooking

ingredients

250 g dried Chinese egg
    noodles

2 large carrots

bunch of spring onions

1 red pepper

1 garlic clove

3 cm piece fresh ginger

2 turkey breasts (see page 179)

3 tbsp sesame or vegetable oil

2 tbsp dry sherry or rice wine

4 tbsp soy sauce

handful of coriander leaves

method

❶ Cook the noodles according to packet instructions, boiling for about 4 minutes. Drain and keep warm.

❷ Peel and trim the carrots. Split lengthways then slice into 5 cm long batons. Trim the onions and slice on the slant into diagonal lengths approximately 2½ cm long. Split the pepper, discard the stem, seeds and any white filament, and slice into batons approximately the same size as the carrot. Peel and finely chop the garlic. Peel and thinly slice the ginger. Slice into skinny batons.

❸ Lay out the turkey breasts and bang a couple of times with the base of a saucepan to flatten slightly. Slice, following the grain of the meat, into ribbons. Cut into approximately 5 cm lengths.

❹ Heat a wok, add the oil and swirl it round the pan to coat the sides. Drop the ginger and spring onion into the hot oil and stir fry vigorously for 1 minute. Push the ingredients to the side, add the carrots, pepper and garlic and stir fry for 2 minutes, then take the onion and ginger back to the middle of the wok and stir fry for 2 more minutes.

❺ Push the vegetables to the side and add the turkey, a little at a time, letting it sizzle briefly on each side before tossing it with the other ingredients for a further 2 minutes.

❻ Pour on the sherry and let it bubble briefly before adding the soy sauce. Add the drained noodles to the stir fry. Toss and mix, adding extra soy sauce and a little water if it seems dry. Scatter over the roughly chopped coriander leaves and serve.

7. rice and grains

Don't be afraid of cooking rice. For everyday rice cooking I would recommend long-grained **basmati rice**. It might not be the cheapest rice but the few extra pence are worth spending because basmati always cooks perfectly, giving fluffy rice that doesn't clump into a sticky, starchy mess. It is perfect for savoury dishes, pilafs, stir fries, salads and stuffings, or served plain. Once you have cracked cooking rice, and it is really very easy and very quick, you won't want to bother with so called 'easy-cook rice' which is either par-boiled or pre-cooked. Both are relatively expensive, particularly canned cooked rice, and won't fill the house with the surprisingly delicious smell that comes from cooking rice properly.

Buy supermarket own brand – often the same as a well-known brand – or, better still, buy from Indian, Chinese and South-east Asian food stores. Go for the biggest bag you can afford and, if possible, transfer it to a glass jar – I use a sweet jar scrounged from a sweet shop – and keep in a cool, dark, dry place.

Round grain Italian **Arborio** or **Vialone Nano**, or Spanish **Carnaroli** is what you need for risotto and paella. This sort of rice can absorb a large amount of liquid without breaking up and some of its starchy exterior layer, which dissolves into the liquid, thickens and gives body to the sauce.

Cous cous and **bulgar**, which are rice alternatives, are even easier. Cous cous is to North Africa what pasta is to Italy. It's a cereal processed from maize and dried and rolled into tiny pellets. Bulgar, which looks like large grains of cous cous, is also popular in North Africa but is a staple in Lebanon and throughout the Middle East. It is made from cracked wheat. Both are sold in a semi-processed state, are widely available, and can be prepared in various ways, the simplest being a brief soak in boiling water.

Polenta is the name of the fine, golden cornmeal cereal that is the staple diet of northern Italy. It is stirred into water and cooked like porridge but enriched with butter and grated Parmesan. It is eaten in its so-called wet state in place of mashed potato, pasta or rice. It is also poured into trays and left to set. It can then be cut into slabs or triangles, smeared with olive oil and griddled or barbecued until it is etched with scorch lines. Grilled polenta is used like bruschetta and piled up with anything and everything from mushrooms to liver and onions. It can also be used like lasagne (see page 150). Convenience versions of both sorts of polenta are now widely available. They are quick and inexpensive. Authentic polenta takes about 45 minutes to prepare and is far cheaper with better flavour.

To Wash or Not to Wash Rice

I rarely bother. But when I do, I notice that although the rice is whiter it lacks flavour. To wash, place the rice in a saucepan and hold it under a gently running cold tap until the water runs clear. Alternatively, place rice in a sieve under a running tap.

Perfect Boiled Basmati

Place 1 quantity of basmati rice to 2 of cold water in an appropriately sized saucepan with a well-fitting lid. Bring the water to the boil, turn the heat very low, cover the pan, and cook for 15 minutes. Turn off the heat. *Do not* remove the lid. Leave the pan untouched for at least 5 minutes so that the rice can finish cooking in its steam. Fluff up with a fork before serving.

What to Do with Leftover Rice

Cooked rice will keep, covered, in the coldest part of the fridge for 3–4 days. It is unwise to keep it longer: cooked rice is susceptible to bacteria that can cause severe stomach upsets. The organism cannot survive in temperatures below 4°C/39°F or above 60°C/140°F. When re-heating rice, make sure the rice is thoroughly hot. The simplest way to do this is to pour boiling water over the rice, breaking up any clumps with a fork. Leave for a few minutes then drain thoroughly in a sieve or colander.

- stir into a cheese sauce and mix with florets of lightly boiled cauliflower or broccoli or grated courgette. Eat risotto-style with grated Parmesan or top with grated Cheddar and brown in the oven.
- mix with yoghurt, sugar and toasted almonds and eat with fruit (*see* page 239).
- mix with a good handful of chopped herbs and vinaigrette. Add cooked peas and/or diced ham or fried chicken or salmon.
- fry a chopped onion with garlic, add cooked prawns, rice, frozen peas and a splash of water or white wine. Boil for 1 minute, stir in a knob of butter.
- freeze it for later use: just pop it into a plastic bag, seal and eat within 1 month.

This is a quick and clever way of making supper that avoids washing up. You can adapt the seasonings and vegetables to produce radically different flavours: go Caribbean by including sliced bell pepper with fresh coriander leaves, Tabasco and lime, or think French with sliced mushrooms, courgette, white wine, olives and fresh herbs.

asian fish in a packet

3 servings
15 minutes preparation
30 minutes cooking

ingredients

200 g basmati rice
6 spring onions
5 cm piece ginger
4 small bok choy, approx 75 g each or 150 g cabbage or spring greens
2 big garlic cloves
pinch of salt
3 tbsp vegetable oil
4 tbsp soy sauce
1 tbsp toasted sesame oil
3 skinned white fish fillets, such as haddock or cod, cut from the middle
you will also need 3 large pieces of tin foil, approx 35 cm x 70 cm

method

❶ Pre-heat the oven to 450°F/230°C/gas mark 8.

❷ Place rice and 400 ml cold water in a medium-sized pan and bring to the boil. Turn the heat down immediately, cover the pan and cook over a very low heat for 10 minutes. Turn off the heat, do not remove the lid, and leave for 5 minutes.

❸ Meanwhile, trim and finely slice the spring onions. Peel and slice the ginger wafer-thin. Quarter the bok choy lengthways, rinse and shake dry. Or shred the cabbage or spring greens.

❹ Peel and finely chop the garlic. Sprinkle with salt and use the flat of a knife to work to a paste. Put this in a bowl. Add 1 tablespoon of vegetable oil, the soy sauce and toasted sesame oil. Whisk together thoroughly.

❺ Lay out the sheets of foil and smear the middle section of each with a little of the vegetable oil. Spoon the cooked rice onto the middle of one half of each sheet. Top with bok choy or spinach, some of the ginger and spring onions, and cover with the fish. Sprinkle with more ginger and spring onions, and douse with the sauce. Fold over the foil and fold the ends and sides a couple of times to make neat, secure packages.

❻ Place the packages on a baking sheet in the middle of the hot oven. Cook for 15 minutes. Serve the packages on plates with chopsticks or forks.

Egg fried rice is perfect instant munch. Instant, that is, if you've got some leftover cooked rice. If you need to cook rice to order, it will still only take about 15 minutes. Anything goes when it comes to fried rice, wrote veteran expert Kenneth Lo in his book *Chinese Vegetable and Vegetarian Cooking*, but 'what must be avoided is a fried rice that is so mixed up that it borders on a mess'. Chicken is the favourite protein add-on, but scraps of bacon, pork or ham are good, too. To be interesting food as opposed to fuel food, you need a smidgin of Tabasco and a generous splash of soy sauce. If you can lay your hands on some fresh coriander to scatter over the top, so much the better.

egg fried rice

method

❶ Wash the rice until the water runs clear then bring to the boil with 400 ml water. Establish a very gentle simmer, cover the pan and cook for 10 minutes. Turn off the heat and leave for 5 minutes without moving the lid. All the water should be absorbed and the grains separate.

❷ Meanwhile, remove the skin and cut the chicken into thin strips. Peel and finely chop the garlic. Trim the spring onions, chop the white and thinly slice the green, keeping separate piles.

❸ Beat the eggs with 1/2 tablespoon of sesame oil, a few drops of Tabasco and half the coriander leaves.

❹ Get a wok very hot, add the remaining oil, and quickly swirl it round. Add the chicken and stir fry continuously until all the chicken has turned white. Adjust the heat, add the garlic and white onion, and cook briefly. Stir in the cooked rice, tossing to mix, then add the peas. Add the egg mixture, stirring vigorously, mixing it through the rice. Add the green spring onion and remaining coriander, toss and tip into bowls. Season to taste with soy sauce etc.

3 servings
10 minutes preparation
10 minutes cooking

ingredients

200 g basmati rice
1 large chicken breast (see
   page 179)
1 garlic clove
8 spring onions
2 eggs
1 tbsp chopped coriander
   leaves
3 tbsp sesame oil
100 g cooked frozen peas
black pepper
Tabasco sauce, soy sauce and
   toasted sesame oil (if
   possible)

Toast is not the only destiny for marmalade. A dollop of it adds an unconventional sweet and sour tanginess to this already choice orange- and saffron-flavoured chicken biryani. Saffron makes this dish. Not only does it colour the rice yellow, it also adds a subtle and exotic flavour which goes surprisingly well with bitter-sharp Seville orange marmalade.

It is expensive but a little goes a long way. You could add it to your Christmas or birthday lists or, if you happen to be on holiday in Spain or Morocco where it is cheap, bring some back with you. Given the choice, buy stamens rather than powder.

Serve this dish with poppadoms and mango chutney.

chicken biryani with orange and saffron

4 servings

25 minutes preparation

30 minutes cooking

ingredients

350 g chicken meat (see page 179)

1 large juicy orange

30 g butter

salt and black pepper

1 tbsp runny honey

1 large onion

3 garlic cloves

2 tbsp vegetable oil

50 g almond flakes

1 bay leaf

250 g basmati rice

1 chicken stock cube dissolved in 600 ml boiling water

method

❶ Slice the chicken into bite-sized pieces. Remove a 5 cm strip of orange zest (no white) from the orange and shred it into small matchsticks.

❷ Melt half the butter in a frying pan and gently brown the chicken. Season with salt and pepper, add honey and squeeze over the orange juice. Bubble up the juices and cook for a minute or two until the chicken is glossy.

❸ Meanwhile, peel, halve and finely slice the onion and garlic.

❹ Heat a medium-sized heavy-bottomed pan over a medium heat. Add ½ tablespoon of the cooking oil and stir fry the almonds until golden. Drain on kitchen paper.

❺ Turn up the heat, add the remaining oil and fry the onions until browned and beginning to crisp. Remove half the onions to drain on kitchen paper. Reduce the heat, add the remaining butter, the garlic and bay leaf. Stir fry for 30 seconds then add the rice, orange zest, half the almonds and ½ teaspoon salt. Cook for a further minute, then add 500 ml stock, the saffron, the chicken and its juices. Bring to the boil, reduce the heat to very low, cover the pan and cook for 10 minutes. Turn off the heat and leave, covered, without removing the lid, for 5 minutes.

6 Meanwhile, simmer the remaining 100 ml stock with the marmalade, cooking until frothy, sticky and reduced to about 3 tablespoons. Swirl the pan as the sauce reduces, adjusting the heat so it doesn't burn. Turn the biryani onto a warmed platter, take out the bay leaf and fork in the reserved almonds and onions. Pass the marmalade sauce through a sieve for a smooth texture, and then dribble it over the biryani. Serve immediately.

pinch of saffron stamens or powder softened in 1 tbsp boiling water

4 tbsp marmalade

Jambalaya is a rice, meat and seafood stew from Louisiana. The name is a jumble of *jambon*, the French word for ham, and *alaya*, which means rice in an African dialect. Consequently the dish usually includes a spicy pork sausage of some sort, although often ends up with ham. Whatever the ingredients, a good jambalaya is always spiked with plenty of chilli.

In order to control the amount of chilli, I have used cayenne at the beginning of the cooking, and added Tabasco – as much or as little as you like – at the end. Don't forget that the pepperoni is quite hot too.

Jambalaya is something that can simmer away gently on top of the stove but to avoid any risk of a crusty bottom (although some people claim that's part of its charm) and to ensure even cooking without soupiness, it is best done in the oven. What you need with this is a good supply of ice cold beer.

jambalaya

3–4 servings
20 minutes preparation
30 minutes cooking

ingredients

2 medium-sized red onions,
    approx 250 g
2 big garlic cloves
1 red pepper
1 celery heart
2 tbsp cooking oil
1 bay leaf
salt and black pepper
½ tsp cayenne pepper
2 plump chicken thighs
2 pepperoni sausages or 100 g
    pepperoni slices

method

❶ Peel and chop the onions and garlic. Core, de-seed and dice the red pepper. Trim and slice the celery, setting aside the leaves, rinse and drain.

❷ Heat the oil in a 2½-litre cast-iron casserole and stir in the onion and garlic. Cook for about 5 minutes then add the red pepper, celery and bay leaf. Season with salt and pepper and cayenne and cook for about 10 minutes while you prepare everything else.

❸ Pre-heat the oven to 375°C/190°C/gas mark 5.

❹ Remove the skin from the chicken thighs and cut the meat from the bone in chunks.

❺ Slice the pepperoni, if using. If the prawns are frozen, slip them into warm water for about 5 minutes to de-frost. Drain the prawns, place in a bowl and toss with the Tabasco. Stir the chicken into the vegetables and when all the pieces have turned white, add the pepperoni, rice and canned tomatoes with their juice. Add the stock. Bring to simmer, cover the pan and cook in the oven or over a low heat for 20 minutes.

6 By now the rice will have absorbed most of the liquid but the jambalaya should be nicely moist. If it isn't add a little more liquid. Stir in the prawns, cover again and cook for 5–10 more minutes depending on whether the prawns are fresh or frozen.

7 Coarsely chop the celery leaves and sprinkle them and the chopped parsley over the top. Serve with lemon wedges and the Tabasco bottle.

200 g peeled raw or cooked prawns
½ tsp Tabasco
250 g basmati rice
400 g can of Italian peeled tomatoes
1 chicken stock cube dissolved in 500 ml boiling water
1 tbsp finely chopped parsley
lemon wedges, to serve

What about Quick-cook Risotto, Cous Cous and Polenta?

All cous cous on sale at the supermarket is quick. Unlike the authentic stuff eaten in North Africa, which needs lengthy steaming, it has been processed so that it just needs to be soaked. However, I don't recommend instant cous cous meals. Why pay double (or more) for less cous cous with a few dried vegetables thrown in? Do it yourself in almost the same amount of time. While the cous cous is hydrating (with stock), fry an onion, toast a few almonds or pine kernels and mix everything together. If you've got grated cheese, a slice of ham, or frozen peas, for example, you are in business.

Instant or quick-cook risotto, however, is another matter. Risotto isn't difficult to make but it is demanding – although there are ways to cheat (see page 140). The best quickie packet risotto is **riso Gallo**. It takes 12 minutes and comes flavoured and coloured with tomato, spinach, saffron and, most spectacularly, with black cuttlefish ink. I also highly recommend **Sacla risotto! risotto!** The little 190 g jar plus a stock cube and 650 ml boiling water and 200 g risotto rice, makes extremely good no-fuss, no-stir risotto in about 15 minutes. The mushroom version is particularly good.

Set polenta – for using like lasagne and bruschetta – is a brilliant store cupboard standby.

It's hardly surprising that so many people think more than twice about making risotto. This lusciously creamy rice dish is shrouded in the sort of epic mystery that used to surround the soufflé and still surrounds gravy making. Well, here's a very simple but anarchic method for effectively eliminating all the hassle from risotto-making at one stroke. Almost all the stock is added in one go right at the beginning.

cheat's risotto

4 servings
30 minutes preparation
40 minutes cooking

ingredients

1 medium-sized onion
50 g butter plus an extra knob
250 g arborio rice
glass of dry white wine
salt and black pepper
generous pinch of saffron
stamens steeped in 1 tbsp
boiling water (see page 137)
1½ vegetable or chicken stock
cubes dissolved in 900 ml
boiling water
50 g freshly grated Parmesan
cheese plus more to serve

method

❶ Choose a heavy-bottomed medium-sized saucepan with a tight-fitting lid. Peel the onion and chop very finely. Melt 30 g of butter and gently soften the onion without browning. Stir in the rice, coating thoroughly with butter.

❷ Pour in the wine and stir constantly until It has almost entirely evaporated. Season with salt and pepper and add the saffron and three-quarters of the stock. Establish a steady, gentle boil, clamp on the lid and immediately turn off the heat. Leave the pan *untouched* for 30 minutes – don't even peek inside. The rice is cooking in its steam and a great deal of heat would be lost if the lid were lifted, even for a moment.

❸ When the time is up, lift the lid off the risotto – it will have absorbed all the liquid but look unpromising. Return it to a low heat and gradually stir in the remaining hot stock and remaining 20 g butter, stirring until the risotto turns creamy and sloppy but not overly wet. Stir in the Parmesan and the knob of butter and serve with extra Parmesan to grate over the top.

other good risotto:

Use the above recipe as a template, but in all cases omit the saffron, which is for that recipe only.

- 2 finely sliced large Spanish onions fried in an extra 50 g butter until really sloppy, adding 1 tablespoon of finely chopped rosemary just before adding Marsala instead of white wine.

- 50 g diced smoked streaky bacon or pancetta, can of rinsed and drained borlotti beans, 1 tablespoon of finely chopped rosemary and 1 tablespoon finely chopped lemon zest. Cook bacon, rosemary and lemon zest with the onion (stage 1 above). Add the beans at the end (stage 3).

- 250 g mushrooms – any type or a mixture – sliced or chopped, plus a handful of chopped thyme and of flat leaf parsley, a splash of Tabasco and a squeeze of lemon. Add the mushrooms, thyme, Tabasco and lemon and an extra 3 tablespoons of olive oil when the onions are cooked (stage 1). Cook, stirring constantly for 5 minutes. Stir in the parsley at the end.

- 3 large unwaxed lemons (zest removed and then chopped as finely as possible and juice squeezed) and 4 tablespoons of mascarpone. Add half the lemon zest and all the lemon juice after the wine has evaporated (stage 2). Stir in the mascarpone, and reserved lemon zest with the butter and Parmesan at the end.

Pilaf is rice with add-ons, begun, usually, like risotto, by frying chopped onion. Unlike risotto, which should end up lava-like and creamy, the rice remains dry with separate grains. Like risotto, however, the rice is imbued with flavour. It's a dish to play around with, adding different textures as well as flavours. This version is made with brown long-grain rice. Brown rice, which is white rice without the husk removed, takes much longer to cook than regular basmati (also long-grain) but you do get rice that tastes gorgeously nutty. To make pilaf with regular basmati, reduce the cooking time and adjust the liquid (*see* Perfect Boiled Basmati on page 133).

Slices of fried mushroom are a good addition to this pilaf. Try it hot, lukewarm or cold. It makes a delicious accompaniment to lamb (roast, chops or kebabs) or roast chicken. Here, it goes down well on its own with a scoop of Greek yoghurt, mango chutney, and a big mound of poppadoms.

brown rice pilaf

4 servings
20 minutes preparation
35 minutes cooking

ingredients

2 tbsp vegetable oil
2 heaped tbsp flaked almonds
handful of broken vermicelli,
    spaghettini or other thin or
    quick-cook short pasta
225 g long-grain brown rice
knob of butter
2 heaped tbsp sultanas or
    raisins
1 vegetable stock cube
    dissolved in 600 ml boiling
    water

method

❶ Heat ½ tablespoon of the vegetable oil in a frying pan and sauté the almonds until uniformly golden. Tip onto kitchen paper to drain. Wipe out the pan and repeat with the vermicelli (this is to brown it not cook it). Tip onto kitchen paper to drain.

❷ In a saucepan with a good-fitting lid, stir fry the rice in the butter and cook until the grains are golden, then add the sultanas, stock or water and the vermicelli. Bring to the boil, cover the pan and simmer over a low heat for about 30 minutes until the rice is *al dente*. Turn off the heat and leave untouched for 5 minutes to finish the cooking.

❸ Meanwhile, peel, halve and finely slice the onions and garlic. Heat the remaining oil in a large frying pan and gently sauté the onions and garlic until limp and tender. Once the onions have flopped slightly, season them with

½ teaspoon of salt (this encourages them to flop and turn juicy rather than crisp and brown). Season with the cinnamon. The onions will take approximately the same time as the rice.

❹ Finish the dish by mixing the onions and almonds into the rice. Serve with a scoop of yoghurt mixed with finely chopped fresh mint, cooked poppadoms and mango chutney.

2 Spanish onions
2 big garlic cloves
salt
1 tsp cinnamon powder
Greek-style natural yoghurt
fresh mint
poppadoms and mango chutney
to serve

Perfect Cous Cous

Pour 2 quantities of boiling liquid – water or stock or stock and vinaigrette – into a decent-sized bowl. Pour 1 quantity of cous cous (say 100 g cous cous to 200 ml liquid) in a gradual stream into the liquid whilst whisking continuously with a fork. Cover the bowl with a plate. Leave for 15 minutes. Remove the plate, fork up to loosen the grains, stir in a knob of butter.

Cous cous is the perfect canvas for creating ever-expanding salads and hot meals. Anything goes. Begin with a handful of toasted almonds or pine kernels, fry some onion until it is soft and floppy or finely slice a bunch of spring onions, chop up a courgette or a handful of green beans, or peas, and cook them quickly in boiling water. Already you have the makings of a meal. Think texture and colour as well as flavour for those continuously evolving cous cous meals. Eat them hot, warm or cold. They will keep, covered, in the fridge for several days.

green cous cous salad with chicken

4 servings
25 minutes preparation
20 minutes cooking

ingredients

6 small, slim leeks, approx
    400 g in total
350 g lean chicken meat (see
    page 179)

method

❶ Bring a large pan of water to the boil. Trim the leeks and cut them into approximately 7 cm lengths. Add to the boiling water with 1 teaspoon of salt. Boil for approximately 4 minutes until tender to the point of a sharp knife. Drain.

❷ Meanwhile, slice the chicken in strips approximately 5 cm x 1 cm wide x 1 cm thick. Place in a dish.

❸ Remove the zest from the lemon in wafer-thin strips.

Squeeze half the lemon juice over the chicken, add
1 tablespoon of olive oil and toss thoroughly.

④ Pour the hot stock into a large serving bowl and add
the cous cous in a steady trickle, stirring with a fork as you
pour. Cover the bowl and leave for about 15 minutes until
all the liquid has been absorbed and the cous cous is
tender. Fluff up with a fork.

⑤ Place watercress, lemon zest and peeled garlic cloves
in the bowl of a food processor. Blitz until everything is
finely chopped; *see* page 20 if you don't own a machine.

⑥ Heat a heavy frying pan over a medium heat and when
hot stir fry the almonds until lightly golden. Tip onto a
plate. Add 1 tablespoon of oil to the empty pan. Brown the
drained chicken in uncrowded batches, cooking for about
45 seconds a side until golden and cooked through.

⑦ Stir the watercress mixture into the cous cous. Taste
and adjust seasoning with salt and pepper. Stir the
almonds and chicken into the cous cous, together with the
chunks of leek.

⑧ Dribble the remaining olive oil and lemon juice over the
top.

1 small unwaxed lemon
4 tbsp olive oil
175 g cous cous
½ chicken stock cube
   dissolved in 350 ml boiling
   water
150 g watercress
2 garlic cloves, preferably new
   season
20 blanched almonds
salt and black pepper

All butchers and some supermarkets sell chicken wings extremely cheaply. Some sell extra big wings – called buffalo wings – and both are excellent Wolf food. Rubbed with oil and laid out on a top shelf in a hot (400°F/200°C/gas mark 6) oven (with a drip tray underneath), their skin will cook up beautifully crisp and each wing will offer several succulent, tender mouthfuls. If you slash them in a couple of places and marinate them first for an hour or so – in the juice of a lemon whisked with an equal amount of olive oil mixed with a crushed garlic clove and the leaves from a small bunch of thyme or rosemary if you have some – they will taste even better.

They can be buried under a can of chopped tomatoes, a chopped onion, a spoonful of honey and a splash of vinegar, then cooked spare-rib style in a moderate oven (350°F/180°C/gas mark 4) for an hour or so, they are a delicious hands-on feast. They are also perfect for making home-made stock after which the meat can be picked off the bones and used in sandwiches, gratins, salads and stuffed tortilla. (For more ideas *see* pages 183, 187 and 189.)

chicken wings with almond cous cous

4 servings
35 minutes preparation
30 minutes cooking

ingredients

FOR THE MARINADE

1 tsp brown sugar
4 tbsp Thai fish sauce (see page 120)
2 tbsp vegetable oil
4 plump garlic cloves
40 g piece fresh ginger
handful of mint leaves
half a handful of basil leaves

method

❶ Dissolve the sugar in the fish sauce and pour into the bowl of a food processor or blender. Add the vegetable oil.

❷ Peel the garlic. Peel the ginger and grate it on the large hole of a cheese grater or roughly chop.

❸ Add garlic and ginger to the other ingredients and add most of the mint, most of the basil and most of the flat leaf parsley. Blitz to make a loose, green paste. (*See* page 20 if you don't own a machine.)

❹ If you've bought buffalo chicken wings, use a sharp knife to joint them in two. Slash down the length of each piece of chicken in a couple of places, cutting through skin and into the flesh. Put all the chicken into a large plastic bag, preferably one that can be sealed and definitely one without holes, and pour in the green marinade. Seal the bag and mulch everything together so the chicken is thoroughly and evenly coated with the paste. Leave for at least 20 minutes and as long as overnight in the fridge.

5 Prepare the cous cous by pouring the stock into a serving bowl. Add the cous cous in a trickle, stirring with a fork as you pour. Give a final stir, cover and leave for 20 minutes.

6 Meanwhile, make a frying pan hot over a medium heat. Add the almonds and stir constantly until patched with brown. Tip onto a plate.

7 Peel, halve and finely slice the onion. Add the oil to the frying pan and stir in the onion. Season generously with salt and cook the onion for about 15 minutes, stirring every now and again, until moist, floppy and uncoloured.

8 Pre-heat the oven to 425°F/220°C/gas mark 7. Fork up the cous cous to loosen the grains, add the butter, onions and almonds. Mix. Make the dipping sauce by stirring the remaining coarsely chopped herbs into the yoghurt with the Tabasco and honey.

9 Ideally you want the chicken to get crisp all over. So, if possible, lay the pieces out on a metal cake rack laid over an oven tray to catch the drips. Otherwise, place directly on the oven shelf with a tray underneath to catch the drips. Place the shelf close to the top of the oven and cook for 15 minutes. Turn the chicken pieces and cook for 15 more minutes or until crisp and cooked through. Serve with the dipping sauce, cous cous and plenty of paper napkins because it is best to eat the chicken wings with your fingers.

handful of flat leaf parsley leaves
1 kg chicken wings or 12 drumsticks
2 tsp Marigold vegetable stock granules or 1 chicken stock cube dissolved in 400 ml boiling water
200 g cous cous
handful of blanched almonds
1 large onion
3 tbsp vegetable oil
salt
knob of butter
6 tbsp thick Greek yoghurt
1 tsp Tabasco
1 scant tsp runny honey

Simple, healthy, quick and easy. Eat hot, lukewarm or cold. It goes particularly well with a scoop of Greek yoghurt stirred with grated cucumber (raita) and toasted pitta bread. Alternatively, team it with fried or grilled fish, with hard-boiled eggs or with barbecued meat and poultry.

lebanese tomato bulgar pilaf

4 servings

20 minutes preparation

25 minutes cooking

ingredients

1 small onion

1 tbsp olive oil

400 g ripe tomatoes or 400 g can of Italian peeled tomatoes

200 g bulgar

½ tsp cinnamon

¼ tsp allspice

salt

method

❶ Peel, halve and finely chop the onion. Heat the oil in a medium-sized pan and cook the onions until pale and transparent.

❷ Meanwhile, place the fresh tomatoes in a bowl and cover with boiling water. Count to 20, drain and peel away the skin. Coarsely chop then add to the onions, stirring a couple of times. Add 300 ml water. Bring to the boil over a medium heat, cover the pan and cook for 5 minutes.

❸ Add the bulgar, cinnamon and allspice and half a teaspoon of salt. Stir thoroughly, reduce the heat to medium-low, cover the pan and cook for about 10 minutes until the bulgar is soft and all the liquid absorbed.

Kibbeh is a Middle Eastern word that describes dishes made with bulgar, the cracked wheat cereal which is sometimes spelt bulghur or burghol. This delicious interpretation is based on a recipe devised by Nigel Slater, whose books will appeal to the Wolf.

baked mushroom kibbeh

method

❶ Peel and chop the onions. Peel and chop the garlic. Heat 2 tbsp of oil in a frying pan over a moderate to low heat and cook the onions until soft and pale gold in colour. Add the garlic and continue cooking for a couple of minutes.

❷ Meanwhile, soak the bulgar in enough cold water to cover it. Pour boiling water over the tomatoes, count to 20, drain, peel and chop. Pick the leaves off the mint and chop coarsely.

❸ Pre-heat the oven to 350°F/180°C/gas mark 4.

❹ Wipe the mushrooms and quarter or halve depending on their size: they should be a bit bigger than bite-size.

❺ Tip half the cooked onions and garlic into the bulgar and return the pan to the stove. Add a little more oil and, when hot, the mushrooms. Season with salt and pepper, cover the pan and cook for 6–7 minutes until tender and juicy. Add the pine nuts, most of the mint and chopped tomatoes and cook for a further 10 minutes. Remove the lid and continue cooking for a couple of minutes until the liquid has almost evaporated but don't let the mixture dry.

❻ Generously butter a shallow baking dish, the size of a small roasting tin. Pile half the onion bulgar in the dish, smooth lightly and tip over the mushroom filling and then top with the remaining bulgar. Dot generously with butter. Bake for 20 minutes and serve with big dollops of the yoghurt mixed with the remaining chopped mint.

4 servings
20 minutes preparation
45 minutes cooking

ingredients

4 medium-sized onions

2 big garlic cloves

4 tbsp olive oil

300 g bulgar

3 medium-sized tomatoes

handful of mint

500 g mushrooms

salt and black pepper

3 tbsp pine nuts

large knob of butter

200 g thick natural yoghurt

Polenta that has been cooked and left to set looks like a glossy slab of compressed yellow pasta. It is sold in this state in vacuum-packed blocks and can be stored like dried goods. Once open it will keep for a few days in the fridge. It is excellent fried or grilled and used like bruschetta (olive oil and garlic toast) but it can also be thinly sliced and used like lasagne for oven dishes. It ends up soft and tender and the edges crisp up a treat.

polenta lasagne with basil

3–4 servings

35 minutes preparation

30 minutes cooking

Ingredients

1 medium-sized red onion

1 garlic clove

400 g can of whole red peppers

3 tbsp olive oil

1 tbsp balsamic or red wine
vinegar

leaves from a small basil plant

400 g can of Italian peeled
tomatoes

salt and black pepper

1/2 tsp sugar

shake of Tabasco

350 g prepared polenta

knob of butter

6 tbsp freshly grated Parmesan

1 or 2 mozzarella cheeses

8 small tomatoes or 16 cherry
tomatoes

method

❶ Pre-heat the oven to 425°F/220°C/gas mark 7.

❷ Peel, halve the onion and slice thinly. Peel the garlic, chop finely. Slice the red peppers into short ribbons.

❸ Heat 2 tablespoons of the oil in a frying pan over a medium heat. Cook the onions, tossing them around every now and again, for about 8 minutes until floppy and browned at the edges. Add the vinegar and let it slowly bubble away. Add the garlic. Stir until aromatic and then add 6 basil leaves, the sliced pepper and the can of tomatoes. Season with salt, pepper and the sugar. Add a shake or two of Tabasco. Bring to the boil then turn down the heat so the sauce cooks at a steady simmer until thick and jammy. This takes 10–15 minutes.

❹ Remove the polenta from its packet and cut 20 thin slices, approximately 1/2 cm thick.

❺ Smear a suitable gratin-type dish with butter and lay out half the polenta. Top with the sauce. Strew a few more basil leaves over the top and sprinkle over a couple of tablespoons of Parmesan. Arrange the rest of the polenta over the top. Slice the mozzarella thinly and lay it over the middle section of the dish. Sprinkle with the remaining Parmesan.

❻ If using small tomatoes, halve them through their middles. Arrange them on top of the mozzarella and smear the cut surface with the reserved olive oil. If using cherry tomatoes, place them in a bowl with the remaining olive oil and toss. 'Plant' the tomatoes on top of the mozzarella.

❼ Cook in the oven for 15–20 minutes until the tomatoes are very soft and juicy, the mozzarella melted, the Parmesan lightly crusted and the edges of the polenta scorched in places. Tear the remaining basil over the top and eat.

Polenta is fine, golden cornmeal porridge. For hundreds of years it was the staple diet of the poorest people in northern Italy. This basic gruel becomes delicious when beaten with plenty of butter and grated Parmesan and has become a fashionable British alternative to mashed potatoes. Authentic polenta demands arduous attention but a quick-cook version is perfect for this.

polenta with garlic and parsley mushrooms

4 servings

20 minutes preparation

20 minutes cooking

ingredients

250 g 1-minute or 5-minute
   polenta

25 g–50 g butter

25 g–50 g grated Parmesan

4 large flat mushrooms

500 g medium-sized
   mushrooms

3 big garlic cloves

1 unwaxed lemon

sprig of thyme

bunch of flat leaf parsley

4 tbsp olive oil

salt and black pepper

extra knob of butter

method

❶ Cook the polenta according to the instructions on the packet. Beat in the butter and Parmesan and cover the pan to keep it warm.

❷ Wipe the mushrooms. Slice the flat mushrooms and quarter the medium-sized mushrooms. Peel and finely chop the garlic. Remove the zest from the lemon and chop it very finely. Chop the thyme. Pick the leaves off the parsley stalks and coarsely chop.

❸ Heat the olive oil in a large frying pan or wide-based pan placed over a medium heat. Add half the garlic and half the parsley, all the mushrooms, lemon zest and thyme. Season generously with salt and pepper. Cook for about 8 minutes, tossing the mushrooms almost constantly, then squeeze over half the lemon juice and increase the heat. Cook for a further 2–3 minutes or until the mushrooms are floppy and tender. Stir in the rest of the parsley and garlic and the extra butter. Taste and adjust the seasoning with salt and pepper.

❹ Serve a mashed potato-sized dollop of polenta and top with the mushrooms. You may need an extra squeeze of lemon to bring out the flavours.

8. potatoes

Pasta might be the first thing that comes to mind for the Wolf on the prowl, looking for a quick, inexpensive meal, but life would be grim without potatoes. Just think for a moment of all the things you can do with potatoes: they can be boiled, mashed, fried, roasted and baked. They are filling, they are comfort food and they are not difficult to cook. Potatoes go with just about everything yet are great on their own. Think wonderful soups, crusty roast potatoes, and big chunky chips with gooey middles. And what about all those creamy potato gratins with their crusty tops? And the joy of cutting into the thick, crisp skin of a properly baked potato giving onto the contrast of its fluffy inside? And how often do you crave one of those spicy Indian potato dishes? Or potato salad, or potato pancakes, or a potato fry up, or a bowl of new potatoes with mint? And what's the point of a good old British stew without mash? Or bangers without mash? And you couldn't make fishcakes without mash. Or shepherd's pie.

Storing Potatoes

Keep potatoes in a cool, dark place but not in the fridge. Ideally, buy little and often and store out of their plastic bag (to discourage sprouting, which organic potatoes tend to do within days anyway).

The fluffiest mash is made from floury, mealy varieties of potato. This is the sort known as old (as opposed to new) potatoes. Basic mash is made with boiled (peeled) potatoes, milk, butter and salt. The more butter you add, the richer the mash will taste. If you add cream instead of milk, it will taste even richer and have a softer texture. If you stir an egg into the mash it will give it more body. Italian mash is stirred with grated Parmesan and a hint of garlic. Either way, Italian mash yearns to be eaten with soft-yolk eggs and, in my book, cooked frozen peas. It is also good with sausages, chops, grilled tomatoes and fried or roast chicken. Never, incidentally, be tempted to 'mash' potatoes in a food processor. This over-works the starch and turns it into thick glue. Hot milk gives the smoothest results.

italian mash gratin

4–6 servings
15 minutes preparation
35 minutes cooking

ingredients

**1 kg floury ('old') variety of
potatoes, such as King
Edward**
salt and black pepper
2 garlic cloves
at least 50 g butter
**50 ml milk, possibly a little
more**
**at least 50 g freshly grated
Parmesan**
2 fresh eggs
freshly grated nutmeg
extra butter

method

❶ Pre-heat the oven to 400°F/200°C/gas mark 6.

❷ Peel the potatoes, cut into even-sized pieces and rinse. Place in a saucepan and cover generously with cold water. Bring the water to the boil, add 1 teaspoon of salt and boil until tender to the point of a knife. Partially covering the pan speeds up the cooking.

❸ Meanwhile, peel the garlic and add whole to the pan when the potatoes have been boiling for about 10 minutes.

❹ Tip the cooked potatoes into a colander to drain. Add the butter and milk to the pan and heat through until the butter has melted. Return the potatoes and garlic to the pan and mash into the buttery milk until smooth. To get a really fluffy mash, beat the potatoes with a wooden spoon a few times.

❺ Crack the eggs into a bowl and whisk together as if for scrambled eggs. Pour the eggs into the potatoes and stir.

Add about three-quarters of the Parmesan and stir that in too. Season with black pepper and nutmeg and stir again.

❻ Butter a suitable oven-proof dish – gratin-style (wide and shallow) is preferable, in order to get plenty of crusty top. Smooth the top, scatter over the remaining cheese and dot with the extra butter.

❼ Place the dish in the hot oven and cook for about 15 minutes or until the top is crusty and golden.

other things to add to mash:

- a handful of grated Cheddar
- a dollop of mustard
- a spoonful of creamed horseradish
- a big mound of chopped parsley
- a bunch of chopped watercress
- chunks of mozzarella
- the juice of a lemon (honestly: *see* page 180)
- a topping of diced tomato, chopped flat leaf parsley and a slug of olive oil
- equal quantities of mashed parsnip, or turnip, or celeriac, or swede

other things to do with mash:

- simmer a chopped bunch of spring onions in milk then use the milk to make mash in the usual way. Stir in the onions with extra butter.
- fry a large, thinly sliced onion very slowly in oil until slippery and golden. Serve on top of mash with toasted pine kernels.
- shred cabbage, boil briefly and stir into mash with soft-fried onion (as above) and extra butter
- soften spinach in butter, stir into mash with a slug of cream. Serve with fried bread. Crisp bacon and fried egg is also good with this.

and for leftover mash:

- mix leftover mash with a little flour and an egg, form into potato cakes then fry in hot oil. Also *see* Tuna Fishcakes (page 49).
- heat a little oil in a frying pan, squash in the potato and leave to cook over a low heat for 15 minutes. Dot the top with butter, use a fish slice to scrape up and turn. Leave for another 15 minutes.
- stir a beaten egg into leftover mash. Form into golf balls and roll in almond flakes and melted butter. Cook in the oven until crisp.

baked potatoes

I don't want to give quantities or timing for baked potatoes.
The quickest and best way to prepare and cook them is like this. Turn the oven to its highest setting and move an oven shelf close to the top of the oven (with enough room for the oven tray that will hold the potatoes). Scrub clean the amount of potatoes you think you will need. Have ready some cooking oil, preferably olive oil, and some Maldon sea salt flakes which you've poured onto a plate. Also have ready an oven tray which you've lined with tinfoil (this eliminates awkward washing up).

Cut the potatoes in half. Pour a little oil into the palm of one hand and roll the potatoes around until they are smeared all over with oil – just plonk them in the sink as you go. Now, dip the cut edge of each potato in salt and lay the potato on its side on the foil-lined baking tray. Continue until all the potatoes are done.

Put the tray on the top shelf (the oven doesn't have to come up to temperature first) and check their doneness with a knife after 30 minutes and up to 1 hour depending on how many you are cooking (the more you cook the longer they take). They are ready when the salted edge appears golden and the rest of the potato looks crusty.

You can 'hold' them by moving the tray to the bottom of the oven and reducing the temperature until 10 minutes before you are ready to eat. Then, whip up the temperature again to re-crisp. Serve them with cold butter, grated cheese, grilled bacon, baked beans, fried eggs etc, etc.

NB: Leftover baked potatoes will keep for a couple of days and can be resuscitated in a hot oven. Give them 10 minutes and they are ready to eat.

A perfect roast potato is crusty on the outside and fluffy on the inside. The way to achieve this is to peel and boil the potatoes first and then rough them up a bit to get a craggy surface. If the potatoes seem over-boiled – by which I mean beginning to break up – so much the better. These make excellent roasties.

It is important to put the potatoes into a hot oven. Before the potatoes go into the roasting pan, pop the pan into the oven with a generous splash of cooking oil or dripping; not too much, just sufficient to coat the potatoes when you roll them around in the pan. Putting the potatoes into hot fat means they will absorb less, require less cooking, won't be greasy and will crisp up better and faster. If you coat the potatoes with the hot oil first, there is no real need for basting, although I would recommend turning the potatoes at least once during cooking so that they roast evenly.

Allow at least 1 hour in a hot oven to cook enough regular-sized, decently crisped potatoes to feed 6. Most often, though, you have to adjust the length of cooking time and oven temperature to suit the joint of meat or bird that the potatoes are cooked with. The smaller you cut the potatoes, the faster they will cook.

Any variety of potato is suitable for roasting but floury varieties such as King Edward, Maris Piper, and Irish or Scottish potatoes are best. New or waxy potatoes make a different type of roast potato. Delicious but different. I would recommend boiling them in their skins, cooling them for a minute or two in cold water and then whipping off the skins.

very crisp roast potatoes

6 servings
15 minutes preparation
80 minutes cooking

ingredients

1 kg floury ('old') variety of potatoes, such as King Edward

method

❶ Pre-heat the oven to 400°F/200°C/gas mark 6.

❷ Peel the potatoes, cut into even-sized pieces. Rinse and boil in salted water until tender. Don't worry if some potatoes begin to collapse (often the case with 'old' potatoes). Drain in a colander.

❸ Drag a fork all over the potatoes making ridges or rough-handle them in the colander.

❹ Put the lard, dripping or oil in a baking tray and heat it up in the hot oven for 5 minutes. Add the potatoes, turning them around in the hot oil so they are evenly coated. Sprinkle lightly with salt. Place the tray on a shelf in the upper part of the oven. Cook for 30 minutes. Turn the potatoes, salt again and cook for a further 30 minutes or until crusted to your liking.

2 tbsp lard, dripping or olive/vegetable oil

salt

other ways to go:

- vary the shape or size of roast potatoes: cut them into dice, slice them into discs or chips, or small chunks.
- drop peeled garlic into boiling water for 2 minutes, drain and add to roast potatoes for the last 15 minutes of cooking. The garlic will be scrumptious to eat, too.
- sprinkle chopped bacon over the potatoes 15 minutes before the end of cooking; finish with chopped parsley if you have some.
- toss potatoes with sliced onion, or with rosemary or thyme, before roasting.
- add sausages or chunks of sausages to the potatoes; turn as they brown.
- cook in hot stock – 600 ml to 1 kg potatoes – instead of oil until the liquid has evaporated.
- wrap boiled and then skinned new potatoes in streaky bacon, and edge the pan with chipolatas. Roast, and eat.

There are two types of potato salad. Or, to be exact, two types of potato salad dressing. Vinaigrette is traditional for French bistro-style potato salads. The potatoes are always sliced and dressed while still hot and are often eaten with so-called poaching or boiling sausage or smoked herring.

But it's the ersatz-mayonnaise-dressed potato salad, made with chopped chives or mint, that I'm going for here. New potatoes or a waxy variety such as Charlotte, or a French, Italian or Moroccan variety, are best for potato salads. That's because these potatoes don't disintegrate when they are boiled and will keep their shape when they are sliced. The reason potato salads are tossed in their dressing while they are hot is to encourage the potatoes to soak up the flavours.

potato salad

4–6 servings
20 minutes preparation
20 minutes cooking

ingredients

750 g evenly sized new or waxy
variety potatoes
salt and black pepper
1 tbsp mayonnaise (preferably
Hellmann's)
1 tbsp wine vinegar
1 tbsp Dijon mustard
4 tbsp vegetable oil
bunch of spring onions
leaves from a small bunch of
mint

method

❶ Scrub or scrape the potatoes. Rinse. Place in a saucepan and cover generously with cold water. Bring the water to the boil, add 1 teaspoon of salt and boil until tender to the point of a knife. Partially covering the pan speeds up the cooking.

❷ Make the dressing by putting the mayonnaise in a serving bowl. Add the vinegar. Dissolve a generous pinch of salt in the vinegar then stir mayo and vinegar together. Season generously with black pepper, add the mustard and stir thoroughly. Add the oil in a thin trickle, beating as you go until smooth and amalgamated. If it seems very thick, slacken the dressing with a little water.

❸ Trim and finely slice the spring onion. Shred the mint. Stir the spring onions and most of the mint into the dressing.

❹ Drain the cooked potatoes. If the potatoes are very small, add them whole. If they are medium-sized, cut them in half. If they are on the large size, cut them into chunky slices.

❺ Toss the potatoes in the dressing and leave for at least 10 minutes before tossing again and sprinkling with the reserved mint. Eat hot, warm or cold.

good things to add to potato salad:

- hard-boiled egg
- a crumble of feta cheese
- black olives and shredded basil
- a crumble of very crisp bacon
- torn roast chicken
- slices of pepperoni or chorizo sausage

When I first started fending for myself, I shared a room in a big flat where nobody could cook. We lived on toast, Fray Bentos steak and kidney pies, fried eggs, bacon, instant coffee and Cornflakes. In no particular order. Nobody washed up and you didn't dare open a cupboard in case a plate of congealed spaghetti fell out. We were also permanently skint, and fags and booze got priority over food. Typical first-time flat dwellers. Out of desperation I discovered that if you grate a potato and fry it in a little hot oil you get a delicious, crisp potato mat. All you need with them is a squirt of ketchup and a pinch of salt. The mat makes a very good sandwich filling. When we got bored with *paillasson* (the real name of what I thought was my invention), we discovered pancakes. And before long the two merged together. We didn't know it, but we were living on latkes. *Latke* is Yiddish for pancake. Eat them hot from the pan or keep them warm while you cook all the batter. Latkes are good on their own and go with everything. Apple sauce and crisp bacon are traditional accompaniments. Latkes re-heat well in a hot oven and will last, cooled and covered, in the fridge for a couple of days. Adding flour to the mixture makes the pancakes firmer and more substantial.

latkes with bacon and apple sauce

4–6 servings
25 minutes preparation
20 minutes cooking

ingredients

1 onion (optional)

1 kg floury ('old') variety of potatoes, such as King Edward

2 large eggs

4 tbsp flour

salt

method

❶ Make the apple sauce first. Peel, quarter, core and quickly chop the apples; the air quickly turns cut apples brown. Place in a pan with about 100 ml water, cover and boil hard until the apples are collapsed, adding a little extra water if necessary. Stir in the butter and sugar.

❷ If including an onion, peel and grate it on the large hole of the cheese grater. Peel the potatoes and then grate them directly into the onion. Then squeeze the mixture dry by pressing the potato between your hands.

❸ Lightly beat the eggs with a generous pinch of salt. Sift over the flour gradually, stirring until the batter is smooth.

Add the potatoes and onion, if using, and stir well.

4 Heat a thickness of about 1 cm of oil in a frying pan. Take spoonfuls of the batter mixture and drop into the hot oil. Flatten a little, and lower the heat so the pancakes cook through evenly. Do not fiddle with the latkes or try to move them yet. After 3 or 4 minutes, when the bottom is golden brown and has formed a thin crust, turn and cook the other side.

5 While the latkes are cooking, pre-heat the grill. Arrange the bacon on the grill pan and cook until crisp before turning to cook the other side.

6 Eat immediately with the apple sauce, which can be hot or cold.

oil for frying

approx 24 rashers streaky bacon

FOR THE APPLE SAUCE

2 Bramley cooking apples

25 g butter

1 tbsp sugar

Take a potato, a pinch of salt and some water and you have the basis of a delicious, subtle, nourishing and inexpensive soup that is quick and easy to make. Add thyme or rosemary, a pat of butter, a sliced onion and a clove or two of garlic and the soup starts getting interesting. Liquidize it and serve it with scraps of grilled bacon and a chunk of crusty bread and you have supper. But potato soups don't always have to be mild and gentle. If you enjoy Thai food, you'll like this one

thai-style potato soup

2 servings

15 minutes preparation

30 minutes cooking

ingredients

1 large shallot or small red
   onion, approx 75 g
2 tbsp vegetable oil
15 g piece of fresh ginger
1 big garlic clove
500 g potatoes, any type
1 small red chilli
1 dsp flour
1 chicken stock cube or 2 tsp
   Marigold vegetable stock
   granules dissolved in 600 ml
   boiling water
1 stalk of lemon grass or ½ an
   unwaxed lemon
handful of coriander leaves
salt and black pepper

method

❶ Peel and finely chop the shallot or red onion. Heat the oil in a heavy-bottomed pan and gently soften the shallot.

❷ Meanwhile, peel the ginger, grate and then chop it as finely as possible. Peel the garlic and chop it very finely. Add both to the shallot.

❸ Peel the potatoes, dice them into approximately 1 cm pieces and rinse thoroughly. Split the chilli, discard stalk and seeds, and chop very finely. (*See* page 21.) Add both to the pan, stirring around to coat the potatoes with oil and to mix with the ginger, garlic and shallot. Continue to stir for a minute or two to prevent the food sticking, then sift over the flour, stirring until it is totally dispersed. Pour on the stock, stirring a couple of times as it comes to the boil.

❹ If using lemon grass, give it a good bash with a rolling pin to partially smash it. If using lemon zest, remove it (no white) from the lemon. Add whichever to the pan with half the chopped coriander. Season with salt and pepper.

❺ Partially cover the pan, establishing a steady simmer, and cook for about 15 minutes until the potatoes are tender. Taste, adjust the seasoning with salt, pepper and lemon juice. Add the remaining coriander, discard the lemon grass or lemon zest, and eat.

Next time you're in the supermarket, slip a packet or two of gnocchi di patate into your basket. Gnocchi are little dumplings and this type are made with potato, egg and flour. Drop them into boiling water and a few minutes later, when they have risen to the top of the pan, they are ready. They taste a bit like compacted mashed potato and are surprisingly sturdy despite being very light and tender.

parmesan gnocchi with pesto and beans

method

❶ Put a large pan of water on to boil. Top and tail the beans and cut them in half. As soon as the water is boiling, add 1 teaspoon of salt and the beans. Bring the water back to the boil and cook for 1 minute. Scoop the beans out of the water and drain in a colander.

❷ Drop the gnocchi into the boiling water and cook for 2–3 minutes until they all rise to the surface.

❸ Drain and toss with the butter in a warmed dish. Dust with half the Parmesan, add the pesto and beans. Toss, dust with the reserved Parmesan and serve.

other ways of serving gnocchi:

- with a cheese sauce (see page 64)
- with double cream heated with a quarter of its weight of grated Parmesan
- with cherry tomatoes splashed with olive oil then grilled until they pop
- grilled under a layer of grated Cheddar
- hidden under chopped tomato and shredded basil
- fried in butter with scraps of crisp bacon and grated hard-boiled egg
- with any tomato or tomato and red pepper sauce

4–6 servings
15 minutes preparation
10 minutes cooking

ingredients

700 g French beans

salt

2 x 400 g gnocchi di patate

25 g butter

4 tbsp Parmesan plus more to serve

4 tbsp pesto (see page 88)

Hash, in culinary terms, means a rough and ready fry-up usually involving leftover boiled potatoes. Corned beef hash is always served with a fried egg, whilst the more intriguingly named red flannel hash utilizes leftover potatoes and roast beef and boiled beetroot. It is also delicious in a different sort of way when made with smoked mackerel. Both types of hash beg to be eaten in Desperate Dan-sized quantities. A well-buttered slice of white bread is the usual accompaniment, with a mug of tea or a glass of milk or a can of beer on the side.

Both these dishes are seriously delicious.

corned beef & red flannel hash

2 servings

20 minutes preparation

20 minutes cooking

ingredients for corned beef hash

500 g potatoes, preferably
  Charlotte or another waxy
  variety

3 tbsp cooking oil, lard or
  dripping

2 small onions or a bunch of
  spring onions

4 medium-sized tomatoes
  (optional) or 2 tbsp tomato
  ketchup

1 large can of corned beef,
  approx 350 g

1 tbsp chopped parsley

2 tbsp Worcestershire sauce

method

❶ Place the unpeeled potatoes in a pan, cover with water, add 1 teaspoon of salt and boil for about 15 minutes until tender.

❷ Meanwhile, peel or trim and finely chop the onions. Add them to a large frying pan with one-third of the cooking oil. Cook for 6–8 minutes over a medium heat until soft and browned in places.

❸ If you are using tomatoes (they make the dish less greasy and it looks prettier), chop them quite small. If you're feeling pernickety, peel and de-seed the tomatoes by placing them in a bowl, covering with boiling water, and leave for 20 seconds. Cut the tomatoes into quarters lengthways, peel off the skins and scoop out the seeds. Chop the flesh.

❹ Chop the corned beef into small kebab-sized chunks. Place the pan with the cooked potatoes under the cold tap and let it run for a couple of minutes. Peel the potatoes, dice slightly smaller than the beef.

❺ Squash the onions against the side of the pan, add

another third of the cooking oil, turn up the heat and add the potatoes. Scoop the onions up over the potatoes and cook for 5 minutes over a brisk heat.

6 Add the corned beef, tomatoes, if using, or the tomato ketchup, half the parsley and the Worcestershire sauce. Season generously with salt and pepper. Stir and leave to cook for 5 minutes. Scoop up the bottom layer so the hash is more or less turned over, and cook for a further 10 minutes. Divide the hash between two hot plates.

7 Add the remaining oil to the pan and quickly fry the eggs. Place an egg on top of each hash and sprinkle with the last of the parsley.

method

1 Peel, halve and chop the onion. Melt half the butter in a heavy or non-stick frying pan and gently soften the onion for a few minutes.

2 Meanwhile, cut the beef into chunks (if using mackerel, flake it off the skin in big chunks). Do likewise with the potatoes and beetroot, keeping everything in approximately the same sized pieces. Or not, as you wish.

3 Crack the egg into a mixing bowl, beat with the milk and horseradish sauce, then stir in the beef or mackerel, potato and beetroot. Season generously with salt and pepper, and lastly stir in the partially cooked onion.

4 Melt the remaining butter and cooking oil in the frying pan over a low heat and spread the mixture evenly in the pan. Cook slowly until cake-like and browned on the bottom. Turn and cook the other side.

salt and black pepper

2 large eggs

ingredients for red flannel hash

1 small onion

25 g butter

4–8 generous slices of cold roast beef or 1 large smoked mackerel fillet

450 g boiled potatoes

2 medium-sized cooked beetroot

1 egg

1 tbsp milk

1 tsp horseradish sauce

salt and black pepper

splash of cooking oil

9. soups, stews and other supper dishes

Soup has always had an image problem. It still epitomizes poverty: soup kitchens dishing out watery gruel smelling of boiled cabbage. Or the other picture, of cupped hands wrapped around a steaming bowl, against an imaginary backdrop of a cosy country kitchen where the fire burns brightly and newly baked bread sits on the table. But the future is suddenly up-tempo for soup. From New York comes a new kind of soup kitchen. A trendy one. These soup kitchens have crossed the Atlantic to London and beyond, and are gradually building momentum, challenging the sandwich bar as somewhere new and interesting to pick up a quick meal.

The menu reflects the true international flavour of soup, with choices as diverse as, for example, Vietnamese noodle soup, Thai curry, American chowder, Italian minestrone, and British boiled beef and carrots. Many of these soups are more like stews. It is easy, of course, to turn soup into a complete meal. You use your imagination and add a few potatoes or noodles, or extra vegetables.

Soup is being claimed as the food of the Millennium. It is definitely on Wolf's menu. It is easy to make, almost anything goes, it can be expanded, altered from one day to the next, it can be made in advance to last over several days, it is healthy and cheap. It is also easy food: easy to serve, easy to eat, low on washing up and quick to re-heat.

Apart from soup, this chapter contains other sorts of food that Wolf likes for supper: shepherd's pie, for example, chorizo and white bean stew, and Irish stew. The recipes are foolproof, easy, and require no special skills or equipment. Most dishes are for several people but you don't need to be a rocket scientist to work out how to make most of them for more or fewer people.

How to Make Chicken Stock

Whenever you roast a chicken, get into the habit of saving the carcass and all the bones. Put them in a large saucepan with at least 1 chopped onion (no need to peel it; the skin gives colour to the stock), a carrot or two and celery if you have it. Add a bay leaf, a pinch of salt, and a few sprigs of thyme. Cover with water. Bring to the boil, reduce the heat and leave to simmer very gently for at least an hour, preferably 1½ hours. Strain the stock into a bowl, discard the debris, cool the stock and then put it, covered, in the fridge overnight.

Next day, remove the layer of congealed fat that will have formed. You have stock, probably jellied stock. Use it within a week. You can concentrate the flavour by simmering the skimmed stock until reduced by about one-third. For a richer, stronger stock, make it with 500 g of fresh chicken wings instead. Don't waste the meat on the bones. Pick it off for sandwiches, salads etc. Use this delicious stock to give body to soup and stews, risotto and sauces. Freeze it in small quantities in yoghurt pots.

But what, I hear you asking, about stock cubes? If you do use fresh stock for soup making, the taste will be richer and more interesting. The soup will also be more nutritious. However, stock cubes, particularly the good ones such as Knorr and Just Bouillon, and Marigold organic vegetable stock powder, gives results that more than pass muster. Anyway, there are plenty of soups that can be made with water.

This is one of those useful recipes that relies on a couple of store cupboard cans and a few inexpensive easy-to-come-by ingredients. You end up with a thick and robustly flavoured satisfying soup: the sort of thing that people used to call a 'rib-sticker'. It is even more special when served with a handful of freshly chopped tender green herbs and a generous grating of Parmesan stirred in right at the end. Watercress, or a mixture of flat leaf parsley, mint and chives, or shredded spinach would be perfect, and will give the soup a noticeable injection of fresh flavour and vivacious colour as well as a healthy dose of iron and vitamins.

boston bean soup with watercress

4 servings
25 minutes preparation
35 minutes cooking

ingredients

6 rashers rindless streaky
    bacon
2 tbsp olive oil
1 large red onion, approx 300 g
2 plump garlic cloves
3 carrots, approx 175 g
salt and black pepper
2 sticks of celery with leaves if
    possible
½ tbsp flour
1 tbsp smooth Dijon mustard
1 chicken stock cube dissolved
    in 600 ml boiling water
400 g can of Italian peeled
    tomatoes
Tabasco

method

❶ Slice across the pile of bacon rashers, to make skinny strips. Heat the oil in a spacious, heavy-bottomed pan over a medium-low heat. Add the bacon and cook until beginning to crisp.

❷ While the bacon is cooking, peel, halve and finely chop the onion, garlic and carrot, keeping separate piles.

❸ When the bacon is ready, stir in the onion and cook for about 6 minutes until floppy. Add the garlic and carrot. Season lightly with salt and generously with pepper. Cover and cook for 5 minutes, stirring occasionally, adjusting the heat so the vegetables sweat rather than brown.

❹ Trim and finely slice the celery and chop its leaves and add to the pot. Cook for a minute or two, remove the lid and sift the flour on the top. Stir thoroughly until it has dissolved and then stir in the mustard and add a little stock, the tomatoes, ½ teaspoon Tabasco and a squeeze of lemon juice. Break up the tomatoes with a wooden spoon. Bring to the boil, gradually adding the rest of the stock.

❺ Tip the beans into a colander, rinse with cold water,

shake dry and add to the pan. Return to simmer and cook for 10 minutes or until the vegetables are tender. Taste and adjust the seasoning.

6 Finely chop the watercress or shred the spinach. Just before serving, stir in watercress or spinach and serve with a spoonful of Parmesan and a splosh of your best olive oil.

squeeze of lemon juice
400 g can of cannellini or
haricot beans
75 g watercress or spinach
4 tbsp freshly grated Parmesan

How to Jazz Up Packet Soups

For an instant fix, nothing beats packet soup. They are all much of a muchness, but particular soups – mushroom, leek and potato, chicken and sweetcorn – are good. Use 2 sachets to slightly less boiling water than suggested on the packet, then stir well and add a splash of Tabasco and any fresh chopped herbs or spare spinach leaves you happen to have. Frozen peas, leftover cooked rice or potatoes, diced beancurd, grated cheese, scraps of ham or cooked chicken and finely chopped raw mushroom are all good additions. Don't season with salt and pepper until you've tasted.

That curious expression 'rib-sticker' seems about right to describe a soup such as this which is so thick with interest and flavour that you will want to go on eating it until you pop. The final and last-minute addition of a handful of spinach and some diced tomato makes the soup. Serve with garlic bread (see page 69) oozing with butter and herbs.

lentil soup with spinach and tomatoes

2–4 servings
20 minutes preparation
40 minutes cooking

ingredients

2 medium-sized onions
1 garlic clove
40 g butter
salt and black pepper
3 carrots
1 celery heart, or 4 sticks from
near the heart
2 small red peppers
½ unwaxed lemon
125 g brown lentils or lentils du
Puy
½ tbsp flour
½ tsp cumin
glass of red or white wine if
possible
1½ chicken or vegetable stock
cubes dissolved in 700 ml
boiling water
4 tomatoes, plum if possible
100 g young leaf spinach

method

❶ Peel, halve and chop the onions. Peel and chop the garlic. Over a medium heat, melt the butter in a spacious, heavy-bottomed pan that can hold all the ingredients. Stir in the onion and garlic, season generously with salt and pepper and leave to soften but not colour.

❷ Meanwhile, trim and peel the carrots. Split lengthways into quarters and chop. Slice across the celery, discarding the root. Rinse and shake dry. Chop the peppers, having discarded the seeds and white filament.

❸ Remove a 5 cm x 1 cm strip of lemon zest (no white) and chop finely. Add carrot, celery, red pepper and zest to the pan and cook for a few minutes before adding the lentils. Stir everything around a few times and leave to cook for a few minutes.

❹ Stir in the flour and cumin until it is absorbed by the buttery juices and add the wine or equivalent amount of stock. Stir as it boils up and then add the (remaining) stock. Adjust the heat so the soup is simmering gently, partially cover and leave for about 30 minutes until the lentils and vegetables are tender. Taste and adjust the seasoning with salt, pepper and the lemon juice. If it seems too thick, add more stock/water.

❺ Skin the tomatoes (see page 21). Chop, saving all the juices. Just before serving, add the spinach and tomatoes with their juices. Bring back to a simmer and serve.

It is hard to believe that such a modest collection of ingredients could produce one of the best quick suppers imaginable. It is a great soup to make, for instance, if you're on your own and don't want to get into a stodge-fest of a baked bean on toast variety. The recipe is based on potage bonne femme and, should you wish, it could be puréed with a little milk or cream, chilled and then served with chives to become vichyssoise. If you want to make it more substantial, serve the soup over a thick slice of toast which you've rubbed with garlic on one side, dribbled with a slick of your best olive oil and topped with a soft poached egg. Alternatively, serve the bruschetta (the garlic and olive oil toast) spread with a smear of mashed anchovy and a dusting of finely grated Parmesan or another hard cheese.

The quantities given here are intended to be enough to satisfy one as a main dish. There will be plenty for two if another dish follows.

leek and potato soup with thyme

method

❶ Trim and slice the leek in thin rounds. Place it in a colander and rinse thoroughly under cold running water. Scrub or peel the potatoes and slice thinly into rounds. Add to the leeks, rinse again and shake dry. Peel and thinly slice the garlic in rounds.

❷ Place leek, potatoes, garlic, bay leaf, thyme and most of the parsley in a small pan. Season generously with salt and pepper. Add half the butter. Cover with 500 ml water and bring to the boil. Simmer vigorously for about 12 minutes until potatoes and leeks are tender. Remove the bay leaf. Taste and adjust the seasoning, perhaps with a dash of Tabasco.

❸ Serve very hot with a knob of cold butter and the rest of the parsley.

1 big serving
15 minutes preparation
15 minutes cooking

ingredients

1 leek
6 medium-sized potatoes, preferably new potatoes
1 garlic clove
1 bay leaf
2 sprigs of fresh thyme
1 tbsp chopped flat leaf parsley
salt and black pepper
40 g cold butter, preferably unsalted
Tabasco (optional)

Chowder is the American name for a rough-and-ready
seafood and potato soup-cum-stew. There are two types. New York-style is
made with tomatoes and water, and New England, which is the inspiration
for this, with milk. The gentle flavours go very well with this ersatz rouille
made with frozen peas, chilli and coriander. A delicious treat which is simple
to make.

haddock chowder with green rouille

2 servings
20 minutes preparation
20 minutes cooking

ingredients

2 rashers rindless streaky
    bacon
bunch of spring onions
4 medium-sized potatoes, any
    type
1 red chilli
2 haddock or cod fillets, approx
    250 g
large knob of butter
1 bay leaf
salt and black pepper
1 heaped tsp flour
approx ½ glass of white wine
400 ml milk
1 garlic clove
150 g frozen peas
2 tbsp coarsely chopped
    coriander
squeeze of lemon juice

method

❶ Slice across the bacon to make thin little strips. Trim
and slice the spring onions, discarding only the very
fibrous green.

❷ Peel the potatoes and chop into 2½ cm chunks. Rinse
and drain. Split the chilli, scrape away the seeds and chop
very finely. Set aside just under half the chilli; see page 21.

❸ Run your index finger down the fillets of haddock to
locate the central bones, and remove with pliers or
tweezers, or catch between your thumb and the blade of
a knife. Cut the fish into 5 cm x 2½ cm pieces.

❹ Melt half the butter in a medium-sized heavy-bottomed
pan over a moderate heat. Cook the bacon for about 5
minutes until beginning to crisp. Add the remaining
butter, all but the equivalent of 2 onions which should be
reserved, the bulk of the chilli, bay leaf and ½ teaspoon of
salt, and allow to soften slightly before adding the
potatoes. Cook without browning, stirring a couple of
times, for 5 minutes. Sprinkle over the flour, stir until it
disappears and mix in the wine. As it bubbles, add the
milk, establishing a simmer. Half-cover the pan and cook,
stirring occasionally to prevent sticking, testing after 10
minutes, until the potato is tender.

❺ Meanwhile, make the rouille by placing the reserved

onion and chilli, peeled and chopped garlic and peas in a
small pan. Add 150 ml water. Season with salt and
pepper. Boil uncovered for 5 minutes. Add half the
coriander and pour the contents of the pan into the bowl
of a food processor. Blitz, adding extra water if necessary,
to make a thick purée. (*See* page 20 if you don't own a
machine.) Taste and adjust seasoning with lemon juice.

6 When the potato is ready, stir in the spinach and push
the chunks of fish under the liquid. Raise the heat slightly
and cook until the fish turns white, 3–5 minutes. Garnish
with the rest of the coriander and serve with a dollop of
rouille.

**handful of young spinach
leaves**

The great thing about gazpacho is that no cooking is
involved. What you do need is a sharp knife, and a food processor. Within
minutes you will be eating a delicious, satisfying and healthy soup. Gazpacho
is as old as the Spanish hills whence it came and original versions would
have been very rough and ready. Some people call it the salad soup because
the ingredients – and that includes the vinaigrette and the bread you might
eat with it – would make a fine salad. The best gazpacho in this country is
made with cherry tomatoes, with plum or vine tomatoes for the garnish, or
very, very ripe tomatoes. Turn gazpacho into a proper meal with a full
complement of garnishes and some crusty bread and butter.

gazpacho

6–8 servings
25 minutes preparation
no cooking

ingredients

4 thick slices white bread
  without crusts, approx 150 g
2 plump garlic cloves
1 cucumber
1 red chilli
2 red peppers
1 red onion
1 kg cherry tomatoes or 1 kg
  very ripe tomatoes
2 tbsp sherry or wine vinegar
about 20 mint leaves
100 ml olive oil plus 2 tbsp
salt and black pepper
squeeze of lemon juice
Tabasco

method

❶ Tear the bread into pieces. Place it and the peeled
garlic in the bowl of a food processor and blitz to make
fine breadcrumbs. (Or crumble finely by hand if you don't
own a machine.)

❷ Peel the cucumber. Halve it horizontally and use a
teaspoon to scrape out the seeds. Chop half of it roughly,
setting aside the rest. Trim and split the chilli. Scrape out
the seeds. (*See* page 21.)

❸ Set aside half of one red pepper and chop the rest
having discarded seeds and white filament. Peel and halve
the onion. Coarsely chop one half and add to the
breadcrumbs together with the chopped cucumber, chilli
and chopped red pepper.

❹ Remove the stalks from the cherry tomatoes and add
them together with the vinegar, 300 ml cold water, most of
the mint, the 100 ml olive oil and ½ teaspoon of salt and a
generous seasoning of black pepper to the other
ingredients. Blitz for several minutes until liquidized.

❺ Meanwhile prepare the garnishes. Keeping separate

piles, finely dice the remaining cucumber and red pepper, and finely chop the remaining red onion. Quarter the plum or vine tomatoes, discard the seeds and finely chop.

6 Taste the gazpacho and adjust the seasoning with salt, pepper, lemon juice and Tabasco. Transfer to a chilled serving bowl and decorate with a swirl of olive oil. Serve with the garnishes in small bowls, adding the rest of the mint to the tomato.

EXTRA GARNISHES

black olives, hard-boiled egg, plum or vine tomatoes, scraps of ham or cooked chicken, canned tuna, mussels, crab etc.

I can honestly say that when I moved into my first flat I couldn't boil an egg. Well, I could, of course, but what I mean is that I had no idea how long it took to end up with the soft yolk that I like. When you are forced to cook for yourself it is surprising how many things you find you can master, and roasting a chicken is usually one of them. I got plenty of practice with that because at the time one of my brothers was doing post-graduate research into chicken feed and how it affected both the egg and its shell, and he regularly turned up with a chicken or two wrapped in newspaper tucked under his arm.

I did what my mother had always done and smeared the chicken with butter, squeezed a lemon over the top and pushed the squeezed out lemon halves inside the cavity. There were no problems with the roast potatoes either. For years I copied her way of cutting them into thick slabs through the length of the potato, arranging the slices round the bird so they ended up imbued with buttery lemon juices and only the edges crisped up. And I still cook roast chicken in much the same way.

However, I want to let you into the secret of another brilliant way of cooking a chicken in the oven. All you need is an impossibly large quantity of onions, some olive oil, salt and pepper. The bird sits on top of the sliced onion in a covered dish. The results are sublime: moist juicy chicken with floppy, sweet and juicy onion 'gravy'. Serve with mashed potato and a green vegetable.

not roast chicken with onions

4–6 servings
20 minutes preparation
90 minutes cooking

ingredients

5 large onions, approx 1 kg in total
1 chicken

method

❶ Pre-heat the oven to 350°F/180°C/gas mark 4.

❷ Peel and halve the onions and slice very thinly. Season generously inside the chicken cavity.

❸ Pour 2 tablespoons of the olive oil into a deep casserole. Add all the onions. Add 2 more tablespoons of oil and season with 1 teaspoon of salt and plenty of pepper.

❹ Place the chicken, breast side down, on top of the onions, pressing it down firmly. Pour the final 2 tablespoons of oil over the top. Position the lid or use foil to make an efficient leak-free lid. Cook in the middle of the oven for 90 minutes. Remove from the oven. Leave covered for 15 minutes before lifting the chicken onto a plate for carving. Serve the chicken topped with some of the onion gravy.

salt and black pepper

6 tbsp olive oil

Buying Poultry Meat

Throughout this section, and elsewhere in the book, there are recipes that use portions of chicken, turkey and, occasionally, duck. Most of the time, the recipe specifies the cut, be it breast fillet, whole leg, drumstick or wing. All the supermarkets and most butchers sell these cuts in various states and, obviously, the more they've done to the meat – removed the skin and bones, or chopped it into pieces – the more expensive it will be. It doesn't take a moment to do any of these chores yourself, so rather than repeat all this with each recipe, I leave the choice up to you. Either pay more for convenience or save a bob or two by doing it yourself.

It goes without saying that the better quality of bird – organic, free range, maize-fed, etc – the more it will cost.

Here's a wizard wheeze for a delicious, quick supper made with chicken breasts. These tender, crisp-shelled escalopes with their hidden flavour burst will go with any potato dish, the plainer the better. Having said that, and it probably sounds very peculiar, I squeeze fresh lemon juice into mashed potato to serve with mine. This is delicious and a perfect accompaniment, being both creamy and soft with a hint of fresh citrus. In fact, you will be squeezing lemon juice over the escalopes and some is bound to get in with the mash, so it's not as odd as it first may seem.

Instead of escalopes, you might prefer to cut the chicken into strips so you end up with goujons of Dijon chicken. These are the perfect TV snack, because you make a great pile (keep them warm on a wire tray over an oven dish in a low oven while you cook the others) and serve them with a creamy dipping sauce or eat with a smear of Hellmann's mustard mayonnaise. Another good idea is to pile the goujons onto thick slices of mayo-buttered very fresh wholemeal bread.

dijon chicken escalopes

2 servings
10 minutes preparation
10 minutes cooking

ingredients

2 skinned chicken breasts
2 tbsp smooth Dijon mustard
salt and black pepper
2 slices wholemeal bread
4 tbsp flour
1 egg
15 g butter
1 tbsp cooking oil
lemon wedges to serve

method

❶ Spread one sheet of greaseproof or cling film on a work surface and lay out the skinned chicken breasts with plenty of space between and around them. Cover with a second piece of paper and gently bash the meat with a rolling pin or similar until flattened and about half as big again. Peel off the top layer of paper/cling film. Smear one side of each escalope with mustard. Season with salt and pepper.

❷ Remove the crusts from the bread, tear into pieces and blitz in the food processor to make fine breadcrumbs. (If you don't have a machine, crumble finely by hand.) Place in a shallow bowl. Sieve 3–4 tablespoons of flour into another bowl and whisk the egg in a third bowl. Dip the escalopes in the flour, shaking off any excess, then in the egg and, finally, press into the breadcrumbs.

❸ About 5 minutes before you're ready to eat, heat together the butter and cooking oil over a medium heat. When good and hot, slip in the escalopes. Cook without moving them for about 2 minutes, flip them over and cook the other side; both sides should be crusted and golden. If not, cook on for a minute or so more. Serve with lemon wedges for squeezing over the top.

you will also need two sheets of greaseproof paper or cling film

This is an adaptation of a famous Scottish soup made with leeks, chicken and prunes. Weird though that might sound it is a surprisingly good mix of textures and flavours, particularly when rice is added to turn it into a meal-in-a-bowl. A slab of brown bread and butter and a nip of whisky would be good accompaniments.

cock-a-leekie

2–3 servings

15 minutes preparation

40 minutes cooking

ingredients

4 chicken thighs, skinned

large bunch flat leaf parsley

1 bay leaf

3 sprigs of thyme

2 garlic cloves

3 medium-sized leeks, approx
   200 g in total

1 small onion

salt and black pepper

100 g basmati rice

10 ready-to-eat dried prunes

method

❶ Place the chicken pieces in a medium-sized pan with 750 ml water. Bring slowly to the boil. Remove the grey scum that forms.

❷ Meanwhile, pick the leaves off the parsley and set aside. Bundle the parsley stalks, bay leaf and thyme together with cotton or string. Crack the garlic cloves with fist or knife, and flake away the skin. Trim the leeks and slice the white part only into 2½ cm rounds. Peel, halve and thinly slice the onion. Add the herb bundle, garlic, leeks and onion to the pan. Add ½ teaspoon of salt and plenty of black pepper. Return to the boil, reduce the heat and simmer gently for 15 minutes.

❸ Meanwhile, finely slice the leek green, discarding only the very fibrous ends. Rinse and shake dry. Remove the stones from the prunes if necessary. Coarsely chop the parsley; you want about 3 tablespoons.

❹ When the cooking time is up, discard the herb bundle and add the rice, letting it trickle under the white leeks (which will float on top). Return to the boil, reduce the heat immediately and simmer for 15 minutes. About 5 minutes before the end of cooking, add the prunes, poking them amongst the now plump rice.

❺ For ease of eating, and to make the chicken go further,

cut the meat off the bones (which add flavour to the broth) before you serve. This is best done now, then add the leek greens and half the parsley. Simmer briskly for 3 minutes – the leek greens should remain *al dente*. Leave to rest for a couple of minutes, then stir in the remaining parsley. Taste and adjust the seasoning.

Things to Do with Leftover Chicken

Portions of cooked chicken – either left over from a roast or bought especially – are versatile and always delicious.

BANG BANG CHICKEN

Mix a shake of Tabasco, squeeze of lemon juice, 1 crushed clove of garlic and a dollop of yoghurt into 3 tablespoons of peanut butter, thinning with a little boiling water if too thick. Make a pile with 2 portions of shredded cooked chicken, 6 shredded spring onions and 1 medium-sized carrot that you have cut into skinny batons. Spoon over the sauce, garnish with a few chopped mint or coriander leaves, and sprinkle with a tablespoon of sesame seeds. Good with boiled new potatoes. Feeds 2, or more with lots of veg.

See also pages 187 and 189 for more ideas.

This is a chuck-everything-in-the-pan-wander-off-and-do-somthing-else-and-come-back-about-thirty-minutes-later sort of dish. It is easily adapted to feed more people or to last a couple of people over several days. It is also infinitely variable within the confines of the basic principles.

All you do is add a chicken leg or two to the cooking pot with a sliced onion, a few potatoes, garlic and some herbs. What you're actually doing is making a quick stock but rather than cooking all the goodness out of the ingredients, you cook them lightly and gently so that they will be delicious to eat when moistened with some of the broth. You want the meat to stay on the bone for this supper because, while the chicken cooks, it is also enriching the broth, and whole legs or big thighs are best for this. To freshen up the flavours and make this boiled dinner much more interesting, both in terms of looks and flavours, a cupful of frozen peas and a handful of shredded spinach are added at the end of cooking.

This dish re-heats beautifully but add extra spinach just before serving. Any leftover broth can be strained and used in other dishes. And, finally, the whole garlic cloves will be as soft as butter. Smear them onto toast to eat with supper.

chicken in the pot

2 servings
20 minutes preparation
35 minutes cooking

ingredients

1 large onion
4 plump garlic cloves
10 small new potatoes
4 chicken thighs
4 medium-sized mushrooms
1 small unwaxed lemon

method

❶ Peel, halve and thickly slice the onion into half moons. Smack the garlic with your fist or the flat of a knife until you hear it crack. Scrape and rinse the potatoes.

❷ If you prefer, skin the chicken. Wipe the mushrooms to remove any dirt and slice quite thinly. Remove the zest (no white) from the lemon and chop into dust. Chop the rosemary leaves similarly finely.

❸ Place all these ingredients in a pan and cover with 600 ml water. Add the wine, if you have some, and the juice of half the lemon. Season with one flat teaspoon of salt and a generous seasoning of black pepper. Bring to the boil, turn down to simmer, partially cover the pan and cook for 30 minutes.

❹ Remove the lid, increase the heat and add the peas. Boil for a couple of minutes or until the peas are tender while you shred the spinach, sorrel or watercress leaves. Taste the broth and adjust the seasoning with salt, pepper and the reserved lemon juice. Stir in the spinach or watercress, turn off the heat and leave for a couple of minutes for the green leaves to soften and the chicken relax.

❺ Serve sprinkled with parsley or persillade, *see* below.

1 tbsp rosemary leaves
glass of white wine if possible
salt and black pepper
200 g frozen peas
handful of spinach or
** watercress leaves**
1 tbsp coarsely chopped flat
** leaf parsley**

Persillade

Parsley is the perfect garnish for many dishes, but why not tease the taste buds with a scattering of parsley which has been chopped finely with garlic? This is called *persillade*, and is a clever French seasoning that smartens up the finished dish whilst adding a fresh, lively zing to every mouthful.

Peel and finely chop 1 big garlic clove then chop it again with the parsley.

It is a useful garnish to know about and is particularly good with fried potatoes or plain boiled foods. The Italians, incidentally, add finely chopped lemon zest, too, and call it *gremolata*.

The idea of cooking honey-sweetened tomatoes with oranges, and seasoning the sauce with cinnamon and a hint of saffron, was inspired by a dish I ate on holiday in Morocco. With chicken added to this 'cook-in' sauce, it becomes a lovely dish for a party; a bit special but easy to prepare and, importantly, one that can be made in advance. It goes equally well with pasta, rice, new potatoes or cous cous. The sauce is delicious on its own with pasta or boiled potatoes. The recipe can be cut in half if you only want to feed 6 people.

moroccan tomato chicken

10–12 servings
30 minutes preparation
45 minutes cooking

ingredients

2 juicy oranges
150 ml white or rosé wine
5 tbsp vegetable cooking oil
1 kg lean chicken meat
4 onions
4 garlic cloves
7½ cm cinnamon stick
pinch of saffron stamens
    softened in 1 tbsp boiling
    water (see page 136)
1 bay leaf
salt and black pepper
4 x 400 g cans of Italian peeled
    tomatoes
2 tbsp runny honey
25 g butter
squeeze of lemon juice

method

❶ Grate the zest off one orange and add it and the juice of both oranges to a bowl. Add the wine and whisk in 1 tablespoon of oil.

❷ Slice the chicken across the grain into strips approximately 5 cm x 1 cm. Mix the chicken into the orange mixture and leave to marinate for at least 30 minutes.

❸ Meanwhile, peel and finely chop the onions and peel and slice the garlic. Cook onions and garlic over a medium heat in 2 tablespoons of oil in a spacious, heavy-bottomed pan. After about 6 minutes, when glossy and softening, add the cinnamon, saffron, bay leaf, 1 teaspoon of salt, a generous seasoning of black pepper, the tomatoes and the honey. Increase the heat for a few minutes while you stir well with a wooden spoon to break up the tomatoes. Leave to simmer for about 30 minutes until thick and jammy.

❹ When the sauce is ready, lift the chicken out of its marinade and add the marinade to the pan, removing the bay leaf first. Continue simmering the sauce while you fry the chicken in uncrowded batches in the butter and remaining oil. Cook it briskly so that it browns and plumps and remove to a plate as you cook each new batch.

5 Add the cooked chicken to the sauce. Simmer for about 10 minutes or until the chicken is completely cooked. Then taste the sauce and adjust the seasoning with salt, pepper, honey and a squeeze of lemon if you think it needs it. Simmer for another couple of minutes.

6 This dish re-heats well and looks very pretty served with a sprinkling of finely chopped parsley or chives.

Another Idea for Leftover Chicken

CHICKEN GRATIN

Stir 1 tablespoon of flour into 1 tablespoon of melted butter then gradually add stock made with ½ chicken stock cube and 250 ml boiling water, stirring until thick and smooth. Add a splash of white wine or a generous squeeze of lemon juice and 3 tablespoons double cream or thick Greek yoghurt. Cook gently without boiling for 5 minutes, stirring often. Season with salt and black pepper, and then stir in 50 g grated cheese and ½ tablespoon Dijon mustard. Simmer until the cheese melts. Pour this over the equivalent of 2 large shredded portions of cooked chicken, top with breadcrumbs made with 2 slices of bread mixed with a knob of melted butter. Bake at 400°F/200°C/gas mark 6 for about 20 minutes until crusty and bubbling. Feeds 2–4.

See also pages 183 and 189 for more ideas.

The authentic version of this Spanish chicken stew is made with a jointed whole chicken, roasted red peppers, about double the peppers' weight in ripe tomatoes, and strips of salty, air-dried Serrano ham. This anglicized, meal-in-a-pot quickie version is pretty damn good, too. It will keep, cooled, covered and in the fridge, for several days.

a sort of pollo al chilindron

8–10 servings
20 minutes preparation
35 minutes cooking

ingredients

1 kg scrubbed new potatoes

350 g frozen peas

2 large red onions

4 tbsp olive oil or another
    cooking oil

salt and black pepper

4 garlic cloves

6 rashers of rindless, smoked,
    streaky bacon

750 g–1 kg lean chicken meat,
    cut into chunks

2 x 400 g cans of whole red
    peppers (pimientos)

400 g can of Italian peeled
    tomatoes

method

❶ Put the potatoes on to boil in plenty of salted water. Cook until tender to the point of a knife. Add the peas, cover the pan but turn off the heat.

❷ Meanwhile, peel, halve and chop the onions. Pour 3 tablespoons of oil in a spacious, heavy-bottomed pan placed over a medium heat. Stir in the onions, add 1 teaspoon of salt and about ½ teaspoon of black pepper. Cook, stirring every now and again, for 5 minutes.

❸ Peel the garlic cloves and slice in thin rounds. Slice across the pile of bacon rashers to make chunky strips. Add both to the onions, stirring vigorously to break up the clumps of bacon. Cook until the bacon fat is beginning to crisp and the bacon lean is cooked.

❹ Scoop the onion mixture out of the pan to a plate or bowl, leaving behind as much of the oil as possible. Increase the heat, add a little of the remaining oil and cook the chicken in batches. You are aiming for the pieces to plump and brown; this should take 3–4 minutes per batch. Remove each batch to the plate or bowl as you go.

❺ Meanwhile, drain one can of peppers. Tip it and the tomatoes with their juices into the bowl of a food processor and blitz. (See page 20.)

❻ Return the onions and all the chicken to the pan. Pour on the blitzed purée and stir as you bring the stew up to the boil.

❼ Drain the remaining can of peppers. Slice the peppers into strips and add them to the pan. Partially cover the pan and cook for about 10 minutes or until the chicken is quite tender. Remove the lid, and if the pan is large enough, add the drained potatoes and peas. If not, drain them and serve them separately. Cook the stew for a further 5 minutes or until the sauce is slightly reduced and thickened. Eat immediately, or cool, cover and refrigerate for up to 5 days.

And Yet Another Idea for Leftover Chicken

CHICKEN FRICASSÉE WITH PEAS AND SPRING ONIONS

Finely slice a bunch of spring onions and soften in a large knob of butter without browning. Stir in 1 flat tablespoon of flour and gradually incorporate 300 ml milk, stirring constantly, to make a smooth sauce. Bring to the boil, reduce the heat immediately and simmer for 6 minutes. Stir in a little mustard, add 250 g frozen peas, season with ½ teaspoon salt and black pepper. Next tear 2 cooked chicken portions into bite-size pieces directly into the sauce. Adjust the seasonings with a squeeze of lemon juice. Serve with boiled potatoes, rice or buttered noodles. Feeds 2.

See also pages 183 and 187 for more ideas.

In the Languedoc, where cassoulet originates, it's a complex, hearty concoction of preserved duck, lamb, pork, sausages and dried butter beans. The stew simmers away for hours and is ready when the meat is meltingly soft and the beans have soaked up all the juices. A crusty topping of breadcrumbs and parsley absorbs any fat and keeps the dish moist.

This relatively quick version is made along the same lines. It is what we might call a 'rib-sticker': gorgeous French stodge. Serve it with lemon wedges to squeeze over the top and lightly cooked French beans.

Quantities could be doubled if you want to make this dish for more people. It re-heats beautifully but is also wonderful cold. You could make this with chicken or turkey and add a few slices of chorizo or pepperoni, too.

cheat's cassoulet

4 servings
30 minutes preparation
60 minutes cooking

ingredients

1 large onion
3 big garlic cloves
2 tbsp cooking oil
salt and black pepper
4 rashers of rindless streaky bacon
1 bay leaf
½ tsp dried thyme
1 tsp dried sage
4 top-quality pork sausages
400 g can of Italian peeled tomatoes

method

❶ Peel, halve and finely slice the onion. Peel and slice 2 garlic cloves.

❷ Heat 1 tablespoon of oil in a large, heavy-bottomed pan until very hot. Stir in the onions. Cook, stirring often, for 4 minutes. Add 1 teaspoon of salt, reduce the heat to low, stir in the garlic, cover the pan and leave to cook for 10 minutes.

❸ Slice the bacon across the rashers and add to the pan with the bay leaf, thyme and sage. Increase the heat slightly and quickly brown the sausages.

❹ Add the tomatoes, breaking them up in the pan, and stock. Season lightly with salt and generously with black pepper. Simmer, uncovered, for 15 minutes, so the sausages poach and the liquid thickens and reduces.

❺ Meanwhile, skin the duck and cut into large bite-size pieces. If using duck legs, cut the meat off the bone in 4 large pieces per portion and then cut it into chunks. Heat the remaining oil in a frying pan and brown the duck. Add duck and juices to the main pan.

6 Tip the beans into a sieve or colander and rinse the beans under cold running water. Shake dry and add them to the pan. Establish a gentle simmer. Stir in 1 tablespoon of parsley. Taste and adjust the seasoning. Remove the bay leaf.

7 Blitz bread and the remaining garlic clove to make the crumbs for the topping. (*See* page 20 if you don't have a machine.) Stir with the remaining parsley. Spread the breadcrumb mixture over the top of the cassoulet, cover the pan and cook for 30 minutes.

8 To finish the dish, pre-heat the grill. Remove the lid, make a criss-cross with a thin stream of olive oil and place the pan under the grill. Cook until crusty and golden but watch it like a hawk to avoid burning. If your pan is too large to fit under the grill, you will need to finish off the dish in a very hot oven for a short time.

½ chicken stock cube dissolved in 300 ml boiling water

4 duck breasts or 4 large duck thighs or drumsticks

400 g can of cannellini or haricot beans

2 tbsp chopped flat leaf parsley

65 g stale crustless bread

1–2 tbsp olive oil

If possible, make this 24 hours in advance. The flavours really mellow and improve when the chili is allowed to go cold and is then re-heated. Traditionally, chili is eaten over rice or with crusty bread but try it rolled up in a hot tortilla or spooned into lightly toasted pitta bread envelopes with soured cream and a dollop of guacamole, and shredded crisp lettuce. Most people think that this dish is called *Chilli* con carne. They are wrong. *Chili* means spice and *carne* means meat.

chili con carne with cheddar tacos

6–8 servings
20 minutes preparation
30 minutes cooking

ingredients

4 rashers rindless streaky bacon
3 tbsp cooking oil
2 medium-sized onions
2 garlic cloves
1 bay leaf
750 g minced beef or lamb
2 tsp chilli powder or 1 tbsp Mexican chili powder
1 heaped tsp ground cumin
small glass of red wine
400 g can of Italian peeled tomatoes
1 heaped tsp oregano
¼ chicken stock cube dissolved in 150 ml boiling water
salt and black pepper

method

❶ Cut the bacon across the rashers into strips. Heat the oil in a spacious, heavy-bottomed pan. Cook the bacon, gently at first then increase the heat, until crisp. Scoop it out of the pan to a plate.

❷ Meanwhile, peel and chop the onions and garlic. Add these with the bay leaf to the pan. Cook for about 10 minutes, stirring often, until the onion begins to soften and colour then transfer to the plate.

❸ Add the meat to the pan. Cook it gently at first as it browns, then increase the heat and continue until it is glossy and almost dry and rubbery-looking. Stir in the chilli or chili, and cumin and cook for 1 minute before returning the onion and bacon. Add the wine and let it bubble away before adding the tomatoes, oregano, 1 teaspoon of salt and the stock. Break up the tomatoes with a wooden spoon.

❹ Cook, uncovered, over a gentle heat until the sauce is thick and most of the liquid reduced. This should take between 20 and 35 minutes. Taste and adjust the seasoning with salt, pepper, Tabasco and lemon juice.

❺ Cook the rice (*see* page 133) while the chili is simmering.

6 Tip the beans into a sieve and rinse. Shake dry and add them to the chili. Cook for a few more minutes until the beans have heated through. Remove the bay leaf.

7 Make the tacos at the last moment. Pre-heat the grill to its highest setting. Lay the tortilla chips out on a sheet of foil placed over the grill pan. Grate the cheese over the chips and cook until the cheese melts and begins to bubble.

8 Serve the chili over rice with a dollop of soured cream garnished with snipped chives. Pass the Cheddar tacos separately.

Tabasco
squeeze of lemon juice
500 g basmati rice
400 g can of red kidney beans
tortilla chips
Cheddar cheese
150 ml soured cream
small bunch of chives

This is what you might call a big bowlful. It is the sort of stew that is welcome at any time of the year and can be altered slightly by adding different seasonal vegetables that have been boiled separately right at the end of cooking. Green beans, for example, in summer and chunks of boiled carrot with a handful of chopped parsley in winter. The mystery ingredient in this delicious lamb stew is anchovy essence which, incidentally, is stocked by most supermarkets. It's a useful secret weapon because it gives fish pies and meat stews a surprising depth of flavour without a hint of fishiness. The dish will keep, cooled and covered in the fridge, for several days. Serve it with boiled potatoes or stir them into the finished stew. It is also good with baked potatoes or crusty bread.

lamb and tomato flageolet

4 servings
20 minutes preparation
45 minutes cooking

ingredients
500 g lamb chump steak
1 large onion (red for
    preference)
2 big garlic cloves
1¹/₂ tbsp olive oil
juice of ¹/₂ lemon
¹/₂ tsp dried thyme
salt and black pepper
400 g can of flageolet beans
1 tsp anchovy essence
    (optional)
400 g can of Italian peeled
    tomatoes

method
❶ If necessary, trim away the band of fat on the meat and slice into large kebab-size pieces.

❷ Peel, halve and finely slice the onion. Peel the garlic and slice in very thin rounds.

❸ Heat 1 tablespoon of oil until very hot in a heavy-bottomed large frying pan or another wide-based pan. Spread out the meat in the hot pan: once it hits the hot pan it will stick so leave for a couple of minutes until the pieces form a crust and can be turned without tearing. Brown both sides of the meat and then remove to a plate. Squeeze the lemon juice over the meat and sprinkle with the thyme.

❹ Add the remaining ¹/₂ tablespoon olive oil to the pan and stir in the onions. Cook, reducing the heat so they cook briskly without burning, before adding the garlic. Season with salt and pepper, reduce the heat and cook for 5 minutes.

⑤ Meanwhile, tip the beans into a colander or sieve and rinse under cold water. Shake dry and add to the pan. Cook for 5 more minutes. Return the meat and its juices to the pan. Stir in the anchovy essence, if using, then the tomatoes and stock. Bring to the boil, breaking up the tomatoes with the back of a wooden spoon, reduce the heat immediately and simmer steadily for about 30 minutes until the stew is thick and juicy and the meat very tender. Taste and adjust the seasoning before serving.

½ chicken stock cube dissolved in 300 ml boiling water

Irish stew is plain food in the extreme. No fancy flavours, no artful cooking technique, just lamb, onions, carrots, potatoes and water cooked with plenty of salt and pepper until everything is tender. Some people say it is important to trim away any big chunks of fat and render it down for frying the meat (and veg) before the stew is left to simmer away on the back-burner. Others don't bother to brown the meat or vegetables which gives the stew more of a boiled dinner flavour. Either way, it is a fatty dish so why, you might wonder, add a dollop of butter at the end of cooking? This gives the gravy sheen and body, and adds a touch of luxurious creaminess.

irish stew

6 servings
20 minutes preparation
90 minutes cooking

ingredients

1 kg lamb cutlets, or lamb
shoulder, or scrag end of
neck, or chump chops
6 large carrots
6 medium-sized onions
12 medium-sized potatoes
salt and black pepper
6 sprigs of thyme
knob of cold butter
3 tbsp finely chopped curly
parsley

method

❶ Trim the bulky fat off the lamb. Peel the carrots and cut in three – you want big chunks. Peel and quarter the onions, then halve each quarter lengthways. Peel the potatoes and leave to soak in cold water.

❷ Put half the meat into your largest casserole or saucepan with a tight-fitting lid. Season generously with salt and pepper, add half the thyme. Spread half the carrots and half the onions over the meat. Season again and repeat with the rest of the meat, carrots and onions.

❸ Pour 600 ml cold water over the stew and bring to the boil. Establish a very low simmer, cover the dish and cook for 40 minutes.

❹ Drain the potatoes, pile over the stew and season thoroughly. Return the lid and cook for another 40 minutes or until the potatoes are tender but firm.

❺ Cut the butter into pieces into the stew. Add most of the parsley and gently stir until the butter has dispersed. Sprinkle over the last of the parsley and serve with frozen peas and hunks of buttered bread.

In Barcelona's famous La Boqueria market, there is a fabulous little stall devoted to beans. White beans, black beans, kidney-shaped beans and oval beans. It's hard to choose which ones to use for the inevitable chorizo stew. They sell cooked beans for quick suppers but we have to make do with a can of cannellini beans for this approximation of Iberian beans on toast. The toast is bruschetta-style – rubbed with garlic and dribbled with olive oil. Alternatively, serve the beans hot from the pan with crusty bread. To make more of this dish, add boiled new potatoes.

chorizo and white bean stew

method

❶ Slice the bacon across the rashers into strips. Peel and chop the onion. Peel and finely chop the garlic.

❷ Heat 1 tablespoon of the olive oil in a heavy-bottomed medium-sized saucepan placed over a medium heat Add the bacon and bay leaf and cook for a couple of minutes until the fat begins to run. Add the onion and cook, stirring frequently, for 3–4 minutes, adjusting the heat slightly so it browns without burning.

❸ Chop the tomatoes and tip the beans into a sieve and rinse thoroughly with cold water. Shake dry.

❹ Add the garlic, rosemary and thyme to the bacon and onions and cook until aromatic. Stir in the paprika then add the tomatoes. Cook, reducing the heat slightly, until the tomatoes have flopped to give a small amount of juice.

❺ While that's happening, slice the chorizo in approximately 1 cm wide pieces. Add them to the pan together with the beans, 1 teaspoon of salt and a generous seasoning of pepper. Pour in 100 ml water. Simmer for 5 minutes. Taste and adjust the seasoning. Stir in the parsley and the final tablespoon of olive oil. This stew will keep, covered, in the fridge for several days.

2 servings
15 minutes preparation
15 minutes cooking

ingredients

2 rashers of rindless streaky bacon
1 onion
2 plump garlic cloves
2 tbsp olive oil
1 bay leaf
2 tomatoes
400 g can of cannellini beans
1 tsp chopped rosemary
½ tsp chopped thyme
1 tsp paprika
3 cm x 10 cm piece cooked chorizo
salt and black pepper
2 tbsp chopped flat leaf parsley

This is one of those useful feed-the-five-thousand sort of dishes that requires very little preparation and more or less cooks itself. Serve it hot or cold with baked or boiled potatoes and a very big green salad. You can make it feed you all week (keep it covered in cling film or tin foil in the fridge).

Ring the changes by:

- slicing it into sandwiches with pickle and lettuce
- add chunks to hot pasta that has been stirred with a dollop of Dijon mustard and frozen peas (which you boiled with the pasta)
- follow the recipe for Corned Beef Hash on page 166 but use squares of meatloaf instead
- fry an onion until slippery and soft and pile it onto toast rubbed with garlic then cover with thin slices of meatloaf
- make another tomato sauce, perhaps adding anchovies, chilli, red pepper or chives, and serve it stirred with chunks of meatloaf

meatloaf and tomato sauce

8–12 servings
15 minutes preparation
60 minutes cooking

ingredients

2 large onions
2 tbsp cooking oil plus a little extra
2 tsp dried thyme or oregano
salt and black pepper
1 kg minced lamb or beef or a mixture of chicken and pork
a decent-sized bunch of parsley, preferably flat leaf
1 egg

method

❶ Pre-heat the oven to 350°F/180°C/gas mark 4.

❷ Peel, halve and finely chop the onions. Pour the cooking oil into a large frying pan placed over a medium heat and stir in the onions. Cook, stirring every so often, for about 10 minutes until beginning to soften. Add half the thyme or oregano, season with salt and pepper and cook, giving everything a couple of stirs, for a further 2 minutes.

❸ Put the meat in a large bowl and break it up with your fingers. Add the onions, scraping all the juices in, too. Coarsely chop the parsley leaves and add them to the bowl with plenty of salt and pepper. Lightly beat the egg and pour it over the top. Mix well, mulching everything together with your hands. Lightly oil a metal or ceramic dish that can hold about 1½ litres. A high-sided oven tin would be ideal. Spread out the mixture in this dish, smoothing the top (making a dome if you wish) with a blunt knife.

❹ Break up the tomatoes with a wooden spoon, and season with salt and pepper, sugar and the rest of the thyme. Tip the tomato mixture over the meatloaf. Make a loose lid with tin foil and punch a few holes so the steam can escape.

❺ Cook in the pre-heated oven for 30 minutes, remove the foil and cook for a further 30 minutes so the top can brown. Test that the meatloaf is ready by inserting a knife in the deepest part of the loaf. Leave it there and count to ten. Pull it out and test it with your tongue. The skewer needs to be hot and the juices should be clear and rosy. The meat will have shrunk away from the sides of the tin, which will have filled up with a clear gravy. Tip this into a jug.

❻ Cut the meat in chunky slices and serve from the dish moistened with a little of the sauce. If leaving the meatloaf (or leftovers) to cool, pour the juices back over the top. They will set into a delicious jelly.

400 g can of Italian peeled tomatoes

½ tsp sugar

A Desert Island dish. Make it properly like this and you are destined to become very popular with your friends. Serve with a big dish of shredded cabbage which you have quickly stir fried in hot oil with a splash of vinegar and a sprinkling of sugar, or frozen peas. And plenty of ketchup to hand.

shepherd's pie

6 servings

20 minutes preparation

60 minutes cooking

ingredients

1 large onion

3 medium-sized carrots

1 celery heart, or 4 sticks taken
   from close to the heart

2 tbsp cooking oil

leaves from 4 sprigs of thyme

1 bay leaf

salt and black pepper

750 g good quality minced lamb

1 tbsp flour

2 tbsp tomato ketchup

1 dsp anchovy essence
   (optional)

FOR THE MASH

1½ kg floury ('old') variety of
   potatoes, such as King
   Edward

salt and black pepper

50 ml milk

50 g butter

method

❶ Peel and chop the onion. Scrape the carrots and grate on the large hole of the cheese grater (or use the appropriate attachment of your food processor). Finely slice the celery.

❷ Heat most of the cooking oil in a heavy casserole and fry the onion over a medium heat for a few minutes. Add the celery, carrot, thyme and bay leaf, season with a little salt and pepper and cook until the vegetables are tender. Transfer to a plate.

❸ Add the remaining oil to the pan and briskly fry the meat, stirring until it changes colour. Some minced lamb produces a stunningly large amount of fat when it is fried. If that is the case, drain it away, carefully tipping the fat directly into the rubbish bin, leaving a maximum of 1 tablespoonful. Sprinkle over the flour, stirring it in thoroughly, add the ketchup, anchovy essence, if using, or a generous seasoning of salt, and then 150 ml water. Cook for a few minutes and then return the vegetables to the pan. Leave to simmer for 30–45 minutes until thick and nicely amalgamated. Remove the bay leaf, and adjust the seasoning.

❹ Remove the pan from the heat, tip the contents into a suitable shallow earthenware dish and leave to cool to avoid the mash sinking when it is added. This is

speeded up by popping the dish in the freezer for about
15 minutes.

5 Meanwhile, make the mash. Peel the potatoes and
cut into even-sized pieces. Rinse and put in a pan with
plenty of water. Bring to the boil, add 1 teaspoon of salt
and boil until tender.

6 Drain the potatoes and mash with the milk and butter to
make a fluffy but firm mash (which must be done by hand
and not in the blender, *see* page 154). Season with black
pepper and nutmeg. Cover to keep warm.

7 Spoon the mashed potatoes over the cooled minced
meat, fork the potato up and dot with butter.

8 Pre-heat the oven to 350°F/180°C/gas mark 4. Bake
the pie for 20 minutes until the top is golden and crusted
and the meat is beginning to bubble up around the edge.

freshly grated nutmeg
extra butter

Imagine, if you will, the smell of a fish pie cooking in your kitchen. When it comes out of the oven, the top will be crusted and golden and as you slide the spoon through the soft mash, it will find big flakes of tender haddock or cod and maybe prawns or mushrooms, all held in a creamy parsley sauce flecked with chopped hard-boiled egg. Definitely worth the effort. Serve with frozen peas. Anchovy essence, incidentally, although not essential, gives the pie a wonderful depth of flavour.

fish pie

6 servings
40 minutes preparation
30 minutes cooking

ingredients

1 small onion
800 ml milk
1 bay leaf
2 cloves
salt and black pepper
1½ kg floury ('old') variety of
    potatoes, such as King
    Edward
4 eggs
750 g thick haddock or cod
    fillet
500 g smoked haddock
100 g butter plus an extra knob
2 tbsp flour
leaves from a large bunch of
    flat leaf parsley
1 dsp anchovy essence
    (optional)

method

❶ Peel and finely chop the onion. Place it in a pan with the milk, bay leaf and cloves. Season with salt and pepper and simmer for 10 minutes. Turn off the heat, cover the pan and leave for 15 minutes.

❷ Meanwhile, peel the potatoes and cut into even-sized chunks. Rinse and place in a saucepan with the eggs. Cover with water, add 1 teaspoon of salt and boil until the potatoes are tender. Drain. Crack the eggs all over and peel under cold running water.

❸ Place the fish, skin-side down, in a single layer in a wide-based pan. Strain the milk over the fish, discarding the onion, cloves and bay leaf. Add a knob of butter and simmer for 5 minutes. Turn the fish and cook for 2 more minutes. Lift the fish onto a plate and leave to cool.

❹ Using 50–100 ml of the milk and 50 g butter, make a firm mash with the potatoes (which must be done by hand and not in the blender; see page 154). Keep warm.

❺ Make the fish sauce by melting 50 g butter in a small pan. Stir in the flour then pour the fishy milk, and any milk leached from the cooling fish, into the roux. Beat continuously, preferably with a wire whisk, as it simmers. Cook for several minutes to make a smooth, thick sauce. Don't be tempted to stint on this cooking. If you do, the sauce will taste of raw flour. Stir in the coarsely chopped parsley and season with anchovy essence or salt and black pepper.

6 Ease the fish off the skin in large flakes, taking care to remove bones. Pile it into a suitable ceramic, glass or earthenware oven-proof dish. Coarsely chop the eggs. Scatter egg over the fish. Pour over the sauce and leave to cool – this is important, otherwise the mash will sink into the mixture when it is added.

7 Pre-heat the oven to 400°F/200°C/gas mark 6.

8 Spoon the warm mash over the fish. Fork up the surface and bake for 30–40 minutes until crusty and gorgeous.

other good things to add to fish pie:

- quartered medium-sized mushrooms fried in butter
- slices of peeled tomato
- cooked mussels (without shells, natch)
- cooked prawns
- sliced leeks that have been softened in butter or milk
- shredded spinach that has been dropped into boiling water to wilt, then squeezed dry in your hands

10. sausages

Succulent, plump, meaty sausages cooked until they're brown and crusty. Who can resist them sizzling in the frying pan?

The British eat six billion fresh sausages a year, an average of 125 per head. By law, sausages must have a total meat content of 65% but only half has to be *lean* meat. That means 50% could be fat, skin, rind, gristle or sinew. The best sausages have at least 85% meat content and there are hundreds of different varieties. A high proportion of them is made with pork but look out for lamb or beef sausages, smoked sausages and vegetarian alternatives.

The very best are hand made, often by your local butcher, with high-quality natural ingredients and no additives. You certainly notice the difference when you eat sausages like these. They don't shrivel and splutter when you cook them and the meat is chunky as opposed to paste-like. The skin is likely to be made with gut casings and the seasonings are chosen to complement rather than disguise. Inevitably, all these sausages are expensive by comparison with a Well-Known Brand whose name I won't mention, but goodness, they're worth it. Check out some of the British regionals such as Kentish Hop (pork, hops and real ale), Scrumpy (pork with apple and rough cider) and deliciously spicy Cumberland. If you are buying from the supermarket, always choose sausages which have a high meat content.

Sausages can be fried, grilled, roasted or poached. Once cooked, they can be sliced, chopped or cut into strips and cooked up again. They can also be unzipped and the meat formed into patties and meatballs. Sausage-meat can be mixed with other things and used in sauces and stews, in stir fries and stuffings. Sausages go with mash, pasta and polenta and with most types of beans and lentils. Sausages and bread have an on-going love affair – any bread, any sausage, hot or cold. Sausages also love mustard and tomato ketchup. And apples.

Who's Who of International Sausages

The great British porker is not the only sausage. Most cultures have their own equivalent and, like ours, it is one of the most economical (and tasty) ways of eating meat. For best value and best quality, buy them from indigenous shops.

BLACK PUDDING, DRISHEEN AND BOUDIN NOIR: blood is the characteristic of black pudding. In the Midlands, the North of England and France, it's pig's blood, while Drisheen (from Ireland) and Scottish black pudding are made from sheep's blood and oats, the latter ingredient giving it crunch. Black pudding is partially cooked and also contains cereal, herbs, spices, onions and fat. The French version, Boudin Noir, is creamier.

In the UK, black pudding is regarded as breakfast food (sliced and fried with eggs and/or bacon, or in a hash with potatoes and onions), but it is very good served French-style with mashed potato or apple sauce. Grill or fry thick slices. Smaller sausages can be cooked whole. It's a matter of choice whether you eat the skin; only if it's crispy is my advice.

CHORIZO: pork and paprika are the distinctive ingredients of these spicy Spanish sausages. Some are smoked, some are completely cooked and can be sliced or left whole and added to cooked dishes. Particularly good in bean stews on account of the strong flavour. **Linguica** is the Portuguese version.

FRANKFURTER: there are two types; the original comes from Germany. Made with a smooth blend of pork and bacon fat, it's smoked then re-heated at home by simmering in water. The American version – **Hot Dog** – is made with beef and pork. Cook the same way. Excellent in a split roll (or door-step) with brown-fried onions, a squirt of ketchup and mustard.

KABANOS: thin, hard, smoked spicy pork sausage from Poland. Slice into vegetable soups or simmer with canned beans or lentils.

LOUKANIKA: spicy, strong-flavoured Greek sausage made with coarsely ground pork and coriander then soaked in red wine. Delicious grilled or fried, with mash, beans, lentils, bread etc.

MERGUEZ: cocktail-size spicy Algerian sausages made with mutton and sometimes goat. Grill or fry. A feature of cous cous and good with harissa or another red-hot chilli paste.

The business! Meaty porkers, cooked until they're almost burnt and eaten with buttery, well-whipped mash, and lashings of highly seasoned thick, dark brown onion gravy. Peas and mustard are essential extras.

bangers and mash with onion gravy

4 servings
25 minutes preparation
45 minutes cooking

ingredients

1 tbsp cooking oil
12 good-quality pork sausages
FOR THE ONION GRAVY
4 medium-sized onions
small knob of butter
1 very scant tbsp cooking oil
salt and black pepper
1 tbsp flour
1/2 glass of red wine, if
    available
1/2 chicken stock cube
    dissolved in 300 ml boiling
    water
1 tbsp tomato purée or ketchup
1–2 tsp made English mustard
    (or more to taste)
dash of Worcestershire sauce
FOR THE MASH
1 kg floury ('old') variety of
    potatoes such as King
    Edward

method

❶ Peel, halve and finely slice the onions. Heat the butter and oil to sizzling in a medium-sized saucepan and stir in the onions. Let them brown in patches stirring occasionally – this is important, both for flavour and for the colour of the gravy – and takes 10–15 minutes. Turn down the heat. Season with 1/2 teaspoon of salt and pepper, cover the pan and cook, stirring every so often to check the onions are moist and not sticking, for 30 minutes. Remove the lid, turn up the heat and evaporate any juices.

❷ Sift the flour into the onions, stir thoroughly and beat in the wine, if using, and stock with a wooden spoon. Establish a simmer, stir in the tomato purée or ketchup, mustard and Worcestershire sauce, and cook for a couple more minutes.

❸ Meanwhile, peel the potatoes and cut them into even-sized chunks. Put the potatoes in a pan, cover generously with water and bring to the boil. Add 1/2 teaspoon of salt and simmer until tender. Drain and mash (do *not* attempt this in the blender, *see* page 154). Have the hot milk and butter ready and, using a wooden spoon, beat half the milk and all the butter into the potatoes, beating for as long as your arm can stand. Rest and do it again. Adjust the consistency with extra milk. Season with black pepper and nutmeg.

❹ While the potatoes are cooking, heat 1 tablespoon of oil in a large frying pan and start cooking the sausages over a moderate heat. This will take about 12–15 minutes, and the sausages are ready when plump, firm, crusty and brown. Serve the sausages with the onion gravy and a big scoop of mashed potato.

75 g butter
salt and black pepper
approx 100 ml hot milk
nutmeg

White Onion Sauce and Bread Sauce

These are two excellent alternative sauces to serve with sausages (or chicken), either alone or with mashed potato.

For white onion sauce, peel and slice a couple of onions and soften them gently in a large knob of butter. When soft and uncoloured – allow at least 15 minutes for this – stir in 1 tablespoon of flour. When it has disappeared, season with ½ teaspoon of salt and gradually add 350 ml of milk, stirring constantly to avoid lumps. Bring to the boil then turn down the heat and simmer gently for 5–10 minutes until thick and gorgeous. Taste and adjust the seasoning with salt and black pepper.

For the bread sauce, finely chop 1 small onion and place it in a pan with 1 bay leaf, 4 cloves, ½ teaspoon of salt and 4 peppercorns. Add 450 ml of milk. Bring to the boil, turn down the heat immediately, simmer for 10 minutes, turn off the heat, cover and leave for at least 30 minutes or until you are almost ready to serve. Strain the milk into a clean saucepan, heat through, then stir in 100 g breadcrumbs and a knob of butter.

This is an excellent way of making sausages go further.
Chunks of sausage meat are cooked in floppy, golden onions with mustard,
sage and a little stock stirred in to make a delicious sauce. The final addition
is frozen peas which are added to the pasta for the last couple of minutes
of cooking and, if you have some, a little chopped parsley to sprinkle over
the top.

caramelized onion and sausage pasta

4–5 servings
15 minutes preparation
20 minutes cooking

ingredients

400–500 g penne or another
chunky pasta
200 g frozen peas
1 large Spanish onion
2 tbsp cooking oil
salt and black pepper
8 good-quality sausages,
approx 500 g
6 sage leaves or 1 tsp chopped
thyme
1 tbsp Dijon mustard, smooth or
grain
1/2 chicken stock cube
dissolved in 150 ml boiling
water
1 tbsp coarsely chopped flat
leaf parsley

method

❶ Put a large pan of water on to boil, add 1 teaspoon salt
and cook the pasta according to the instructions on the
packet. Add the peas to the boiling pasta water a couple
of minutes before the end of cooking. When the peas are
tender, drain pasta and peas, return to the cooking
saucepan and cover to keep warm.

❷ Meanwhile, peel, halve and slice the onion into chunky
wedges. Heat the oil in a large frying pan or similar. When
hot, stir in the onions, tossing them around for a few
minutes as they begin to brown and wilt. Adjust the heat
so the onions don't burn, season with 1/2 teaspoon of
salt, cover and leave to soften, turn juicy and colour
slightly.

❸ Meanwhile, slash down the length of the sausages with
a sharp knife to cut through the skin. Peel away the skin
and discard. Pinch off lumps of sausage meat to make
four roughly shaped balls out of each sausage. Shred the
sage, if using.

❹ When the onions are slippery, tender and nicely
browned, add the sausage balls and sage or thyme to the
pan. Ideally, you want all the sausage balls to fit in one
layer but it doesn't matter if they are a bit cramped. Let
the balls cook for a couple of minutes before carefully

turning them around and continue frying, adjusting the heat as necessary, for 10–15 minutes until cooked through with nice crusty edges.

❺ Stir the mustard into the pan, add the stock and let everything bubble up together to make a thick sauce. Taste and adjust the seasoning with salt and pepper. Tip the sausage sauce into the cooked pasta. Stir and garnish with parsley.

Anyone born and raised in Dublin will know exactly what is meant by Dublin Coddle. When made with creamy but densely textured Irish potatoes, decent rashers of home-cured bacon and plump, meaty porkers, it is hard to believe that there is nothing else in the pot apart from onions and water.

Although you will be lucky to find Irish potatoes outside Ireland, it is possible to make a very good version of Dublin Coddle if you chop carefully. Good-quality sausages with a high meat content are essential and streaky bacon will give the best flavour. Don't be tempted to add extra flavouring in the way of garlic but frozen peas or shredded spring greens are great additions. The required accompaniment, apart from a bottle of stout, is bottled HP or brown sauce. Delicious.

dublin coddle

4 servings
15 minutes preparation
60 minutes cooking

ingredients

4 medium-sized onions, approx 450 g
8 good-sized potatoes, any type
8 rashers rindless streaky bacon
8 good-quality pork sausages
salt and black pepper
200 g spring greens or 200 g frozen peas
handful of flat leaf parsley
50 g cold butter

method

❶ Peel, halve and finely chop the onions. Peel the potatoes and rinse. Place onions and potatoes in a 1-litre capacity heavy-bottomed saucepan.

❷ Cut the bacon rashers into pieces and add them too. Season generously with black pepper, add 600 ml cold water and lay the sausages on top. Place the pan over a high heat and bring to the boil. Reduce the heat immediately, establish a steady but gentle simmer, cover the pan and cook for 45 minutes. Remove the lid, increase the heat and simmer vigorously for 10 minutes.

❸ Meanwhile, finely shred the spring greens, if using, place in a colander and rinse thoroughly with cold water. Shake dry. Pick the leaves off the parsley stalks and chop the leaves. Add the spring greens or frozen peas to the pan, poking them down under the liquid. Cook for 5 minutes. Stir the parsley into the pan. Taste the liquid and add salt if necessary. Serve in wide soup bowls. Add a little knob of cold butter to each and pass the HP sauce.

What you're aiming at with this old-fashioned British favourite is nicely browned meaty sausages partially hidden under puffed and swollen Yorkshire pudding with deep golden brown crusty edges. Properly made sausages with a high meat content are what you really want for this, but if you are making Toad with less than brilliant sausages (which, frankly, is likely) or with skinny chipolatas (highly recommended), it is essential to fry them quickly first. All over, until browned. If you want to cheat with the Yorkshire pudding, there are plenty of batter mixes available. Add a whisked egg and a dollop of mustard to improve the flavour.

toad in the hole

method

❶ Pre-heat the oven to 425°F/220°C/gas mark 7.

❷ Heat the oil in a frying pan placed over a medium heat. Fry the sausages or chipolatas until browned all over. Drain on kitchen paper, leave to cool while you make the batter, then smear generously with mustard or ketchup.

❸ Put the eggs into a mixing bowl and whisk or beat until really thick (or use an electric hand whisk/blender); the more you whisk, the lighter the pudding. Add a little of the flour and then some of the milk to loosen the batter. Alternate these two ingredients until used up and continue whisking until smooth: it *will* happen. If you can't get rid of the lumps, pour and push the batter through a sieve. Season, using plenty of pepper, and then mix in 75 ml water. Leave to rest for 15 minutes.

❹ Take a roasting tin that can accommodate the sausages in a single layer, place on a high heat and heat up the chosen fat until smoking. Pour in the batter, all in one go, and immediately arrange the mustard- or ketchup-smeared sausages into it.

❺ Put the dish in the centre of the oven and bake for about 30 minutes until puffed, crisp and a rich golden brown. Serve without delay, with extra ketchup if desired.

4 servings

20 minutes preparation

30 minutes cooking

ingredients

2 tbsp cooking oil

12 good-quality pork sausages or 20 chipolatas

3 tbsp mustard or 4 tbsp tomato ketchup

2 small eggs

100 g plain flour

100 ml milk

salt and black pepper

3 tbsp dripping, bacon fat or cooking oil

I wish I could take credit for this sensible and delicious recipe. So simple, so obvious, all ingredients that go together. I discovered it in Jane Grigson's *Vegetable Book* (Penguin) and it comes from Justin de Blank, who pioneered the real-food movement in the seventies with a delicatessen, and a bakery. Only worth making with decent sausages.

sausages in the dutch style

6 servings
20 minutes preparation
35 minutes cooking

ingredients

750 g good-quality pork sausages
a little lard or oil
1 large Dutch or Savoy cabbage
salt and pepper
2 heaped tbsp flour
425 ml milk
2 heaped tbsp each grated Parmesan or Cheddar, and Gruyère

method

❶ Pre-heat the oven to 350°F/180°C/gas mark 4 and put a large pan of water on to boil.

❷ Prick the sausages and lay them out in a baking dish which you've greased with lard or oil. Cook in the oven for about 20 minutes, turning occasionally, until brown all over and cooked through. Drain the sausages but save 3 tablespoons of the fat.

❸ Meanwhile slice the cabbage, discarding the hard core, and drop it into the boiling water with 1 teaspoon of salt. Boil for 1 minute – you want it crisp – tip into a colander, and shake well to drain thoroughly.

❹ Mix the sausages and cabbage together in a gratin dish and return them to the oven while you make a thick sauce. Place the 3 tablespoons of fat in a small saucepan, stir in the flour and when smooth, add the milk gradually, stirring constantly to avoid lumps. Simmer gently for 10 minutes, stirring most of the time. The sauce has to be very thick, as the cabbage will still be exuding some moisture however well you drained it.

❺ Season the sauce and add most of the cheese. Pour it over the cabbage and sausage, mixing everything gently together. Scatter the top with the remaining cheese and return the dish to the oven. Turn the heat to 425°F/220°C/gas mark 7 to brown it. It is ready when it is bubbling hot.

11. curries

We used to think that the hotter you could take your curry and the more pints of lager you could put away to quench its heat was a sign of something. Quite what I'm not sure. Those days are past. More or less. Curry doesn't have to be mouth-burningly hot to be worthy of attention. In fact, it is the subtle Indian curries, those spiced with care and thought, so the flavours are mellow and multi-faceted, that are really worth getting excited about. Our passion for Thai food, with its balance of chilli-hot, sweet, sour and creamy flavours, has broadened our curry horizons and indirectly made us more aware of layers of flavour that are possible to build in a relatively hot curry.

Obviously, the proportion and balance of spices are what give a curry its distinctive flavour, but the stage at which you choose to add them to the pot is equally important. There are a variety of ingredients that can be used to thicken, colour and flavour the base sauce. Ingredients like coconut, onions, tomatoes, nuts and seeds not only thicken but also create layers of flavour. This sort of detail makes curry-making sound complicated and hard work. That is *so* not true. It is no more difficult to make very good Indian and Thai curries at home than it is to make a shepherd's pie or an old-fashioned British stew. For a curry to be authentic, however, it requires stocking up the store cupboard with a range of spices and other ingredients like coconut milk, lemon grass, fresh ginger and certain nuts and seeds. And the best flavours will come from buying these ingredients little and often.

When shopping for curries, the best quality and often best value comes from shopping at indigenous shops or markets. Choosing whole spices rather than powders, for example, and grinding them at home will noticeably affect the end result. The Wolf hasn't always got time for such attention to detail. Fortunately, a perfectly good although more ubiquitous curry flavour – both Indian and

Thai – is quickly and easily achieved from a wide range of ready-made curry products. They come in bottles, packets and individual portion sachets. And fresh coriander, ginger and a range of chillies, albeit of dubious strength, are stocked by all supermarkets and some corner shops.

The results will be good enough using these products but if you bother to make a curry using your own spice mix, you will notice the difference immediately. Not only will the flavours have a freshness and vivacity which is impossible with processed spice mixes, you will also increase your new-found popularity stakes (everyone loves people who make a good curry). Another advantage about perfecting a curry or two is that when you are entertaining, it is easy to turn a relatively simply made curry into an event. Just make sure you provide a full range of complementary trimmings such as mango chutney, lime pickle, a pot of thick natural yoghurt (add chopped cucumber and a garnish of ground chilli and it becomes raita), poppadoms and hot nan bread or chapati (tortilla or pitta bread, incidentally, make good alternatives), plus the inevitable rice.

Remember that the longer you cook chilli the softer its flavour becomes. You never lose all the heat but it mellows and becomes harmonious with the other flavourings. If, however, you need to tone down chilli-heat, add coconut milk or natural yoghurt. If you do have the misfortune to burn your lips or mouth with raw chilli, *see* page 21.

As a general rule, curries, like soups and stews, improve if left to go cold – preferably overnight. Reheat before serving. A can of ready-made curry is useful when you're in a hurry (even better if you add it to minced meat or chunks of chicken fried with a chopped onion) but fresh can be quick too. Read on.

Thai Curry Pastes

Thais like their curries hot, fearsomely hot. The heat comes from chillies and garlic, which are pounded with galangal or ginger, lemon grass, and masses of fresh coriander, to make a stiff green or red paste. The paste is the starting point of every Thai curry. You can buy authentic, freshly made curry pastes – with industrial chilli strength – at any Thai food shop. They are sold in small plastic pots with sufficient paste to make a couple of large curries, and will keep in the fridge for several days before the flavours begin to fade.

Supermarkets sell various brands of sachets and bottles of Thai curry paste. They don't compare well with the Real Thing but are a useful way of injecting Thai seasonings into a curry or stir fry. If you use them, and you probably will, improve the flavours by adding a whole chilli (which will be removed at the end of cooking), a generous splash of Thai fish sauce (see page 108), and plenty of fresh coriander to the dish. The best brand is Merchant Gourmet in the Asian Home Gourmet Spice Paste range.

So What is Garam Masala?

Garam masala is an Indian blend of spices that have been ground into a powder. Usually the spices have been roasted (dry-fried) whole and then ground to a powder. It is generally added towards the end of cooking or sprinkled over the top of the food as a last-minute seasoning. Mixtures of spices vary from region to region and cook to cook but the intention is to add fragrance – cardamom, coriander, cumin, cinnamon, cloves, nutmeg and black peppercorns – rather than chilli heat. Buy it in packets or bottles or beg a little from your favourite Indian restaurant. Like all spices, ground ones in particular, flavours fade gradually in the packet. It's easy enough to make your own; any Indian cook book will give several recipes.

One of the essential components of an Indian meal is a bowl of steaming dhal or dal. It should come heavily laced with browned onions and garlic, smell strongly of cumin, and be flecked with bright green coriander. The exact texture of dhal can be tailored to taste at home, but may be somewhat variable at your local Indian restaurant. That's because the age as well as the type of lentil or split pea – which is what dhal is made from makes a huge difference to the finished dish

For a quickie dhal, the thing to use is tiny red split lentils. They require no soaking, and turn fluffy and tender, as well as several shades lighter, after only thirty minutes' cooking. They won't give the same depth of earthy flavour as the larger, plumper yellow split peas, but they work well in this interesting take on masoor dhal.

It is made with an unusually large quantity of onions, plenty of aromatic cumin, a hint of chilli, and lots of fresh mint stirred in at the end. For a soothing sort of supper, serve it with boiled rice, hard-boiled eggs and mango chutney. It is also a very good accompaniment to any lamb curry.

masoor dhal with mint and onions

4 servings
15 minutes preparation
40 minutes cooking

ingredients

2 medium-sized onions
3 large garlic cloves
3 tbsp vegetable oil
generous pinch cayenne
175 g red split lentils
1 tsp ground cumin
salt and black pepper
squeeze of lemon juice
about 30 mint leaves

method

❶ Peel, halve and chop the onions. Peel and chop the garlic. Heat the oil in a spacious, heavy-bottomed saucepan over a high heat. Add the onions and stir constantly for several minutes until they begin to sweat and then turn brown.

❷ Reduce the heat, stir in the garlic and cook for a couple of minutes before adding the cayenne, the split lentils and half the cumin. Stir well, then add 600 ml water. Bring to the boil, reduce the heat, cover the pan and simmer gently for about 25 minutes or until the dhal is thick and the lentils tender.

❸ Stir in ½ teaspoon each of salt and pepper, the reserved cumin and some lemon juice. Taste and adjust

the seasoning. Cover the dhal while you chop the mint.
Stir in the mint and serve.

NB: If left to cool, dhal will thicken. You may need to
reheat with a little extra water. If making this ahead, don't
stir in the mint until you are ready to serve.

Serve this excellent dish with boiled rice and a big scoop
of garlicky cucumber (raita), and it qualifies as a main course in its own
right. If there is a poppadom or two in the offing, and some stingingly hot
lime pickle, so much the better. As a side dish, it goes with any curry.

french beans with cumin tomatoes

method

❶ Keeping everything in separate piles, peel and halve the
onion and chop finely. Peel the garlic and chop finely.

❷ Trim the beans and chop in half. Chop up the
tomatoes.

❸ Heat a large frying pan or wok over a medium heat.
Add the oil and stir in the onions. Cook briskly for about 8
minutes until the onion begins to soften and colour, then
add the garlic, 1 teaspoon of cumin, a generous pinch of
salt and the chilli powder. Cook for 2–3 more minutes until
the onions are nicely brown. Increase the heat and add the
beans. Stir fry for 2 minutes before adding the tomatoes.
Toss for a minute or two, stir in the coriander, remove
from the heat and serve sprinkled with ground cumin.
Serve hot, tepid or cold.

2 servings as a main dish
or 4–6 servings as a side
dish

15 minutes preparation
20 minutes cooking

ingredients

1 large onion
3 garlic cloves
250 g French beans
4 medium-sized tomatoes
1 tbsp cooking oil
1 tsp ground cumin plus a
    little extra
salt
generous pinch of chilli powder
1 tbsp coarsely chopped
    coriander leaves

A simple but effective way to spice up cabbage. If you don't particularly like crunchy white cabbage, choose another variety. I like this with sausages but remember it when the piggy bank is almost empty and serve with curried potatoes.

masala cabbage

4–6 servings

15 minutes preparation

20 minutes cooking

ingredients

1 small or ½ large white
    cabbage, approx 750 g

1 onion

5 cm piece fresh ginger

2 tbsp cooking oil

1 tsp turmeric

1 tsp salt

1 tsp paprika or another chilli
    powder

juice of ½ a lemon

1 tsp garam masala

method

❶ Halve or quarter the cabbage and cut out the core. Shred, rinse in a colander and shake dry. Trim, halve and finely slice the onion. Peel the ginger. Either grate it on the large hole of a cheese grater, or slice thinly, cut the slices into matchsticks and then chop finely.

❷ Heat the oil in a large frying pan or similarly wide-based pan placed over a medium heat. Add the onion and ginger and cook, stirring often, until tender and beginning to brown.

❸ Add the turmeric, salt and paprika, and cook for 1 minute, stirring often, then add the cabbage. Stir well and cook for a couple of minutes before reducing the heat slightly. Cover the pan and cook, stirring every so often, for about 15 minutes or until the cabbage is tender but still has a bite to it.

❹ Squeeze over the lemon juice, sprinkle with the garam masala and cook, stirring constantly, for 1 more minute. Serve immediately. This re-heats well.

Muglai aloo is one of those moreish curried potato dishes that you will find under various names on almost any Indian curry house menu. This version is based on a less healthy dish I invented for In Praise of the Potato and is possibly even better eaten cold the next day. The potatoes end up bathed in a pale yellow aromatic cream, laced with silky strands of wilted onion and fresh coriander leaves. It is interesting enough to serve on its own, or with rice, pickles and poppadoms, but works well as part of a curry blow-out.

curried potatoes

method

❶ Cook the potatoes in boiling salted water without bothering to peel them, until just tender. Drain, cool under running cold water, then drain again and skin.

❷ While the potatoes are cooking, peel, halve and finely slice the onion. Melt the butter in a frying pan over a medium-low heat and add the onion. Stir until thoroughly coated with butter. Season with salt, cover the pan, reduce the heat and cook, stirring every so often, until wilted, juicy and lightly coloured. Allow at least 15 minutes for this.

❸ Meanwhile, split the chillies and use a teaspoon to scrape away the seeds. (*See* page 21.) Chop. Peel the ginger and chop. Peel the garlic and chop. Blitz these ingredients into a smooth paste in the food processor, adding a little water. (If you don't own a machine, *see* page 20.)

❹ Stir the paste into the yoghurt, along with the ground cloves, cumin, coriander and turmeric. Pour the yoghurt into the softened onions, add 50 ml water and the potatoes. Stir well and simmer for at least 10 minutes. Adjust the seasoning with salt and pepper, stir in the fresh coriander and serve.

6 servings
25 minutes preparation
25 minutes cooking

ingredients

1 kg small salad potatoes such as Charlotte
salt and black pepper
1 large onion
40 g butter
2 green chillies
5 cm piece fresh ginger
3 large garlic cloves
200 g Greek yoghurt
1 tsp each ground cloves, cumin and coriander
½ tsp turmeric
2 tbsp chopped coriander

This is a very good example of the sort of gently scented, aromatic kind of curry that it is possible to make using curry powder and the last-minute addition of the spice mixture garam masala. Apart from looking very attractive, this curry is a good contrast of textures as well as flavours, with lightly cooked beans contributing much-needed crunch. Served with basmati rice, the quantities given are overly generous for four people but with nan bread or chapatis, there is plenty for six. Of course, you will also need mango chutney, raita and poppadoms etc etc.

If you are feeling flush or are making this recipe for a special occasion, try it with 400 g prawns rather than half prawns and half mushrooms. A good vegetarian version could be made with 200 g kebab-sized chunks of tofu.

fragrant mushroom curry

4–6 servings
20 minutes preparation
25 minutes cooking

ingredients

1 large onion
2 tbsp vegetable oil
1 large mild red chilli
200 g French beans
2 rounded tsp curry powder
200 ml carton of coconut cream
½ chicken stock cube dissolved in 250 ml boiling water
2 medium-sized tomatoes
200 g button mushrooms or quartered medium-sized mushrooms

method

❶ Peel, halve and finely chop the onion. Add the oil and then the onion to a spacious, wide-based, heavy-bottomed pan placed over a medium-low heat. Cook, stirring often, for 10–15 minutes until the onion is soft but uncoloured.

❷ Meanwhile, trim and split the chilli and scrape away the seeds. Chop into tiny dice. (*See* page 21.) Stir the chilli into the soft onions and cook for a couple of minutes while you top and tail the beans and cut them in half.

❸ Stir the curry powder into the onions and cook, stirring constantly, for 2 more minutes. Add the beans to the pan, increase the heat slightly and cook, stirring every so often, for 3 minutes.

❹ Add the coconut cream and the stock, give the dish a good stir, and leave to simmer while you chop the tomatoes.

❺ Add the tomatoes to the pan and, 2 minutes later, the mushrooms. Cook for about 6 minutes and then add the prawns. Cook for a few more minutes until warmed through. Now taste the gravy and adjust the seasoning with salt, pepper and lemon juice.

❻ Sprinkle over the garam masala, cook for a further minute or so before serving strewn with coriander leaves.

200 g cooked, peeled large
    prawns
squeeze of lemon juice
salt and black pepper
1 rounded tsp garam masala
    (see page 215)
handful of coriander leaves
    (optional)

A Word about Coconut Milk Products

Coconut, in its various processed forms, has all sorts of uses in curries.

COCONUT MILK: often thought to be the watery liquid inside the coconut but actually extracted from the flesh of the coconut. You can make your own from desiccated or fresh coconut but it is a laborious and time-consuming job. Buy coconut milk in 400 ml cans. Give the can a shake before use because coconut milk separates if left to stand. Unless specified, canned coconut milk is unseasoned. It is also thick, very white and reminiscent of evaporated milk. It does not keep well once the can is opened; a maximum of 2 days in the fridge.

COCONUT CREAM: thicker than coconut milk, sold in 200 ml long-life cartons and is useful on account of its size.

CREAMED COCONUT: a curious ingredient. It looks a bit like a block of frozen lard, but it's a useful thing to have in the store cupboard. You can grate it directly into stir fries and stewed dishes, or dissolve it in warm water, milk or stock to make a substitute for coconut milk or coconut cream.

OK, so we know that the best Indian curries are made

with whole spices that have been carefully chosen then roasted and ground into a powder that will insinuate the food to give hauntingly interesting flavours. This simplified tandoori-style kebab relies on curry paste and these days there are plenty of good ones around, *see* page 215.

And another thing: you don't need to own a wood-burning tandoor, the spectacular pot-bellied clay oven that gives the dish its name, to cook this recipe. In the summer the barbecue would be the best alternative, but the rest of the time the simplest way to cook a quantity of kebabs is in a very hot oven. If you prefer, the cooking can be done in batches, either on a ridged griddle or under the grill. If you use a grill, make sure it is very hot before you start and place the kebabs close to the heat but watch like a hawk to avoid the marinade burning and thus tasting bitter.

A distinctive feature of tandoori food is the yoghurt marinade. This is seasoned with garlic, ginger and the spice garam masala. Restaurant versions are always bright red – usually coloured with food dye – but turmeric turns this one a beautiful tint of pale yellow. If, incidentally, your store cupboard doesn't run to turmeric, leave it out. The curry powder will have some in it anyway and the flavour will hardly be affected. Serve this with raita and rice or, instead of rice, roll it up in toasted tortilla or pile it into hot pitta bread envelopes.

turkey tikka with cucumber raita

4 generous servings
25 minutes preparation plus
    30 minutes marinade
10 minutes cooking

ingredients
750 g lean turkey meat (see
    page 179)

method
❶ Cut the turkey into chunks slightly smaller than usual kebab size.

❷ Peel the garlic and ginger and coarsely chop. Place both in the bowl of a food processor. Add the garam masala, curry paste, turmeric, salt, lime juice and half the yoghurt. Blitz until smooth, transfer to a bowl, beat in the remaining yoghurt and stir in the turkey. Cover then pop in the fridge for at least 30 minutes or as long as overnight.

❸ If you are using a barbecue, get the coals very hot and covered with ash before you start cooking. If using an oven, pre-heat it to 450°F/230°C/gas mark 8 and line a flat baking tray with tinfoil. Thread the turkey kebabs onto the skewers and lay out on the prepared tray. Cook near the top of the oven for 8–10 minutes, turning once during cooking.

❹ To make the raita, mix the first 4 ingredients, then sprinkle with cumin and chilli.

6 garlic cloves

5 cm piece of fresh ginger

1 tsp garam masala (see page 215)

1 tbsp curry paste

1 tsp ground turmeric

½ tsp salt

2 tbsp lime juice

150 g thick natural yoghurt

FOR THE RAITA

150 g thick natural yoghurt

1 seeded and chopped tomato

½ grated cucumber

1 tbsp coarsely chopped coriander or mint

pinch of cumin

pinch of chilli powder

you will also need a packet of wooden skewers which should be soaked in cold water (to prevent them burning as the food cooks) while you prepare the food

This is a very quick simplified version of an authentic Thai green curry. The preparations are all done first, in much the same way as you would if you were making a stir fry. It is a semi-cheat's recipe, made with a mixture of fresh and preserved ingredients but relies on a commercially made Thai curry paste – see page 215. I have bumped up the flavours, whilst giving the gravy a fresher taste, with extra ingredients. Additional coriander – which, along with green chillies, is the green in the curry paste – is vital and so too is a slug of Thai fish sauce. If you miss out this, nam pla or nuoc nam, as it's called in Vietnam, a vital component of the sour chilli creamy flavour which is essential to this particular curry will be lost. Vile though it smells, nam pla lifts the flavours with its salty savoury tang.

Serve the curry with boiled basmati rice.

thai green chicken curry

6–8 servings
35 minutes preparation
30 minutes cooking

ingredients

800 g chicken meat (see page 179)
1 medium-sized red onion
1 garlic clove
1 lemon grass stalk
2¹/₂ cm piece fresh ginger
2 lemons (one should be unwaxed)
2 tbsp cooking oil
2 sachets of Thai green curry paste
400 ml can of coconut milk

method

❶ Cut the chicken into bite-size pieces, either kebab style or longer and skinnier.

❷ Meanwhile, peel and finely chop the onion. Peel and finely chop the garlic. Peel away the outer layers of the lemon grass to locate the tender inner shoot, cut into 3 pieces. Peel the ginger, chop finely. Using a potato peeler, remove 2 strips of lemon zest (no white) from the unwaxed lemon.

❸ Heat the oil in a pan that can hold the complete curry; a wok would be fine. Add the onion, garlic and ginger, stir fry over a medium heat until the onion is tender and the garlic and ginger aromatic. Add the lemon grass and lemon zest. Stir in the curry paste with 2 tablespoons of coconut milk. Cook, stirring constantly, for a minute or so. Add the rest of the can of coconut milk and the stock. Bring to the boil then season with a splash of Tabasco, the fish sauce, 1/2 teaspoon salt and a little pepper. Squeeze in the juice from 1 lemon. Taste and fine-tune the seasoning with salt, more lemon juice and Tabasco. Simmer gently for about 10 minutes.

❹ Meanwhile, bring a pan of water to the boil. Top and tail the beans and cut them in half. Add the beans to the now salted boiling water, bring back to the boil and cook for 30 seconds. Drain.

❺ Drain and rinse the bamboo shoots and add to the sauce. Bring back to simmer and add the chicken. Cook for 10 minutes. Stir in the coconut cream, add the prepared beans and most of the coriander. Bring back to simmer, cook for a couple more minutes, taste and adjust the seasoning with lemon juice, salt and possibly Tabasco. Serve garnished with the reserved coriander leaves.

1/2 chicken stock cube dissolved in 250 ml boiling water

Tabasco

2 tbsp Thai fish sauce (see page 108)

salt and black pepper

200 g French beans

225 g can of bamboo shoots in water

200 ml carton of coconut cream

2 tbsp coarsely chopped coriander leaves

Delicious, very filling and quick and easy to make. Serve with rice, poppadoms and mango chutney. For a special occasion, garnish the curry with toasted flaked almonds.

potato and chicken curry with spinach

4–6 servings
20 minutes preparation
25 minutes cooking

ingredients

500 g small new potatoes or a
   waxy variety such as
   Charlotte
2 onions, approx 250 g
2 big garlic cloves
2 red chillies or 1 tsp chilli
   powder
2 tbsp vegetable oil
750 g chicken meat (see page
   179)
3 heaped tsp curry powder
200 ml carton of coconut
   cream or canned coconut
   milk
½ chicken stock cube
   dissolved in 250 ml boiling
   water
2 medium-sized tomatoes
salt and black pepper
squeeze of lemon juice
1 heaped tsp garam masala
   (see page 215)
150 g young spinach leaves

method

❶ Cook the potatoes in boiling salted water until tender. Cool under cold running water then drain and peel. Cut the potatoes in half, leave very small potatoes whole.

❷ Meanwhile, peel, halve and finely chop the onion. Peel and finely chop the garlic. Trim and split the chilli, if using, and scrape away the seeds. Chop into tiny dice. (*See* page 21.)

❸ Add the oil and then the onion to a spacious, wide-based, heavy-bottomed pan placed over a medium heat. Cook, stirring often, for about 10 minutes until the onion begins to brown and soften. Don't let it burn. Reduce the heat and add the garlic and chopped chilli or chilli powder. Cook for 2 more minutes stirring constantly.

❹ Meanwhile, cut the chicken into kebab-sized chunks.

❺ Now go back to the onions and stir in the curry powder. Cook stirring constantly, for 2 more minutes. Add the chicken to the onions, increase the heat slightly and stir constantly until all the pieces have turned from pink to white (apart, that is, from the coating of curry powder).

❻ Add the coconut cream or milk and the stock. Give the dish a good stir and leave to simmer while you peel then chop the tomatoes. Peeling is quickly done by immersing the tomatoes in boiling water for 20 seconds. Check the skin is ready to peel away by stabbing with a small, sharp knife. Discard the skin and chop the tomatoes.

❼ Add the potatoes to the pan and simmer for about 15 minutes until the chicken is cooked through. Check a piece and cook for a few more minutes if necessary. Now taste the gravy and adjust the seasoning with salt, pepper and lemon juice.

❽ Sprinkle over the garam masala, stir in the tomatoes and cook for a further minute. Now add the spinach. Push it down under the bubbling curry; it will wilt almost before your eyes. Don't overcook; it will only take a few seconds before it's ready. Loosely stir in the yoghurt (garnish with the almonds, if using) and serve over rice.

150 g Greek-style yoghurt
2 tbsp toasted almonds
(optional)

Don't let the long list of ingredients put you off. This is a brilliant recipe: quick, low fat, delicious and it makes a surprisingly large quantity. Serve it with boiled basmati, cucumber raita and chutneys or roll up in hot chapati or tortilla. Alternatively, spoon onto chapati or tortilla and 'garnish' with thick natural yoghurt or raita and a dribble of chutney, and eat pizza style. Leftovers are excellent the next day.

pork keema curry with peas

6 servings
15 minutes preparation
20 minutes cooking

ingredients

2 onions, approx 250 g
4 cardamom pods
2 plump garlic cloves
5 cm piece fresh ginger
salt
1 tbsp cooking oil
1 large green chilli with a low
   heat rating
1 tsp ground turmeric
1 tsp paprika or other chilli
   powder
2 heaped tbsp Greek-style
   yoghurt
500 g extra lean minced pork,
   preferably organic
2 fresh red chillies
1 tsp ground cumin
2 tsp ground coriander
200 g frozen peas
1 tbsp tomato purée

method

❶ Peel, halve and finely chop the onions. Place in a pan and cover with 250 ml water. Lightly bash the cardamom pods and add them. Bring to the boil, turn down the heat, cover the pan and cook for 15–20 minutes until the onion is tender.

❷ Meanwhile, peel and chop the garlic. If you have a liquidizer, add the garlic to the bowl together with the peeled and grated ginger, ½ teaspoon of salt, the oil and 1 tablespoon of water. Blitz to liquidize into a thick cream. (If you don't own a liquidizer, sprinkle the chopped garlic with ½ teaspoon of salt and use the flat of a knife to pulverize into a juicy paste. Peel the ginger and grate. Mix the ginger into the garlic paste and chop and pound until smooth. Mix with the oil and water and tip into a mixing bowl.)

❸ Trim and finely chop the green chilli. Add the chopped chilli, turmeric, paprika or chilli powder and yoghurt to the bowl and stir thoroughly. Add the meat, mix well and leave for 30 minutes.

❹ If you own a liquidizer, don't wash it after blitzing the garlic and ginger paste. Pick the cardamom pods out of the onions and then pour onion and water into the liquidizer. Blitz to make a cream sauce. (If you don't own a liquidizer, pass the onions and water through a sieve into a bowl and force the onions (without the cardamom) through the sieve with the back of a wooden spoon. Mix well.)

5 Tip the pork mixture into a large frying pan or similarly wide-based saucepan and place it over a medium-high heat. Cook for 7–8 minutes, stirring regularly, until the meat is brown and the mixture dry.

6 Meanwhile, trim and finely chop the red chillies. (*See* page 21.) Add the cumin, coriander and red chilli to the pan. Cook for a further minute before adding the onion purée and 1 teaspoon of salt. Cook for 5 minutes, stirring regularly.

7 Add the peas and tomato purée. Stir well and simmer for 10 minutes until the peas are just tender and the curry is moist and thick. Stir in the garam masala and the coriander leaves. Cook for 1 minute. Taste and adjust the seasoning with lemon juice and salt. Serve without delay.

1 tsp garam masala (see page 215)

3 tbsp chopped coriander or mint leaves or mixture of both

squeeze of lemon juice

12. puddings

If you reach for a bowl of cereal rather than toast and Marmite when you are hungry, you are probably a pudding person. Perhaps you have your own repertoire of quick pudding ideas. When the store cupboard is full, that's easy. Pouring runny honey over Greek yoghurt, for example, or knocking up a banana custard with a carton of fresh custard from the supermarket couldn't be simpler.

Both of these quick puds have potential for elaboration. How about serving the yoghurt over stewed fruit like plums or apricots, and turning banana custard into a trifle with whipped cream and toasted almonds? And talking of plums, have you tried cutting them in half and arranging the plums, cut side up, on a thick slice of buttered bread, sprinkling it lavishly with sugar and baking it in the oven until the plums weep into the crusty bread? This is gorgeous with something thick and creamy. And if you like yoghurt, why not make a sort of fruit fool with whatever soft fruit is in season? Just crush or quickly soften the fruit with a squeeze of lemon juice, dust with sugar and fold into the yoghurt.

Fruit salads are my particular weakness. If you can't be bothered to actually make one, what about a de-constructed fruit salad? Peel an orange, unzip a banana and select an apple or a small bunch of grapes. Take alternate mouthfuls. With slightly more trouble – i.e. slicing the fruit and arranging it attractively on a platter, decorated, perhaps, with sprigs of mint and a dusting of sugar – de-constructed fruit salad makes a great end to a meal. Particularly after curry or a stew.

And do you know that childhood favourite of whisking up a can of evaporated milk until it is very frothy and mixing it with a fruit jelly diluted at quarter strength? Chill it in the fridge and serve with runny cream. Or posh it up with a mound of strawberries or whatever soft fruit is in season.

Pudding used to be a normal part of the main meal of the day. It used to have equal status with the main course and was often just as filling as the savoury dish. Fruit crumble and custard, for instance, or rice pudding and a dollop of strawberry jam. Many of our traditional puddings are economy-led as well as being filling. Bread and butter pudding, for example, was a way of using up stale bread, and fruit tarts were often made with windfalls and berries plucked from the hedgerow. Nothing wrong with that. In fact, these sorts of puds can be very quick and easy to make. They are also very filling. After all, why shouldn't a particularly gorgeous apple tart or a huge fruit salad sometimes *be* supper?

The Wolf likes short cuts to pudding pleasure, so instant individual trifles, baked apples, fruit crumbles and tarts using ready-made puff pastry are the order of the day. And don't chuck out that stale bread or leftover rice. Read on and find out how to turn them into delicious easy puddings.

In Morocco, a salad of oranges is flavoured with orange blossom water and decorated with ground cinnamon. It is often eaten with cold rice pudding. Their rice pudding isn't like the British version; it is cooked in almond-flavoured milk with spices and decorated with nuts. Here's a good cheat's version. The orange blossom water is available from supermarkets.

moroccan orange salad

4 servings

15 minutes preparation

3 minutes cooking

ingredients

knob of butter or ½ tbsp
   cooking oil

2 tbsp almond flakes

6 medium-sized seedless
   oranges

2 tbsp icing sugar

2 tbsp orange blossom water
   (optional)

ground cinnamon

400 g can of Ambrosia creamed
   rice

method

❶ Melt the knob of butter or heat the oil in a frying pan. Add the almond flakes and toss until golden. Drain on absorbent kitchen paper.

❷ Slice the peel off the oranges removing all the pith. Cut the oranges in chunky slices and place in a bowl.

❸ Scoop the juice from the chopping board into a bowl or jug. Sift 1 tablespoon of icing sugar into the orange juice, stir in 1 tablespoon of orange blossom water (if using) and pour over the oranges. Chill and dust with about ½ teaspoon of cinnamon and remaining icing sugar before serving. Sprigs of mint make the salad look very pretty if you are making this for a special occasion.

❹ Turn the rice pudding into an attractive bowl. If using orange blossom water, stir in the second tablespoon. Dust with a few lines of cinnamon and decorate with the toasted almonds.

You can use any combination of green fruit you fancy for this salad. Regard the quantities given as a guideline, adding more of one fruit or omitting another as you wish. The surprise element is a clever idea I picked up in Spain. Variations on the theme of sweetened, creamed avocado – for that's the surprise – are common in Brazil. There they use lime instead of lemon juice and add a tot of port to jolly things along.

green fruit salad surprise

method

❶ Prepare the fruit over or near a bowl so you can catch as much juice as possible. Cut the melon into eight, then cut the flesh off the skin in bite-size chunks. Halve the grapes. Peel, core and chop the pears into chunks slightly smaller than the melon. Peel the kiwi fruit, halve lengthways and then halve each half. Cut out the central core if it's hard and slice each piece into four slices. Mix everything together.

❷ And now the avocado cream. It's difficult to give precise amounts of sugar and milk to make this because it will depend on the sweetness and size of the fruit. Begin by halving the avocados and winkling out the stone. Cut out any black bits of flesh then mash flesh with a fork, either in its shell or a bowl. Tip into a bowl and sift over a tablespoon of icing sugar and 6 tablespoons of milk. Mash and whip to a smooth purée (you could do this in a blender or Mouli-légumes, fine blade). Taste, add more sugar and/or milk and adjust the flavour with a little lemon juice. You are aiming to achieve the consistency of thick, whipped cream.

❸ Spoon the avocado cream into bowls or one big bowl and top with the fruit.

4–6 servings
20 minutes preparation
no cooking

ingredients

½ ripe Galia melon

225 g seedless white grapes

3 firm but ripe Conference
   pears

3 ripe kiwi fruit

2 ripe avocados

icing sugar

milk

lemon juice

It is the soft chewy centre hidden inside a crisp shell that makes meringues worth eating. I never tire of eating them with whipped cream or thick Greek yoghurt and often match them with any soft fruit you care to mention. Raspberries, over-ripe strawberries and peaches are particularly good but so too are apricots that have been stewed with fresh orange juice and honey. For the occasions when you want one of these quick desserts to look a bit smarter, use a second fruit to make a purée to dribble over the top – strawberries with a raspberry sauce or raspberries with a strawberry sauce. Suit yourself. Alternatively, beat a little whisky or rum into the cream and call it Caledonia or Barbados cream. You can buy meringue nests in most supermarkets.

strawberry meringues

4 servings

15 minutes preparation

no cooking

ingredients

450 g strawberries, preferably small English ones

1 tbsp caster sugar

150 g raspberries

1 tbsp icing sugar

squeeze of lemon juice

142 g whipping cream

4 meringue nests

method

❶ Rinse the strawberries and remove their stalks. Cut them in half lengthways and place in a bowl. Sprinkle with the caster sugar and leave to turn juicy.

❷ Tip the raspberries into a sieve placed over a bowl. Using the back of a spoon, press the fruit through the sieve, leaving the (vast quantities) of pips behind. Sift the icing sugar over the top, stir into the vivid, thick juice and season with a squeeze of lemon juice. If the icing sugar turns lumpy, pour the sauce into a saucepan and gently heat through whilst stirring to dissolve the sugar.

❸ Pour the cream into a mixing bowl and whisk until it forms soft, floppy peaks. Arrange the meringues on a serving platter or plates, spoon a dollop of cream on top of each meringue and pile the strawberries and their juices over the top. Cover with another spoonful of cream and pour the raspberry sauce over the top. Serve immediately.

Don't be alarmed by the word trifle. Jelly is not involved. This trifle is very simple to make and absolutely delicious and has the added advantage of being easy to adapt for as few or as many people as required.

Soft almond macaroons (my branch of Sainsbury's keeps them with biscuits but you may have to ask) have a wonderfully dense but light creamy texture and a gorgeous almond flavour. A firm sponge cake, such as all-butter Madeira cake, is a good alternative. If you are making this for a party, have everything ready and assemble the trifle at the last moment, either in individual bowls or one big one. Ice cream, incidentally, is the surprise. You may prefer to leave it out and increase the quantity of yoghurt or custard instead.

plum and amaretti trifle surprise

method

1 Cut the plums off their stones in big chunks. Put the flesh in a pan with the wine or water and half the sugar. Cover the pan and simmer vigorously for 5–6 minutes until the pieces of plum are tender. Taste and if necessary add extra sugar, stirring until dissolved. Tip into a dish and leave to chill or pop dish into the freezer for about 10 minutes to cool.

2 Meanwhile, heat the oil in a frying pan placed over a medium heat and when hot add the almonds. Toss constantly until lightly golden. Tip onto kitchen paper to drain.

3 Quarter the macaroons or cut the cake into 2½ cm chunks. Place in individual dishes, spoon over some of the plum mixture to partially saturate, and top with a scoop of ice cream (if using), then cover with yoghurt or custard. Spoon over some more of the plums, top with more yoghurt and sprinkle with toasted almonds. Serve immediately. Yum.

4 6 servings

15 minutes preparation

10 minutes cooking plus

15 minutes cooling

ingredients

500 g ripe red plums

glass of white wine or water,
approx 150 ml

2–4 tbsp sugar

50 g flaked almonds

1 tbsp vegetable oil or butter

150 g soft almond macaroons
(Corsini, Amaretti Morbidi) or
150 g all-butter Madeira cake

4 scoops of vanilla ice cream
(optional)

200–300 g Greek yoghurt or
bought fresh egg custard

Don't. Buy it ready made. It freezes brilliantly.

One of the most useful things to keep in the freezer is a packet of frozen puff pastry. It defrosts quickly and, when rolled quite thinly, it is the perfect base for savoury and fruit tarts and pizzas. A very good wheeze is to cook a sheet of puff pastry, let it cool, spread it with thick Greek yoghurt or crème fraîche, and pile it up with fresh fruit. I've done it to great effect with strawberries – cutting them into quarters and dusting them with icing sugar – and with grapes and toasted almond flakes. It would be delicious too with apricots stewed in orange juice and honey, or gooseberries with elderflower cordial. The most impressive version, however, is made with a mixture of soft red fruit all stirred together so their juices mingle.

You can tailor the shape and size of tart you make according to whim. I usually go for an oblong shape because that happens to be the shape of my favourite flat baking sheet. If you prefer, make two oblong tarts, or cut out a large circle, or make a number of individual round, square or oblong tarts. Whatever you choose, the principle is the same.

soft summer fruit tart

6 servings
15 minutes preparation
15 minutes cooking

ingredients

250 g puff pastry
approx 1 tbsp flour

method

❶ Pre-heat the oven to 400°F/200°C/gas mark 6.

❷ Oil a flat baking sheet or upturned oven dish. Dust a work surface with flour and roll out the pastry into an oblong approx 30 cm x 20 cm. Lay pastry out on the oiled flat baking sheet, prick it all over with a fork, and place it near the top of the oven. Cook for about 10 minutes until partially puffed. Remove the sheet from the oven and use a fish slice or palette knife to turn the pastry. Return to the oven for a further 5 minutes to puff what was the base. Don't worry if it hasn't risen evenly or if it looks rough. Transfer to a cake tray to cool.

3 Meanwhile, rinse all the fruit and shake dry. Remove the stalks from the strawberries and cut into chunks or slices. Place the pieces in a mixing bowl.

4 Pull the redcurrants off their stalks. De-stone the cherries by splitting them in half. Add both fruits to the bowl and add the blueberries.

5 Halve the passion fruit through their middles and scrape the seeds and their juices into the fruit. Halve or slice the grapes. Toss all the fruit together.

6 Make the sauce by rinsing the redcurrants. Don't bother to pick them off the stalk. Place them in a pan with 4 tablespoons of water. Bring to the boil and stir in the icing sugar. Pass through a small sieve into a little jug Add the squeeze of lemon

7 By now the pastry will have cooled. Transfer to a suitable serving platter, tray or chopping board. Spread thickly with yoghurt, crème fraîche or cream right to the edges. Arrange the fruit in a haphazard heap over the cream entirely covering it. Dust generously with icing sugar. Serve with the cooled sauce.

NB: The cream topping could be flavoured with fruit juice or a nip of Marsala or balsamic vinegar or cassis, if you happened to have one or another of these.

250 g strawberries

150 g redcurrants

200 g large dark cherries

50 g blueberries

2 passion fruit

100 g red seedless grapes

4–6 tbsp thick Greek yoghurt, crème fraîche or double cream

icing sugar

FOR THE SAUCE

200 g red currants

3 tbsp icing sugar

squeeze of lemon juice

Clafoutis is a wonderful pudding to learn to master and is no more than a sugary, thick egg batter, poured over plums or another soft fruit, and cooked in a gratin-style dish. It emerges from the oven looking like a low-rise soufflé and has a lovely wobbly, soft texture which will be stained in places with fruit juices. Traditionally, it is made with black cherries from Limousin but try it with gooseberries or raspberries, stewed dried apricots or, as here, plums.

The batter is rich and soft when made with single cream but half and half (cream and milk) is pretty good, too.

plum clafoutis

4–6 servings

20 minutes preparation

30 minutes cooking

ingredients

10 large or 18 smaller ripe red
   plums or greengages

knob of butter

4 fresh eggs

100 g caster sugar

50 g flour

300 ml single cream or half
   cream and half milk

caster sugar and cream or
   Greek yoghurt, to serve

method

❶ Pre-heat the oven to 350°F/180°C/gas mark 4. Use the butter to grease generously a 23 x 30 cm gratin-type ceramic dish.

❷ Rinse the plums and quarter lengthways, cutting them off their stones. If using greengages, cut them in half and remove the stones. Lay the fruit out in the buttered dish.

❸ Make the batter by whisking the eggs in a large bowl, then stir in the sugar. When it is completely amalgamated, sieve over the flour, a little at a time. Carry on whisking or beating with a wooden spoon until the mixture is smooth. It will happen. Now add the cream, or cream and milk, whisking or beating until mixed. Pour the batter over the fruit.

❹ Bake the clafoutis in the oven for 30 minutes or until the egg mixture has set and the plums are tender and weeping slightly. Turn off the oven and, if you can bear it, leave the clafoutis for up to 30 minutes before serving. Although it will deflate slightly, it will taste better eaten lukewarm. Serve with caster sugar and cream or Greek yoghurt. It is also wonderful cold. Perfect morning-after-the-night-before food. But it rarely hangs around that long.

If you like rice pudding, you'll love this quick way of making it. The rice – stirred with Greek yoghurt and sugar – is good with any stewed or juicy fresh fruit. Try it with stewed rhubarb or gooseberries cooked with a slug of elderflower cordial, or halved greengages poached in sugary water. I like it with chunks of very ripe peeled peach or with strawberries and passion fruit. If the strawberries are low on flavour, sprinkle them with sugar and, when melted, toss them with a little balsamic vinegar or red wine.

strawberry and almond yoghurt rice

method

❶ Place the rice in a small saucepan with 400 ml water. Bring to the boil, reduce the heat to very low and cover the pan. Cook without lifting the lid for 10 minutes. Turn off the heat and leave, still covered, for a further 5 minutes. Use a fork to break up the rice and spread it out in a bowl to cool slightly.

❷ Meanwhile, if the almonds aren't already toasted, heat a small frying pan and when hot add the almonds, tossing them around constantly for a couple of minutes until lightly toasted. Tip onto plate to arrest cooking and cool.

❸ Remove the stalks from the strawberries and if very large cut them lengthways in quarters, if medium-sized halve them, if small, leave them whole. Peel the peach if using. Ripe peaches are usually easy to peel, but if reluctant, immerse in boiling water for 20 seconds first.

❹ Sprinkle half the sugar over the tepid rice and add 2 tablespoons of the yoghurt. Stir loosely to mix.

❺ Add the strawberries and most of the almonds and stir again. If using a peach, chop it into chunks directly over the rice. Sprinkle over the remaining sugar.

❻ Cut the passion fruit in half through the middle and scrape the seeds and juice over the rice. Spoon small dollops of the remaining yoghurt over the top and strew with the last of the almonds. Serve immediately.

4 servings
15 minutes preparation
10 minutes cooking

ingredients

200 g basmati rice

25 g flaked almonds (or toasted flaked almonds)

250 g ripe strawberries or 2 large ripe peaches

1 tbsp caster sugar

6 tbsp Greek yoghurt

2 passion fruit

Everyone loves baked apples. They will puff and fluff in the oven, ending up ready puréed and begging to be eaten with custard or thick cream or Greek yoghurt and a dribble of honey or Golden Syrup.

Baked apples are usually stuffed, and the traditional filling is mincemeat, a knob of butter and a coating of Golden Syrup which caramelizes into a luscious sauce as it cooks. Even simpler is stuffing the cavity with sultanas soaked in rum or whisky, a smear of butter and yet more syrup. Or, try sugar cubes alternated with lumps of butter; the two will merge into a luscious, molten, caramelized sauce.

Almost any fruit goes well with apple. Ready-to-eat dried fruit, such as apricots or prunes, which plump as the apple cooks, always work well. And if the fruit is soaked first in black tea, or citrus fruit juice or brandy, or a combination of all three, as is almost the case in this recipe, it can't fail to go down well.

Piping hot baked apples go wonderfully well with cold custard, but have you tried them cooled very slightly and eaten with vanilla ice cream *and* hot custard?

baked apples with spiced fruit

4 servings
15 minutes preparation
45 minutes cooking

ingredients

4 large Bramley cooking apples
25 g butter
2 tbsp raisins or sultanas
2 tbsp rum, brandy or whisky
seeds from 1 cardamom pod
6 ready-to-eat dried prunes or
  apricots
1 small orange

method

❶ Pre-heat the oven to 350°F/180°C/gas mark 4.

❷ Rinse the apples, then use an apple corer, potato peeler or small sharp knife to remove the core in one neat piece. Run the point of the knife around the circumference of the apple (this will create a fluffy band between the halves of skin as the apple cooks).

❸ Divide the butter into four chunks and 'plant' the apples on the butter which you have placed on a suitable oven-proof dish; anything will do, so long as the apples have space around them.

❹ Now prepare the filling by placing the raisins or sultanas in a small saucepan with 1 tablespoon of water, alcohol and cardamom seeds. Simmer very gently until almost all the liquid has evaporated.

❺ Meanwhile, chop the prunes or apricots. Remove the zest from the orange and chop finely. Blanch the chopped zest in boiling water for 30 seconds and drain. Halve the orange and squeeze out its juice. Add the chopped prunes or apricots, orange juice and chopped zest to the raisins and simmer gently until everything is nicely juicy and most of the orange juice taken up by the fruit. Chop the stem ginger and stir it into the mixture with a dribble of its juices.

❻ Spoon the fruit mixture into the apple core cavities, packing it down gently. Over the apples dribble the remaining stem ginger juice and then a spoonful of Golden Syrup.

❼ Bake for approximately 45 minutes until the apples are fluffy and puffed. Serve with extra Golden Syrup.

2 pieces of stem ginger plus 1 tbsp juice

4 tbsp Golden Syrup

Recipes that include the name Betty, and they tend to be turn-of-the-century British dishes, always involve bread; and stale bread is perfect. Here, breadcrumbs are layered with thin slices of cooking apple seasoned with cinnamon, sugar and butter. While the dish cooks in the oven, the bread and apple merge into an extraordinarily succulent, soft and light yet mysterious mixture which seems to assume some of the flavour of the last-minute topping of butter-tossed flaked almonds. It is wonderful eaten while the apple still seethes in the dish but it is also very good lukewarm or cold. Serve with thick cream or Greek yoghurt, and extra sugar.

apple betty with almond crisp

4–6 servings

20 minutes preparation

50 minutes cooking

ingredients

70 g butter

juice of 1 lemon

3 large Bramley cooking apples
 or 2 x 490 g bottles of
 Bramley apple sauce

4 tbsp demerara sugar

1 tsp ground cinnamon

120 g fine fresh white
 breadcrumbs

50 g more butter

3 heaped tbsp flaked almonds

method

❶ Pre-heat the oven to 350°F/180°C/gas mark 4.

❷ Use a knob of the 70 g of butter to smear the base and sides of a dish sized approximately 25 cm x 18 cm that is at least 5 cm deep. Divide the rest of the first measurement of butter into three and reserve.

❸ Squeeze the lemon juice into a bowl that can hold all the apple when it has been cut into slices, and pour on about 300 ml water. Quarter, core and peel the apples. Slice them thinly into the acidulated water as you go. This has the double effect of stopping the apple discolouring, which happens almost instantly with Bramleys, and adding a slight lemon tang to the flavours.

❹ Tip the apples into a colander and shake vigorously to dry. Scoop half the apples into the dish, spreading them flat. Sprinkle with 1½ tablespoons of demerara sugar and half the cinnamon. Cut scraps from the first third of the reserved butter over the top. Cover with half the breadcrumbs. Now make a second layer of apple, this time pressing down evenly. Sprinkle over another 1½ tablespoons of demerara, the remaining cinnamon and scraps of the next third of butter. Top with the rest of the breadcrumbs and the final third of butter cut into scraps.

❺ Place a sheet of foil over the top and cook for 35 minutes. Remove the dish from the oven. Remove the foil and turn the oven up to 400°F/200°C/gas mark 6.

❻ Meanwhile, melt the second amount (50 g) of butter in a small pan and stir in the almonds. Spoon this evenly over the top of the dish, sprinkle with the remaining demerara and cook for a further 15 minutes or until the top is caramelized and crusty. Serve with cream or Greek yoghurt.

More Quick Puddings to Make with Bottled Apple Sauce

- Spread thickly on hot pancakes (use a mix or buy ready made), roll up and eat with Greek yoghurt or vanilla ice cream.
- Make Dutch Apple by soaking a handful of sultanas in black tea or whisky then simmer with the apple. Eat hot with cold custard or ice cream. Or cold with hot custard.
- Make apple crumble (see pages 245–7 for recipes).
- Spoon onto hot buttered toast, sprinkle with sugar and flash under the grill to caramelize.

Every now and again there is a restaurant dish that is so quick and easy that it translates to the domestic kitchen without trouble. One such dish, with the extra bonus of being very economical, is variously known as Tarte aux Pommes Minute and, at fashionable Le Caprice, Tarte aux Pommes Chantilly. This tart takes 10 minutes or so to cook, and is an individual Normandy-style apple tart on a wafer-thin pastry base.

quick apple tart

4 servings

20 minutes preparation

10 minutes cooking

ingredients

flour for dusting

250 g puff pastry (see page 236)

1 tsp cooking oil

1 lemon

1 tbsp caster sugar

4 medium-sized Cox's apples

2 tbsp icing sugar

knob of butter

150 g whipping cream

2–3 tbsp whisky or Calvados (optional)

method

❶ Pre-heat the oven to its highest setting: probably 475°F/240°C/gas mark 9.

❷ Dust a suitable flat surface with flour and roll out the puff pastry very, very thinly. Cut out 4 circles using a saucer as a guide. Sprinkle a little water on an oiled baking sheet and lay out the circles of pastry. Lightly prick the pastry all over with the tines of a fork to stop it rising as it cooks and pushing off the apples.

❸ Squeeze the lemon juice into a mixing bowl and stir in the caster sugar. Peel, core and slice the apple into thin segments. As you work, place the slices in the sweetened lemon juice to stop them from discolouring. Cover the pastry with the slices in overlapping concentric circles. Then dredge each tart with icing sugar and dot with a little butter.

❹ Place the baking sheet in the hot oven and cook for 10 minutes or until the pastry is crisp and golden and the apples are tender and scorched in places. Serve hot, warm or cold with the cream, whipped if you like, with whisky. To be authentic it would be Calvados.

Oranges go very well with rhubarb, and in this recipe their sweetened juices poach the rhubarb for a crumble that preserves this fragile fruit in buttery chunks under a particularly crisp topping. You should use tender forced rhubarb since chunks of old rhubarb take ages to cook.

rhubarb and orange crumble

method

❶ Pre-heat the oven to 375°F/190°C/gas mark 5.

❷ Use about half the 25 g of butter to generously smear the base and sides of a ceramic, earthenware or glass gratin dish with a capacity of approximately 1⅕ litres. Cut the rhubarb into chunks approximately 3 cm long, discarding any root and silky strands that come away as you slice. Rinse and shake dry. Add to the dish.

❸ Grate (or finely chop) the equivalent of a 3 cm piece of zest (no white) from one of the oranges. Squeeze 200 ml orange juice into a jug. Stir in the caster sugar until dissolved and add the orange zest. Pour the juice over the rhubarb. Cut the remaining butter into scraps and scatter it over the surface.

❹ Sift the flour into a bowl and cut the 75 g butter into small pieces over the top. Add the oats, demerara sugar, salt and cinnamon. Rub the butter into the dry ingredients until it resembles irregular gravel.

❺ Scatter the crumble over the rhubarb making sure it is completely hidden. Cook in the middle of the oven for 35 minutes until the crumble is brown and crisp and the juices are bubbling round the edge. Serve the crumble hot, warm or cold with cream or custard. You may also need extra sugar; caster sugar would be best.

4–6 servings
20 minutes preparation
35 minutes cooking

ingredients

25 g butter
approx 500 g rhubarb stalks without leaves
2–3 medium-sized oranges
3 tbsp caster sugar
FOR THE CRUMBLE
40 g plain flour
75 g butter
75 g porridge oats
40 g demerara sugar
pinch salt
1 heaped tsp ground cinnamon

Make this crumble at the end of summer when the first chill of autumn sends shivers down the spine, and plums are at their most bountiful and at give-away prices. If you are lucky enough to be able to lay your hands on windfall apples and know a flourishing blackberry bush where you might be able to pick the last of its fruit, the crumble will be food for free. I have therefore included quantities and directions for that as well.

You may even be able to pick cobnuts (a variety of hazelnut grown in Kent) to use in the crumble. Just crack the green husk to reveal a plump, sweet and juicy kernel that is soft enough to hand chop. It is a good idea, incidentally, if you are cooking a two-course meal, particularly if you are using the oven for the main course, to cook the crumble first and leave it on the side to eat warm or cold.

Whipped cream, crème fraîche, Greek yoghurt or custard all go with this. But so does vanilla ice cream (with or without one of the others). If you don't want to include nuts in the crumble, just increase the quantity of flour.

plum hazelnut crumble

6–8 servings
20 minutes preparation
40 minutes cooking

ingredients

50 g fresh shelled cobnuts or
   40 g chopped hazelnuts
75 g wholemeal flour
75 g chilled butter
pinch of salt
1 tsp cinnamon, or 1 tsp ground
   nutmeg or 1 tsp mixed spice
65 g plus 3 tbsp demerara
   sugar
juice of ½ lemon

method

❶ Pre-heat the oven to 350°F/180°C/gas mark 4.

❷ If using fresh cobnuts, remove them from their husks and hand chop or toss into the bowl of a food processor and blitz briefly to chop into small pieces.

❸ Put the flour into a mixing bowl then add 50 g of the butter cut into chunks. Using your finger tips, rub the butter into the flour until it resembles damp breadcrumbs. Add the cinnamon, nutmeg or mixed spice, chopped nuts and 65 g of the sugar. Stir to mix.

❹ If using plums, cut them lengthways into quarters and discard the stone. If going for a blackberry and apple crumble, squeeze the lemon juice into a second bowl. Peel, quarter and chop the apple into chunks and toss them in the lemon juice with a little water as you work.

This stops the apple from discolouring and also adds an agreeable freshness to the flavours. Drain the liquid, then add the blackberries and toss together.

❺ Use a knob of the remaining butter to smear a 1⅕ litre capacity oven-proof gratin-style or deep pie dish – your choice will depend on whether you like a thick, dense crumble and deep layer of fruit or a thinner crunchier crumble. Tip the fruit into the dish, smooth the surface, sprinkle with the remaining sugar and dot with scraps of the remaining butter. Spoon over the crumble to completely cover the fruit. Place in the middle of the oven and cook for 40 minutes or until the crumble is golden and crusty and the plum or blackberry juice is bubbling up round the edge. Serve with cream or cold custard.

750 g plums
or 2 large Bramley cooking
apples (approx 500 g) and
250 g blackberries

Everyone is always very impressed by upside-down apple tart. Peeled and halved apples are nestled up close to each other in sugar melted with butter then covered and tucked up with pastry. When the tart emerges from the oven, the pan is inverted and hey presto! The apples are now glistening and golden brown and sitting in a gorgeously gooey caramel-smeared crisp pastry. It is the distinctive burnt flavour that is so addictive. Serve it hot from the oven with crème fraîche or thick Greek yoghurt.

tarte tatin (upside-down apple tart)

4 servings

30 minutes preparation

30 minutes cooking

ingredients

50 g butter

4 heaped tbsp caster sugar, approx 100 g

generous squeeze of lemon juice

8 small Cox's apples

175 g puff pastry (see page 236)

method

❶ Pre-heat the oven to 400°F/200°C/gas mark 6.

❷ Over a moderate heat, melt the butter in a sturdy metal flan tin, frying pan or similar, measuring approximately 24 cm x 4 cm deep. Sprinkle on the sugar and keep stirring as it melts, froths and gradually turns through shades of amber to dark brown. For my first efforts I was wary of letting it go too dark and ending up with a bitter caramel, but the colour and thus intensity of the burnt flavour are a matter of taste you will only discover by trial and error. If the sugar turns to crystals, which it sometimes does, don't worry, this is the time to add the lemon juice. If the mixture appears not to want to caramelize, keep going. It will eventually. When you're satisfied, remove the pan from the heat.

❸ Quarter, core and peel the apples. Plant them, rounded side down, in the toffee (don't worry if it turns hard), fitting them snugly into one layer.

❹ Roll out the pastry and cut a circle to fit inside the tin or pan. Press it lightly over the apples, tucking it down the sides.

❺ As soon as the oven is ready, cook for 30 minutes until the pastry is puffed and golden. Remove from the oven and run a knife round the inside edge of the tin. Cover the tart with a large plate and quickly invert the tin, watching out for the juices which will inevitably run. Divide into four and eat with plenty of crème fraîche or Greek yoghurt.

Poshed-up Cake

No need for a recipe here. This is just a reminder that all manner of delicious quick puddings can be made with cake.

- Take Victoria sponge, for example. Serve a slice with fruit compote (bought in a carton from M&S or made at home) with a dollop of whipped cream. Or quarter some strawberries, dredge them with sugar and a squeeze of orange juice, wait until the sugar has melted, toss and serve over Greek yoghurt with a slice of cake.
- Slices from a block of cake, such as Madeira cake or Battenberg cake, can be turned into quick trifles (see page 235) or covered with soft fruit such as strawberries and raspberries or served with whipped cream covered with a fruit purée (just force strawberries or raspberries through a sieve and adjust the seasoning with lemon juice and sugar) and a garnish of toasted almonds or hazelnuts.
- What about cutting thin slices of jam Swiss roll to line a glass bowl, anchor it with soft fruit and cover with jelly? Let it set (in the fridge for a couple of hours) then decorate the top with whipped cream and silver balls.
- Ice cream goes well with these sorts of puds.
- And what's wrong with cake and custard?

And, finally. This is one of the best and simplest ways of making a treat of a perfect peach. The white English or Italian peaches are best of all, but a beautiful yellow peach will still be delicious. All you need is one ripe peach per person and enough fizzy white wine to cover it. In Italy, they would choose Prosecco, but Champagne or any fizzy white wine works its magic. And so does red wine, port or amontillado sherry.

peaches in fizzy white wine

4 servings
15 minutes preparation
no cooking

ingredients

4 perfect ripe peaches
2 tbsp caster sugar
1 bottle of chilled fizzy white
   wine

method

❶ Put the kettle on to boil. Place the peaches in a bowl. Pour boiling water over the top to cover; count to 20. Gently drain the peaches in a colander and splash with cold water. With a small sharp knife, carefully peel away the skin.

❷ There are two choices here: either slice the peaches directly into 4 tall-stemmed wine glasses. Or, place a whole peach in a suitable glass. Either way, sprinkle the fruit with a little caster sugar and cover with the wine, pouring with care so the fizz doesn't bubble over.

❸ Look at it.   Drink it.   Eat the peach.

and thanks to Terry

index